Tony Moynihan

Coping with IS/IT Risk Management

The Recipes of Experienced Project Managers

 Springer

Tony Moynihan
School of Computer Applications
Dublin City University
Dublin 9, Ireland

British Library Cataloguing in Publication Data
Moynihan, Tony
    Coping with IS/IT risk management: the recipes of experienced project managers.
    (Practitioner series) 1. Industrial project management 2. Information
    resources management 3. Risk Management
    I. Title.
    658.4'04
    ISBN 1–85233–555–6

Library of Congress Cataloging-in-Publication Data
Moynihan, Tony, 1939-
    Coping with IS/IT risk management : the recipes of experienced project managers/
    Tony Moynihan
        p. cm. – (Practitioner series)
    Includes bibliographical reference and index
    ISBN 1–85233–555–6 (alk.paper)
    1. Industrial project management 2. Information resources management
    3. Risk Management. I. Title. II Series.
    T58.5 .M69 2002
    658.4'038–dc21   2001054265

Practitioner series ISSN 1439–9245
ISBN 1–85233–555–6 Springer-Verlag London Berlin Heidelberg
a member of BertelsmannSpringer Science+Business Media GmbH
http://www.springer.co.uk

© Springer-Verlag London Limited 2002
Printed in Great Britain

Typeset by Florence Production Ltd, Stoodleigh, Devon, England
Printed and bound by the Athenæum Press Ltd, Gateshead, Tyne & Wear, England
34/3830–543210 Printed on acid-free paper SPIN 10853748

Practitioner Series

LIBRARY

Tel: 01244 375444   Ext: 3301

CHESTER COLLEGE

Springer
London
Berlin
Heidelberg
New York
Barcelona
Hong Kong
Milan
Paris
Singapore
Tokyo

Other Titles in This Series:

Series Editor's Foreword

This is only the fifth book in the 21 volume Practitioner Book Series to be over 300 pages long. But, as before, for good reason. Tony Moynihan has persuaded 30 project managers, all experienced in IT/IS, to talk about how they manage project risk. So a major component of the size of the book is these project managers talking (in a structured way). And since IS/IT projects seem to observe one of Dwight D. Eisenhower's favourite maxims

"When preparing for battle I have always found that plans are useless, but that planning is indispensable."
(R. Andrews (2000) *The New Penguin Dictionary of Modern Quotations*, page 123, reference 6).

I welcome a book that provides us with the 'recipes' of the successful battles conducted by these IT solution providers.

Tony Moynihan deals with the problem of eliciting the project managers' recipes (similar to riding a bicycle, easier to do than to describe to someone else) in a series of phases. In the first phase, 14 experienced project managers were interviewed to determine the factors they take into account when deciding on how to "shape" and manage new projects for new clients. These factors were used in the next phase to create a set of hypothetical project profiles. Twenty experienced IS/IT project managers then discussed (in full in the book) these profiles and how they would handle the situation.

The third phase in the book analyses the 20 conversations to determine the project managers' theories of action. These 'theories' were then examined through a series of theoretical lenses derived from the appropriate literature.

Clearly this book is intended for Practitioners, and in particular, IS/IT/software project managers. But it is also a goldmine for researchers (so much rich source material) and for students (well written descriptions of real life). All in all, a classic example of where the intended Practitioner audience for the book will be greatly increased by the unplanned-for addition of a wide variety of non-Practitioners. This book makes a timely and welcome contribution to the advance of knowledge and understanding in IS/IT.

Ray Paul

Preface and Acknowledgements

There are thousands of books and articles written about managing information systems projects. Most of these books and articles make at least some reference to project risk, and what to do about it. This is another one of those books. So, why bother? What have I got to add to what's already on offer?

I think that what's unique about this book is its approach. I get successful, experienced IS/IT project managers to talk about how they manage risk . . . not about what they are urged to do in books and on training courses . . . but what they ACTUALLY do (or **think** they do!). The bigger part of the book is just people talking. In fact, my biggest fear for the book is that the reader will feel that there is **too much** talking . . . and too little "theory"!

There are people I want to thank. My colleagues at DCU for their feedback and advice. Particularly John Hurley, Rory O'Connor, Chris Curran and Howard Duncan. My wife Nuala for her patience. The University for giving me the time and resources.

But my biggest debt is to the thirty project managers who gave me their time and commitment, and who made this book possible. In the book, I refer to each by his/her first name only. Not because they asked me to, but because it makes me feel more comfortable, and because I told each at the outset that this is how I would do it.

I want to dedicate the book to Owen, one of my thirty "guinea pigs". Owen gave me a lot of honest feedback after my interview sessions with him, and he helped me to debug my interviewing approach. Sadly, Owen died recently. He was held in the highest regard in the Irish IT community, and beyond. He will be remembered with affection.

Tony Moynihan
Dublin City University
July, 2001

Contents

Part 3: Distilling Out the Theories-of-Action

Part 4: "So, It Works in Practice . . . But Will It Work in Theory?"

Appendices

Introduction

Over a decade ago, Studs Terkel wrote a now famous book called *Working*. It has recently been reprinted (Terkel, 1997). In the book, dozens of people take a chapter each to talk about their daily experiences of their jobs . . . as cab drivers, engineers, nurses, secretaries, call-girls . . . a wide canvas! Studs allowed people to talk into his tape recorder . . . no steering, no prompting, no interruptions . . . at least that's how it seems to the reader. Almost pure stream-of-consciousness stuff. When I first read *Working*, I thought "That's a neat idea. Write a book by getting other people to do all the work! No analysis, no interpretation, no conclusion . . . just get people talking, and write it all down."

This book is a bit like *Working*. Most of it consists of people talking about their work . . . but in a structured way. And I do have some analysis, and a lot of interpretation. Like Studs, I don't try to come to firm conclusions.

The people I get talking are not cab drivers or nurses. They are men and women who manage information systems development projects for external clients. They work in software houses, IT consultancies, or whatever. They act as problem diagnosers, system designers, system implementers for their clients. In the words of the trade, they are *IT solution providers*.

What do they talk about in this book? They talk about their "recipes" for managing projects . . . particularly their ways of handling potentially serious problems like unrealistic client expectations, lack of real project ownership, and the like. In fancier language, they talk about their *theories-of-action*.

Argyris and Schön (1978) invented the term *theory-of-action*. They define a theory-of-action thus: "A full schema for a theory-of-action would be as follows: in situation S, if you want to achieve consequence C, under assumptions a, . . . n, do A." (10). So, this book is about situations, actions, consequences and assumptions in managing IS/IT projects . . . as seen by experienced IS/IT project managers (PMs).

Another way to describe this book is in terms of Gluch's notion of a *project-risk-element* (Gluch, 1994). A project-risk-element consists of three components: a risk condition, a default project transition, and a default project consequence. A risk condition is an aspect of the current state of the project that gives cause for concern. A default transition is the likely sequence of states the project will move through if no action is taken to deal with the risk condition. A default consequence is the likely ultimate adverse outcome resulting from the default transition. This book is about IS/IT project-risk-elements, and the strategies that experienced PMs claim to use to cope with these.

The task of eliciting peoples' theories-of-action is not at all straightforward. Schön discusses this problem in the context of how professionals such as consultants, engineers and managers think in action: "When a practicioner displays artistry, his intuitive knowing is always richer in information than any (external) description of it. Further, the internal representation strategy, embodied in the practicioner's feel for artistic performance, is frequently incongruent with the strategies he/she uses to construct external descriptions of it. Because of this incongruity, for example, people who do things well often give what appear to be good descriptions of their procedures which others cannot follow. Everyone who has tried to learn from a book how to ski or write a story knows how difficult it can be to act from such a description" (Schön, 1983: 276).

Even if the expert is willing and able to explain "how he/she does it", there is the question of the validity of the information being volunteered. ". . . activity is context bound and to study any human activity divorced from its context is to study it divorced of its meaning" (Bell and Hardiman, 1988: 57). In other words, the "algorithm" elicited from an expert in an artificial setting, or while the expert is working on a contrived task, may not be the algorithm used "in the real heat of battle".

Not encouraging! So, how did I set about the task?

I broke the study into three phases. In Phase 1, I tried to answer the question: What factors do experienced IS/IT project managers take into account when deciding on how to "shape" and manage new projects for new clients? By factors, I mean things like the characteristics of the system to be built, the nature of the client organization, the sorts of people involved, the technology to be used, the politics of the situation . . . whatever. In Argyris and Schön's terms, the variety of *(S)ituations* to be dealt with. In Gluch's terms, the variety of *risk-conditions* to be removed or managed around. To answer this question, I interviewed fourteen experienced project managers. I asked each PM to choose some recent projects that he/she had managed. Then I asked the PM to compare and contrast these projects with one another, in terms of factors that had differed across the projects, and that had led to differences in the ways in which he/she had "shaped" and run these projects. In Part 1 of this book, I explain how I did all of this. I show examples of some of the interview transcripts, to bring the process I used to life. Then I show the results I obtained.

In Phase 2 of the study, I used the factors I identified in Phase 1 to create a set of hypothetical project profiles. I then talked through these profiles with a further set of twenty IS/IT project managers. I explored with each of these PMs how he/she would handle a project with the particular profile I had chosen (randomly) for him/her. In Argyris and Schön's terms, I defined a set of hypothetical project (S)ituations, and I had the PMs describe how they would handle these situations. In other words, to describe the (A)ctions they would take to handle these situations. In Part 2 of the book, I explain how I did this, and I show the transcripts of all twenty conversations in full. These conversations make up the larger part of the book. This is the Studs Terkel-like piece!

In Phase 3 of the study, I analyzed the twenty conversations. My aim was to distill out the project managers' theories-of-action. I explain how I did this, and I show the results I obtained, in Part 3.

The project managers who helped me in this study are all very experienced and successful people. So, their opinions on how to do things carry a lot of weight. Nevertheless, I felt that I should make an independent effort to demonstrate the "rationality" (or otherwise!) of their theories. This I tried to do in Phase 4 of the study, in which I looked at their theories through a series of theoretical "lenses" that I had selected from the management and organizational literature. These efforts form the bulk of Part 4 of the book.

Who are my target readers? My primary intended readers are IS/IT/software project managers. But I think the book is of relevance to **any** professional who makes his/her living by bringing specialist skills to bear on solving problems for client organizations. Particularly if the problems to be solved are ill-defined, and the solutions entail organizational change. I also hope the book will be read by researchers and students of information systems and software engineering project management.

PART 1

"What Makes Different Projects Different?"

How Project Managers Construe Projects

2

2.1 Introduction and Method

In this part of the book, I try to answer the question: What factors do experienced IS/IT project managers take into account when deciding on how to "shape" and manage new projects for new clients? In Argyris and Schön's terms, the variety of *(S)ituations* that PMs have to deal with in the early, strategic phase of new projects. In Gluch's terms, the potential *risk-conditions* that PMs have to manage.

A group of fourteen experienced IS/IT project managers (PMs) helped me to answer this question. All fourteen PMs had at least eight years' experience of running projects for external clients. All but one were men. All were in the range 35–55 years of age. Ten of the fourteen PMs were owner-directors of their companies. The remaining four PMs reported to an owner-director. The numbers of developers employed in their companies ranged from two to ten persons. The scale of the projects they typically managed fell within the ranges:

Project duration: 2–18 months;

Project effort: 2–36 man-months;

Project team size: 1–6 people.

All worked with mainstream, current technology. All were in the business of providing information systems "solutions" to commercial clients.

I used the technique of *personal construct elicitation* (see Stewart and Stewart, 1981 or Bannister and Fransella, 1989). A personal construct is a bi-polar distinction, or scale, which a person uses when contrasting different people, objects, situations, and so on. For example, for me, an important distinction between dogs is the likelihood that a dog will bite me! So, when comparing dogs, or thinking about a particular dog, I am likely to think in terms of "will he/won't he bite me?" People tend to have multiple sets of many interacting constructs to help them to make sense of the world. The task of identifying the set of constructs used by a person in a particular context is called *personal construct elicitation*. The technique I describe below is one of the standard approaches to construct elicitation.

I began the session with each PM by gathering some basic information about the PM and his company. I then asked the PM to make a list of the systems development projects he/she had worked on as project manager. I explained that the projects need not be very recent, nor need they yet have been completed, nor need they have been undertaken in the PM's current organization. If he/she could identify more than nine projects, I asked him/her to choose the three that were the most successful, the three that were the least successful, and three "in-between."

I then said: *Projects can differ from one another in terms of situational factors that developers must take into account when planning and running them. These factors could relate to the client, the "deliverable", the resources available, or whatever.*

I then randomly chose three projects from the list and said: *Tell me in what important ways two of these three projects were the same, but different from the third, in terms of important situational factors you had to deal with. Particularly factors that created risk.*

I asked the PM to repeat this task with different triads of projects, until no new situational constructs were being elicited (or boredom/exhaustion had set in!).

Finally I asked: *Can you think of any other situational factors that you had to take into account when planning these projects?*

A typical construct elicitation session lasted for about one hour. The shortest session was about thirty minutes. The longest session was about ninety minutes. The minimum number of projects chosen by a PM was four. The maximum number of projects chosen was six. Most PMs chose five projects. Most sessions went very well. Most respondents said they found the exercise intriguing. Boredom was not apparent!

In the next section, I show the verbatim interview teamscripts for five of the PMs: Doug, John, Martin, Rene and Dick. My questions, interjections, and so on, are shown in bold type. I hope these transcripts will help to bring to life the interview process I used.

2.2 "So, What Are the Differences?"

DOUG

I'm going to call my projects A, B, C, D and E.

OK. Now compare C, D and E with one another. What are the important differences?

In D and E we were able to build complete prototypes. We couldn't do this with C because of the nature of the system. In D and E the clients saw the prototype and understood the limitations, so expectations were met 100 per cent In C, we had to carry the can if we didn't analyze the requirements properly. I really don't like not being able to show the client a prototype. If we are not able to do even the simplest prototype or mock-up, we feel very uncomfortable. In fact, if this happened to day, we'd bail out of the project.

Also, in C we weren't implementing on our standard platform, because of client insistence. We were led to believe that everything was OK on the platform to be used. But there was too much learning involved for us. Not a happy experience!

In C there was a change of personnel also. The person who "bought" the system, the accountant, left the company. So it became a "reselling" job again.

B, D and E?

In all three cases we were dealing with the accounts department. D and E didn't have a separate IT department. B was a bank and did. That's both good and bad. The good point of having an IT department is that users' expectations are more realistic. They have a much better understanding of timescales and what's "doable." The existence of an IT department gives more structure to the whole process. Regular meetings and so on. The bad point about IT departments is that they can slow you down, and they can be wedded to old technology.

B, C and E?

C and E stand out because they were much smaller companies with just one or two accounts staff. B had about twenty accounts staff. In B the scope of what we were doing was very narrow – just creditors' accounting. In C and E we were looking at everything – receivables, payables and stock control. We like doing narrow-scope jobs in departments of big companies, not broad-scope jobs in small companies. The expectation of small companies these days, with all the hype about fancy PCs and networks, is that they should be able to get everything of the shelf on a very tight budget. But in larger companies, where you are dealing with only one module within a large central system, they expect to spend much more on it.

B, C and D?

In B and D we were dealing with people who knew what they wanted. In C we were dealing with a marketing guy who didn't seem to know what he wanted, and who didn't appreciate the full scope of the business. B and D involved upgrading existing systems, so we had a framework to work with. C was a green-field job.

A, D and E?

In A and D we were dealing with good accountants. E was a half-baked accountant. We had to spend a lot of time educating people in E to show them what they should be getting from a good system. I find that in smaller companies a major part of the job is educating people to show them what they could be getting, or should be getting from a system. This is true even in the pre-sale phase . . . telling them what they should be looking for in a good system. It can help kill the competition!

D and E were more self-sufficient from a technical point of view . . . running networks, servers, housekeeping and so on. A needed a lot of technical hand-holding at implementation stage. We regularly had to wheel in our engineers to sort things out.

A, C and E?

A and C were totally dependent on us. They just sat back and waited for us to initiate everything. E had a lot more "go" and energy. They were much more self-sufficient and were much more receptive to training. Once the people in E were shown what had to be done, that was the end of the story, whereas the other two were constantly having to be shown what had to be done, and to be held by the hand. Partially, this had to do with staff volatility. Staff were moving all the time in both these companies. New people constantly having to be trained on the system. It ended up that anything that had to be done, they asked us to do it. This business of too much dependency is a hard one to suss out before you get to know a company.

Looking at the whole set of projects, any other big differences?

One of the first things I ask myself at the very start of a new project is, are we dealing with the real decision makers, or are the people we're dealing with just runners for the real decision makers. Then I look to see if there are the real users involved also. The successful projects are those that involve the real decision makers and the real users getting together in one room at the very start of the project.

Then I go through the standard things like: realistic timescales and budget, any signs of hidden agendas, can they afford to pay for the system, what expectations do they have? That's just sussing out your client. Then you pick your players for the game: will they be able to handle this job? Will they be able to handle the client? If the client is going to be very awkward, you want somebody strong to head up your team. Kicking off the project is the next most vital thing. As I said, getting your team together with the client and the users in the one room at the one table. Both key decision makers and the real users. If you don't get this right, your project will go all over the place. Over the years, our bad projects have always been the ones that had bad kick-offs. With a good kick-off meeting, you are well on your way.

JOHN

My projects are Dermot, Fred, Billy, Heather, Ann and Emer.

What about Dermot, Fred and Billy?

Fred stands out here. It was the only project where we suffered a bad debt in all the years I've been running the company. With the benefit of hindsight, there were a number of things about this client which should have set the alarm bells off. The premises were in a not particularly nice place and weren't well maintained. Then I discovered that their product was somewhat unethical. As a company, they did not have the ethics that I would insist on now if I was to do business with them. I suppose I learnt this one the hard way! You need to deal with companies that you feel comfortable to work with. Dermot and Billy were fine. That's the big difference between these three projects.

Billy, Heather and Dermot?

Billy was a project done through their IT department, which meant that the communications structure was much cleaner. The other two were done directly for end-users, which meant that, not only had we to take into account the whole development and implementation process, but we also had to educate people about designing systems, costing them, and how to manage their own participation in the project. Ben was one of the systems that I really cut my teeth on, and on which we very nearly lost our shirt. It was the first big system that I ever managed. And it was in the area of production monitoring. Heather and Dermot were just database applications, and as such you could really scope out the potential downside risks. Because they are fairly straightforward. The production monitoring system was heavily based on doing calculations which were quite complex. Production engineers would be very au fait with the sorts of sums involved, but not computer people. For example, one of the things that needed to be calculated by the system was the percentage diamond usage on a grinding wheel. This sounds very straightforward, but to do it you had to take various factors into account. And it meant that to get the formula right took two or three visits to the plant. Then we had the problem of testing our "recipe". If you are in a situation where someone says "I want that report sorted by surname", you can do it and test it yourself. But we couldn't do this in Ben. So we had to depend on users and engineers for huge input and testing.

Any other differences here?

Heather was done for a foreign national who didn't speak good English. That added a few complexities to the problem. But you just have to deal with these kinds of things on a personal basis.

Heather, Ann and Fred?

I want to separate Ann from the other two. One of the mistakes we made with Ann was that we allowed ourselves to be sucked in to a wide-scope turnkey solution. We were to provide the network, software and services, and support on the network and the software and the hardware. In hindsight I would fight tooth and nail in the future to insist on splitting the software, the network and the hardware into separate projects because these three need different skill-sets. Unless you are specializing in hardware sales you can't really afford to look after it and maintain it, so that's when you need the likes of XXX and YYY to just come in with you and supply the hardware and maintain it and have a separate contract with the client. We found that sending out a programmer to deal with networking solutions took twice the time of a real network guy. The skill-sets are very different. You just can't take a programmer and say he is an all-round animal. It's horses for courses.

Another thing about Ann. Ann didn't have a real project sponsor on the client's side. I have often said jokingly, but very much mean it, that "The best projects we have delivered have had the best clients." When the client knows what they want and how to go about getting it, and are insistent that we give it to them, typically produces the best results. It sounds so obvious! Sometimes clients are only too willing to delegate the entire project to you. You could argue that, if that's what they want – fine. And to a certain extent in the sales process I would agree with you. But when it comes to actually implementing the project you need the client to buy in with you and get really involved. Strong clients good projects, weak clients – fifty-fifty whether you will have a good project.

Fred, Dermot and Emer?

This brings me back to Fred! The one blot on my financial notebook as I see it. It was one of the projects that I had the least technical input into as there was a project leader looking after it and I left him running on his own. In hindsight there were a number of things which should have flagged to me that things weren't going right. The project initially was fixed-price. Then we had two or three extensions to it which they agreed to pay retrospectively. So the . . . anyway, that one went badly wrong.

What about Ann, Fred and Dermot?

In two of these projects we were working directly with the client, not an IT department. And these two projects had ultimately far more problems. The final solutions were neither as elegant or as well done as they could have been. Working directly with the client, you're less likely to hit the right solution with the first design. I say to people "It's not just about moving the mountain to where the client says he wants it, you must put the mountain on wheels so you can move it again when he changes his mind!" The concept of putting the mountain on wheels is the kind of design that I try to get people to do when working directly with clients. But it doesn't yield elegant solutions.

Any other big differences? Between any of the projects?

Yes. Some of these are single-person projects. In my experience, one person can do 100 per cent, two people can do about 80 per cent each. It slides enormously as you have to break a project up. Version control gets harder, communication between people gets harder . . . anyway, we all know that.

I'm trying to think through my mental process of what I do when I scope out a new bespoke project. I suppose I look at the organization itself to see if it can afford the type of solution they are looking for. If someone is asking me to rewrite an accounts system because they want particular features specific to them, in all conscience I have to ask myself "should I not just tell them to buy . . . (off-the-shelf)". I also look at the way they are organized. If I walk into a guy's office and it's in a total mess, and he will be our main point of contact, I would add a couple of grand to the project. Then I look at anything we might have to do for the first time. If we're trying to sell a system that we don't know we can do, I defer things, go home and do some prototyping. I come in the next morning and say "Yes – we can do it."

MARTIN

OK, I've picked five projects. they're all pretty different from each other. I'll call them A, B, C, D and E.

Let's start with projects A, B and C. The big differences you had to take into account?

A and B were somewhat similar in so far as what was to be done was well known from the word go. It became a technical delivery job at an early stage. In C, the requirements were very fuzzy from the start. The biggest part of the job was to define the requirements.

Any other big differences between any two?

No.

What about A, B and D?

Again requirements for A and B were reasonably well defined. D was a bit like C in that the requirements were not too obvious at the start. But also the choice of the technology component of the solution for D was not as obvious as in the other projects, and the most likely technology to be used was pretty much new.

Any other differences?

In D, as well as being unable to foresee requirements and being into new technology, we also used new methods for the analysis and design phase of the project. This project brought a lot of difficult things together. While A was one we knew we could do from the outset. It was old technology, well-known requirements and used a well-known methodology.

Any other differences before we move on?

No.

Let's try C, D and A.

There was one big difference here. In C the part of the system we were working on was a relatively small part of a long-term plan which involved five other future systems. So we had to build a system which was doable in a reasonable timescale, but which would mesh in with these future systems. So we had to design all the systems together. D and A were really stand-alone systems.

B, D and E?

B was a very well-defined project as regards what had to be done, so even though it was bigger than the other two, it was simple to manage. E was different from the other two because it was extremely complex both math-ematically and scope-wise. I'd almost say it was probably too complex to be run as one project. It went in as a single system but I really believe that you should keep deliverables to more manageable proportions. We just got away with it.

What do you mean by complex?

The large number of different screens to support a function was incredible. There was no obvious hierarchy in these because there were so many combinations needed. There were hundreds and hundreds of screens, all interacting together. The real hard bit was to get the users to agree on what they wanted because the whole system was almost too much for any one person to understand.

B, C and D?

C and B technology-wise had nothing hugely new about them. D had a lot of new technology coming into it. Also, I hadn't thought of this one before, D had a huge impact at the user end – on workflow and work procedures. Much more than B and C. In B and C it was changing something that already existed and not much change at that. In D, what we designed was going to totally change the way the company operated. And in B and C, if things went wrong during conversion, the old system could carry on. D had to go right first time. That's it with these three.

A, D and E?

D and E have a lot in common. They are both to do with multi-currency transaction processing. A was much more a database application. A did not have a major user-impact. Once the database was designed properly, we were a fair bit down the line. With D and E we had to go heavily into how users use information and the work procedures that went with this. Maybe the real difference between D and E and A is that D and E were both real-time systems that affected how the company operated, so getting the user-interfaces correct and usable was vitally important.

A, C and E?

E was a complex online system that the organization involved really wanted very badly. And all the people working on it really wanted it. Their level of input to the project was incredible and they wanted to be involved at all stages. With A, the system was being imposed on the company because of legislation changes. That definitely made managing the project different. With A, you had to bring the users with you in so far as you weren't giving them any perceived added value. In E everyone came with you and wanted to come with you. In A the project was seen primarily as a nuisance. They knew it had to happen, but it wasn't going to affect their day-to-day productivity. This meant that you had to be sure that, when people said they agreed with you, that they actually meant it, and didn't just want to get rid of you.

E, D and C?

D was going to really change how the company was going to operate. People at the top really wanted it. But the people directly affected by it had very opposite feelings because of uncertainty about changes to their jobs. So the politics were heavy going.

How about standing back and looking at the WHOLE set of projects. Any other big differences?

Even though A was not addressing a complex system, it had a very tight timescale to it because of the planned legislation changes. It could easily have missed the deadline if things hadn't been done right. It went right mainly because there was one very strong person on the client's side who knew what he wanted, and why he wanted it. I wouldn't say that it couldn't have happened without him, but it was a major help having him there. He stuck with it all the way. So it was very much a hands-on collaboration, rather than his just saying "Get on with it and I hope it works out."

In B, we had to do the pushing. The client was very passive and left things to us to shape up and move along. But this didn't matter too much because we knew what was needed from the word go.

There's one difference that hasn't come up so far. I've already said that E was very complex as regards calculations and screens. But it also needed a number of analysts working on it. For all the other projects we've looked at, you are talking about teams of less than five analysts. E had more than that and I always find that if the analysis level gets big, project management gets very tough. It's very easy to get five or six different sub-systems analyzed . . . but getting them "meshed" together properly is one of the most complex parts of managing a project. E certainly stands out on that one.

Another difference that I see across the projects is that, for some projects, we were able to break the project up into easily "measurable" and manageable modules. This lets you measure where you are. With project A we had very large modules. People on the project were always saying "we are three-quarters through program X . . .". But one could have no level of confidence in this statement. If I was doing that project again, I would break it into more modules. This would have taken extra manpower, but from a risk point of view it would have been worth it.

RENE

I'm calling mine A, B, C, D, E and F.

A, B and C?

B and C were totally custom-built solutions . . . built from scratch. A used one of our existing products, with a custom-built user-interface added. So, in A we were more restricted in what we could offer, in that we had to compromise between what the client wanted and what we could offer. Whereas in B and C, which were built from the ground up, we could give them more or less anything they wanted.

B is somewhat different from the other two in that it was replacing an existing system written by another company. Basically, they wanted a lot of the functionality of the original system, but they weren't happy with its stability . . . its reliability. Performance was very slow, and parts weren't well written.

A is different also in that the specification we drew up was changed several times by the client during the process of development. Their organization was still in its start-up phase, and they kept making internal changes to the organization that affected the product we were building. Even before we gave them the first release, it had deviated from the original specification. Happily, our code was well structured and because of this it was easier to change. Still, we had to cope with this.

Let's try A, B and D.

D is somewhat similar to A in that it was a customization of one of our existing products. D was basically computerizing some existing manual forms. So there were very few changes to the initial specification. Whereas in A they were "growing" their procedures as we went along because they were a new start-up. In D, the manual forms were very well established and had been refined internally before we got involved . . . So they were very clear about what they wanted.

F, C and E?

All of these were built from scratch. E would be different in that it had to link to software that someone else wrote. Also, there was a hardware aspect to E. We had to communicate directly with a bit of custom-built hardware. We made up the hardware ourselves with the help of an engineer. We had to work out our own communications protocol. It was no-way an off-the-shelf solution. It was interesting and it was fun.

C presented different problems in terms of the software. It involved real-time reporting on a stream of incoming information. It needed graphics and was quite tricky in terms of processing. For example, our software had to interpret gaps in the incoming data stream and take appropriate action. We didn't have to buy in any skills for this one, nor did we have to learn new tricks. I had covered the mathematical ideas needed in my computing degree course. F was a very straightforward database system.

C is different from E and F in that C had their own computer department and had a heavy investment in computers. They had a mainframe on site and they had people knowledgeable about computers. Whereas E and F were much less technically-minded, end-user types, especially E who were very naïve on what computers could possibly do for them. In the early discussions with E , we had to work hard to find out exactly what they were looking for. We would ask questions like "Give me your ideal solution?" and "What exactly happens when . . .?" Then we'd say "The computer can do this for you", and they'd say "great!". Then a little later on they'd keep coming up with changes. With C, they had more set ideas. They knew what computers could do, and said what they wanted. Another difference . . . C dictated the pace of the project to us. Whereas in E we had to dictate the pace, and take the responsibility for telling them what computers could do for them.

Can I try A, C, F?

Sure.

A were quite specific on deadlines and dates. We had to meet their deadlines for the various stages of the project. They wanted beta versions on time for them to test. They had listed their own test schedules and the acceptance tests the software had to pass. C and F took the software when WE said it was ready and began running it immediately. If there were subsequent problems, they would give us a phone call. Another thing . . . C and F were single-developer projects, whereas A involved more developers.

I want to bring in D. D is different from A, C and F in that the system in D was specified by someone who didn't end up actually writing the system. It was "speced" by one of our people and developed by another of our people. C and F were "speced" and developed by the same person. I think the person who actually speaks directly with the customer has a much clearer understanding of exactly what's required. No matter how good the spec you pass the developer is, there will be understandings that just aren't conveyed properly. I insist that the person who does the spec checks the work as it progresses . . . and would hopefully spot problems.

Do you prefer that the person who does the spec also does the development?

Yes. But on larger projects it can't always be like this. So, I always set up a direct interface between the programmers and the client. Sometimes even the person who "speced" the project can't answer programmers' questions. So we let them talk to the client directly.

Looking across the whole set of projects, any other big differences?

They are all happy customers!

DICK

I'll call the projects A, B, C, D and E.

D, E and C?

D and E were larger projects. They involved innovative systems and software, at least in terms of our experience. C was really a "commodity" job. D and E were absolutely tailored, one-off situations. In C we half hoped we could turn the solution into a product that could be used in several other situations. D and E were done for big organizations . . . a government body and a large manufacturer/exporter. C was done for a small general medical practice.

Did the scale difference make a difference to the way you had to think about the projects?

With the benefit of hindsight, I would have handled all the projects differently. C proved to be the most troublesome, in so far as we took a very simplistic approach to it. We didn't realize at the start that the client was totally unsophisticated. Even though we produced an early spec and got agreement on it, when it came towards implementation the goalposts kept moving and moving. Their ideas on requirements got more and more refined as they thought more about it . . . so we were chasing a moving target. The users in D and E were much more sophisticated . . . they were much more articulate in defining what they wanted. They were used to formalizing the steps in a project.

We had a meeting this morning about our projects generally and our approach for next year. We feel that dealing with the "lower end" of the market . . . with computer illiterates . . . has enormous costs for us and that clients here have an over-optimistic . . . over-simplistic . . . view . . . some of them can hardly cope if they have to press more than one button! We have now more or less made a rule that we won't get involved in that lower end again because it is too troublesome. There is too much client education involved in bringing a client who is in no way computer literate to being computer-literate . . . and we have to carry that overhead.

We are also learning that, because of the powerful development software available now, we can skip the classical stages like doing a written system specification. We can do a prototype . . . the client can come in, he can see and feel it . . . tell us if he likes it or not . . . we can say "make any modifications you want because it's easy to do . . . you'll be happier in the end". From a selling point of view this is very attractive to the client. But it means we must follow a much more formal route . . . or else we could get into an infinite loop.

B, D and E?

D and E were big database-type projects. We did ground-up systems for these which were totally written by us. In E we had to interface with some other software. There was a big overhead on this because we couldn't get at the source code . . . we literally had to experiment with the interface. We could put pure database people on B and D. On E we needed someone who could get down to almost machine-code level.

B, C and E?

Performance was a big factor in B. It wasn't so important in C and E. We had to change the implementation language in B because we just couldn't get the performance out of it. This was made even worse because our hands were tied initially on the platform that we were writing for. B was very troublesome for us, because they behaved like a trade union. The management knew nothing about computers . . . but they were brilliant negotiators, so every little extra was squeezed out of us. We eventually drew the line and this was the best thing we ever did. The politics there were fierce. There were no politics in E. They were pleasant to work for . . . .the people we dealt with were very bright and computer-literate. They understood where we were coming from, and if we had problems they helped us rather than berate us.

B, C and D?

The key thing about D is that they are a multinational company. So they are quite prepared to spend money to get the best, and had a good understanding of what they wanted done. B were penny-pinchers. Always conscious of the price . . . moaning that they weren't getting value for money. They had the attitude "We can go out and buy EXCEL for $300 and it does a whole lot of things . . . with big screens and a big manual. Your little piece of software does about one tenth of what EXCEL does, and it costs ten-times as much."

A, D and E?

A was an oddball accounting application. They were a charity that had to carefully account for income and expenditure. There were no such notions as profits, value added tax, nominal ledgers, or things like that. We had to invent a new type of accounting system for them.

A, C and E?

A and C were one-man projects. E was much bigger. The client there was more sophisticated and more articulate about requirements. In C, it was the opposite so we had a much bigger overhead and a big cost overrun.

A, B and E?

A was a single-person project. B and E were multi-person projects.

It's interesting . . . putting all these projects in front of me and asking me about differences. It's giving me a framework of the factors that I worry about in projects. Things like . . . computer literacy . . . knowledge of the user about requirements . . . the type of system . . . I feel I'm getting repetitious now . . .

2.3 Analysing the Transcripts

The fourteen interview sessions were tape-recorded and then transcribed onto "hard copy". From the transcripts, I extracted the constructs used by the PMs. In most cases, it was possible to document the constructs verbatim from the transcript. In some cases, it was necessary to do some minor editing of the transcript to remove hesitations, etc. In all cases, the respondents were shown the final wording of their constructs, for approval or amendment. In almost all cases, the respondents said they were happy with the wording, so few amendments were required.

I collected a total of 201 constructs from the 14 PMs. The mean number of constructs identified by the PMs was 14.4. The minimum number identified was 10. The maximum was 19. The modal number of constructs identified was 13.

There was a considerable level of apparent overlap of constructs across the PMs. In the light of this, I collected together constructs that, on the surface at least, seemed to be "saying the same thing". In this way, I formed sets of constructs. If I was at all unsure about including a construct in a set, I allowed it to constitute a set of one. For each set of constructs, I attempted to construct a single, surrogate construct which I felt captured the common meaning underlying the constructs in the set. When I had completed this exercise, I gave each PM a list of his/her original constructs, which he/she had already approved, together with the corresponding surrogate constructs. I asked the PM to confirm, or otherwise, that the wording of the surrogate constructs captured precisely the intended meaning of his/her own constructs. In the great majority of cases, respondents confirmed their happiness with the surrogate constructs. Where the PM felt that a surrogate construct did not accurately capture the intended meaning of one of his/her constructs, I removed his/her construct from its set, and allowed it to stand alone with the original wording. This exercise of replacing sets of seemingly identical constructs with single surrogate constructs reduced the total number of constructs from 201 to 113.

In Table 2.1, I show the reduced set of 113 different constructs, together with the frequency of mention of each construct. The surrogate constructs are those with a frequency of mention greater than one. For the purpose of

Table 2.1 The constructs

#			
	Need to integrate/interface with other systems		**19**
#	**With existing systems:**		
1	We will be developing the application from scratch	The application will be building on a current system (not ours)	3
2	This will be a 'green-field' exercise	We will be inheriting existing technology and systems	1
3	We don't have to change other developer's code	We have to change other developer's code	3
4	We won't have to do any tricky interfacing with existing applications written by others	We will have to do some tricky interfacing with existing applications written by others	4
5	Our system need not integrate closely with any unfamiliar third-party system or product	Our system will have to integrate closely with an unfamiliar third-party system or product	2
6	We won't have to link/communicate directly with unfamiliar hardware devices	Our system will have to communicate directly with an unfamiliar hardware device	1
	With future systems:		
7	The new system doesn't have to be particularly adaptable to future needs	The system must be adaptable enough to cope with unknown future needs	3
8	The system probably won't need to interface with as yet unspecified future systems	The system must be able to interface with as yet unspecified future systems	2
	The existence/competence/seniority/commitment of the project 'patron'		**17**
9	The client/sponsor is a clearly identifiable person	The client/sponsor is diffuse (e.g. a committee)	3
10	We are dealing directly with the key decision-maker	We are dealing with people who can't make the big decisions	2
11	Someone in the client organisation has taken clear, committed ownership of the project	Nobody seems to want to 'own' the project	3
12	The project 'owner' is high enough up the hierarchy to give cover and help if needed	There is no powerful person we can look to for cover and help if needed	1
13	The project 'owner' has a big stake in the success of the project	The project 'owner' has nothing much to lose if the project fails	1
14	The client/sponsor seems to be well able to manage any politics around the project	Our client could be ineffectual in handling any politics around the project	2

15 The person handling the project on the client's side has the time, skill and authority needed	The primary person on the client's side lacks the time, skill or authority to do the job	4
16 Our main point of contact seems to be an organized, competent guy	Our main point of contact seems to be "all over the place"	1
Scale/coordination complexity of the project		**16**
Scale:		
17 This will be a one-person project	This will be a multi-person project	2
18 We will need only one or two people on the project	We will need three or more people on the project	2
19 We will need fewer than five analyst/ designers on the project	We will need five or more analyst/designers on the project	1
20 The project will take three months or less	The project will take more than three months	2
21 The project is less than one man-year	The project is more than one man-year	2
Coordination complexity:		
22 I will have the people/skills needed working full time on the project	The people/skills I need will have to be shared across other projects	1
23 The project will involve managing just a few disciplines	The project will involve managing a lot of different disciplines	2
24 The people who "spec" the requirements with the client will also write the system	The people who "spec" the requirements with the client won't be the writers of the system	1
25 We can do it all ourselves	We will have to do significant subcontracting	3
Level of change for the client		**15**
26 We are just computerizing existing procedures/systems	The procedures/system we design will be new to the client	3
27 We are just upgrading an existing system	We are replacing an existing system with a very different one	2
28 The functionality will not be new to the client	The functionality will be radically new to the client	2
29 There will be no major changes to workflow or procedures	There will be major changes to the customer's workflow/procedures	2
30 The system won't mean a lot of change to the customer's organization structure	The new system will mean a lot of change to the customer's organization structure	1
31 The system won't involve integrating functions now done in different offices	The system will integrate functions now done in different offices	1
32 The system involves just a single functional area	The system will span a number of different functional areas	3
33 The project won't require major skills transfer to the customer	The project will require major skills transfer to the customer	1

Client's knowledge/understanding of requirements		14
34 They seem to have thought out their requirements	They haven't thought out their requirements	3
35 We are dealing with skilled people who know what they want	We are dealing with people who don't know what they want	2
36 They have a good understanding of the problems they want solved	We will have to work with them to identify the problems	2
37 The client knows what he wants and it makes sense	We will have to "educate" the client to show them what they really need	2
38 They know what they want and how to go about getting it	They seem to want to "delegate" the whole project to us	2
39 The client is able to define the problem in IT addressable terms	We will have to define the problem	2
40 It will become clear early on what's needed	This will have to be a "prototype a bit" and then move on from there sort of project	1
IT competence and experience of customer/users		**14**
41 We are dealing with computer-literate users	The users are computer-illiterate	2
42 We are dealing with experienced computer users	We are dealing with people with little or no computer experience	2
43 We are dealing with skilled people who know what is possible/impossible	We are dealing with people who don't know what is possible/impossible	2
44 The client has realistic expectations about time, cost and what's "doable"	The client has unrealistic expectations	4
45 The customer is experienced in running computer projects	The customer is not experienced in running computer projects	2
46 We have an educated customer who knows what's involved in IT projects	We will have to educate the customer about running IT projects	1
47 The people involved know enough to manage their participation in the project	We will have to educate people about how to manage their participation in the project	1
Main source of control over the project		**14**
48 "Structuring" of the project will be driven by the client	"Structuring" will have to be driven by us	1
49 The client has the skills so we can safely share control with them	The client lacks the skills so we will have to take control	1
50 We will have enough control to ensure that what has to be done is done	We will be dependent of what the client's people are willingly prepared to do	1
51 We will have some influence over the requirements	The requirements seem to be already set in stone	1

52 If I feel uncomfortable, I'll be able to say "stop" while the problem is addressed	If I become uncomfortable during the project, I won't be able to say "stop"	1
53 We will be able to juggle a bit with timescales	We are working to a tight client-imposed timescale	3
54 The client is setting firm checkpoints and deadlines	The client is leaving it up to us to set the pace	2
55 We won't have to share control of the project with a third party	We will have to share control of the project with a third party (e.g. other consultants)	2
56 We won't be relying on third parties for critical, non-standard hardware or software	We will be relying on a third party for critical, non-standard hardware or software	1
57 We won't be in the hands of any subcontractors	We will be depending heavily on subcontractors	1
Enthusiasm/support/energy for the project		**12**
58 There seems to be genuine support for the project at all levels	There is support for the project at some levels but not at others	2
59 The people we are dealing with will stick with the project through thick and thin	If things go wrong, we are on our own!	1
60 The users have a real commitment to getting it right	There are no specific users who have a vested interest in getting it right	1
61 The client is willing to put a lot of commitment into the project	The client is not really very committed to the project	3
62 The client is very passive and will leave things to us to push along	The client is very active and will help pull the project along	2
63 The people most affected seem to genuinely welcome the system	The people most affected don't seem to want the system	2
64 There is no reason to think people will be hostile to the project	The people most affected are hostile to the project	1
Developer's experience of the application		**8**
65 We have experience of this application	The application is new to us	5
66 We have all the needed skills in-house	The project needs skills we don't have in-house	2
67 We've done it all before	We will be delivering functionality which is new to us	1
Number of disparate groups to be satisfied		**7**
68 We only have to satisfy a single group of similar users	Our solution has to satisfy multiple groups of users with different needs	4
69 There seems to be no serious internal conflict about what's needed	There seems to be serious internal conflict about what's needed	1

70	The project involves only a single interest group	The system involves conflicting interest groups	1
71	There seems to be no hidden agenda	The "real" agenda is hidden from us	1
	Developer's familiarity with the platform/environment/methods to be used		7
72	The platform/environment is new to us	The platform/environment is familiar	3
73	The development methods to be used are new to us	We will be using familiar development methods	4
	Who we will be mainly dealing with . . .		7
74	We will be dealing mainly with a single individual	We will be working mainly through a group or committee	2
75	We will be dealing directly with the users	We won't be dealing directly with the users	3
76	We will be working through the client's DP department	The project will be done directly for users	2
	Logical complexity of the application		6
77	The application is straightforward	The application is complex	3
78	The processing logic/algorithms are not complex	The processing logic/algorithms are complex	2
79	The system is small/simple enough for one person to get his head around it	The system is too complex for one person to get his head around it	1
	Criticality/reversibility of roll-out of new system		5
80	We can pilot the new system until we get it right	The new system has to go right first time	2
81	If our system fails, they can fall back onto the old system	There is no fall-back if our system fails	1
82	The project has a phased implementation	The whole system must go "live" on a single date	2
	Developer's understanding of the business sector		4
83	The challenges will be mainly technical ones	The challenge will mainly be to understand the client's business	2
84	We know this business sector	This is a business sector we are not familiar with	2
	Maturity of the technology		4
85	We will be implementing on technology which is not very new	We will be implementing on technology which is pretty much new	3
86	The technology to be used is less than leading-edge	We will be using some "frothy" leading-edge technology	1
	Ease of validation of the solution		4
87	We will be able to show the client an early prototype/mock-up	We won't be able to show the client an early prototype/mock-up	3

88	We can validly test our solution before showing it to the client	We need a lot of input from the client to test our solution	1

Client's willingness/capability to handle implementation — 4

89	The client has the willingness and skills to manage implementation issues	We will have to sort out/drive implementation	3
90	The client is competent from an implementation point of view (e.g. managing networks, PCs)	The client needs a lot of technical hand-holding and training for implementation	1

Freedom of choice of platform/development environment — 3

91	We can choose the platform/environment	The platform/environment is a "given"	2
92	We will be defining the technical architecture	The technical architecture is pre-defined for us	1

Developer's knowledge of country/culture/language — 2

93	We know the country/culture	We will be working in an unfamiliar country/culture	1
94	No language problems	We are dealing with people who don't speak good English	1

Stability of client's business environment — 2

95	The client's organization is stable	The client's organization is going through a period of rapid change	1
96	The client's business environment is relatively stable	The client's business environment is changing rapidly	1

Other constructs — 17

97	The decision makers are also the users	The decision makers are not the users	1
98	The users will have a lot of input into the design	The system will be "thrust" on the users without their input	1
99	They are quite prepared for innovative solutions	The solution will have to be a safe, cautious one	1
100	The client's goal seems to be to get the best possible deal out of us	The client seems to view us as a partner in solving the problem	1
101	We can safely use this project to try new things and learn new skills	We must be careful to stick with the tried and tested	1
102	The client will do their own acceptance testing	The client will leave it up to us to test the system and say when it's OK	1
103	It's a batch system	It's a real-time system	1
104	The primary objective is to improve a business process	It's a DSS/EIS/MIS-type system	1
105	The system is mission-critical	The system is not mission-critical	1

106 The client has had good experiences with IT in the past	The client has had big disappointments with IT in the past	1
107 The client's premises are in good shape and in a nice district	The client's premises are in bad shape or in a bad district	1
108 They look like they can afford to pay	It could be hard to get money out of them!	1
109 The client has a forward-looking IT department	The client's IT department acts as a brake	1
110 The client is a single-person or very small company	The client is a larger company	1
111 We are dealing with straightforward, factual, down-to-earth people	The client has a lot of the "aul Irish" about them	1
112 They are cautious people who want everything checked and cross-checked	They will let us get on with it without any unnecessary double-checking	1
113 They insist on everything being "speced out" to the last detail	We aren't tormented with unnecessary bureaucracy	1

providing structure in Table 2.1, I have grouped together constructs which seem to closely share a common theme. I show the themes I identified in decreasing order of the frequency of mention of the constructs under the theme. This categorization is obviously a subjective one. In my defence, I tried to stay as close to the constructs as possible in compiling the categories.

Table 2.2 shows, for each theme, the number of managers mentioning at least one construct under that theme, and the total number of constructs under that theme (many managers had multiple constructs under the same theme.)

2.4 Some Obvious Questions . . .

At this point, a question may have occurred to the reader . . . Are fourteen PMs enough? Would I have identified more constructs and more themes had I conducted elicitation sessions with more PMs? Table 2.3 suggests that this is unlikely. No new themes seemed to emerge after the tenth elicitation session. Would more constructs have been elicited? The answer must surely be "yes", but one's intuition is that any new constructs would overlap a lot with those already elicited.

Here's a second question . . . One would expect that the PMs' theories-of-action would include a lot of "received wisdom" from the IS and software project management literature. Is this the case?

Table 2.2 Number of managers having at least one construct under each theme and the total number of constructs under each theme

#	Theme	Number of managers having at least one construct under the theme	Total number of constructs under the theme
1	The client's knowledge/understanding/clarity regarding the requirements/problem to be solved	12	14
2	The existence/competence/seniority/committment of the project "patron"/"owner"	9	17
3	Level of IT competence and experience of the customer/users	9	14
4	Need to integrate/interface with other systems	9	19
5	Scale/coordination complexity of the project (numbers of disciplines, need to share resources, need to subcontract, etc.)	8	16
6	Main source of control over the project (developer versus client versus third parties)	8	14
7	Level of change to be experienced by the client (to procedures, work flow, structures, etc.)	7	15
8	The need to satisfy multiple groups of disparate users versus the need to satisfy one group of similar users	7	7
9	"Who we will be working through . . . (through users versus the IT department; through individuals versus committees)"	7	7
10	Developer's familiarity with platform/environment/methods	7	7
11	Developer's previous experience of the application	6	8
12	Level of enthusiasm/support/"energy" for the project in the client's organization	5	12
13	Logical complexity of the application	5	6
14	Ease of validation of the solution (e.g. possibility of prototyping)	4	4
15	Client's willingness/capability to handle implementation	3	4
16	Freedom of choice of platform/development environment	3	3
17	Criticality/reversibility of the roll-out of the new system	2	5
18	Maturity of the technology to be used	2	4

19	Developer's knowledge of country/culture/language	2	2
20	Stability of the client's business environment	2	2
21	Developer's knowledge of client's business sector	2	4
22	Other constructs (hard to classify)	8	17
	Total		**201**

Table 2.3 *Cumulative number of themes mentioned by number of elicitation sessions completed*

Number of sessions	1	2	3	4	5	6	7	8	9	10	11	12	13	14
Cumulative number of themes	9	13	17	17	17	19	20	20	20	21	21	21	21	21

And a third one . . . Since all the PMs work at much the same business, one would expect to find a lot of overlap across their theories-of-action, and hence the situational factors they see to be important. Is this the case? In other words, do different project managers characterize project contexts in much the same way? Or do different project managers tend to use different "lenses" when "viewing" projects?

I will try to answer both these questions in the next chapter.

A Closer Look at Their Constructs

3

Now let's try to answer those two questions.

How do the PMs' constructs relate to the risk factors identified in the IS/software project management literature?

Barki, Rivard and Talbot (1993) conducted a wide review of the literature with the aim of building an inventory of IS and software development project risk variables. The literature they reviewed covered both in-house development and custom-development for external clients. Their review included Boehm's work on software project risk items (Boehm, 1989). They identified thirty-five variables, which they subsequently used as the basis for scales in a project risk-assessment instrument. In the same vein, the Software Engineering Institute (SEI) at Carnegie Mellon University published the SEI taxonomy-based risk identification instrument (Carr et al., 1993). This risk-assessment instrument contains 194 questions. Taken together, these two sources cover the ground of project risk factors in a very comprehensive way.

There seems to be a lot of overlap across the constructs I elicited from the PMs, Barki's risk variables, and the questions in the SEI risk-assessment instrument. In fact, there are quite a number of almost one-to-one correspondences. This is reassuring! However, both the constructs, Barki's risk variables and the SEI questions vary over a wide range of levels of abstraction. So it's impossible to make strict one-to-one comparisons across the three. In Table 3.1, I assign Barki's risk variables and, where I could find close correspondences, a selection of the SEI questions, to the various themes in the personal constructs. I have added a final row to Table 3.1 to capture risk variables and topics in the SEI instrument which do not seem to fit under any of the construct themes.

When matched with the personal constructs, there seem to be a number of "gaps" in Barki's list of risk variables. Perhaps the most striking omission is the absence of risk variables measuring the level of the client's understanding of their requirements. Fourteen personal constructs fall under this theme. Of Barki's risk variables, the closest in spirit to this theme seems to be *the complexity of the task to be computerised.*

Table 3.1 Comparison of the construct themes, Barki's risk variables and questions in the SEI risk taxonomy

Construct Themes	Barki risk variables	Some SEI risk questions
The client's knowledge/understanding/clarity regarding the requirements/problem to be solved		Are requirements changing as the product is being produced? Are requirements missing or incompletely specified?
The existence/competence/seniority/commitment of the project "patron"/"owner"	Lack of top management support	
IT competence and experience of customer/users	Lack of user IT experience	Does the customer understand software? Does the customer understand the technical aspects of the system?
Need to integrate/interface with other systems	Number of links to existing systems; number of links to future systems; extent of linkage of system to other organizations	Are the external interfaces completely defined?
Scale/coordination complexity of the project (numbers of disciplines, need to share resources, need to subcontract, etc.)	Number of hardware suppliers; number of software suppliers; number of people on the team; relative project size; team diversity	Do requirements specify a larger/more complex product or require a larger team than the developer is used to?
Main source of control over the project (developer versus client versus third parties)		Does the program have any dependencies on outside products/services?
Level of change to be experienced by the client (to procedures, work flow, structures, etc.)	Extent of changes (to user tasks, organization structure, etc.); degree of computerization of the present system	
The need to satisfy multiple groups of disparate users versus the need to satisfy one group of similar users	Number of users outside the organization; number of users inside the organization; number of departments involved; number of hierarchical levels occupied by users	

Construct Themes	Barki risk variables	Some SEI risk questions
"Who we will be working through . . . (users versus the IT department; individuals versus committees)"		Is there a poor interface with customer, other contractors, senior/peer managers? Are all customer factions involved in reaching agreements?
Developer's familiarity with platform/environment/methods	Lack of development expertise in the team (regarding platform, methods, tools)	Is there prior company or project member experience with the development system?
Developer's previous experience of the application	Team's lack of experience with the application; team's lack of experience with the task (to be computerized)	Do the requirements specify something never done before, or that your company has not done before? Is the staff lacking domain knowledge?
Level of enthusiasm/support/"energy" for the project in the client's organization	Lack of user support	
Logical complexity of the application	Task complexity (of the task to be computerized)	
Ease of validation of the solution (e.g. possibility of prototyping)		Is there any problem with developing realistic scenarios and test data to demonstrate conformance with requirements? Is the product difficult or impossible to test?
Client's willingness/capability to handle implementation		
Freedom of choice of platform/development environment		
Criticality/reversibility of the roll-out of the new system		
Maturity of the technology to be used	Need for new hardware; need for new software	Any state-of-the-art requirements for technologies, languages, hardware, etc.?

Construct Themes	Barki rish variables	Some SEI risk questions
Developer's knowledge of country/culture/language		
Stability of the client's business environment		
Developer's knowledge of client's business sector		
Aspects which don't seem to be covered in the personal constructs	Team's lack of general expertise; leader lack of familiarity with the team; dependence on a few key people; project leader's experience; technical complexity (hardware, software, database); resource insufficiency (money, time, people); intensity of conflict within the team; lack of clarity of role definitions; quality of software supplier support; quality of hardware supplier support	Product design (e.g. internal interfaces, performance constraints); coding and testing; maintainability, reliability requirements; development process (e.g. configuration management); management methods and process (e.g. quality assurance); work environment (e.g. team spirit); programme constraints (e.g. on budget, staffing); contractual issues

Barki has no risk variable relating to the extent of the PM's control over the project. Some examples of personal constructs on this theme are: *"We will have some influence over the requirements/The requirements seem to be already set in stone"; "If I feel uncomfortable at any point, I'll be able to say 'stop' while the problem is addressed/If I feel uncomfortable at any point, I won't be able to say 'stop'"; "The client is setting firm checkpoints and deadlines/The client is leaving it to us to set the pace."*

Barki's risk variables do not address the nature of the "interface" to the client organization through which the project manager must work. Examples of constructs on this theme are: *"We will be dealing mainly with a single individual/We will be working mainly through a committee"; "We will be working through the client's DP department/The project will be done directly for users."*

Four of the fourteen PMs in our study mentioned constructs dealing with the possibility (or otherwise) of validating and testing the "solution" before unveiling it to the client. Examples of these constructs are: *"We will be able to show the client an early prototype or mock-up of the solution/We won't be able to show the client an early prototype or mock-up"; "We can validly test our solution before showing it to the client/We will need a lot of input from the client to test our solution."* There appear to be no corresponding risk variables on Barki's list.

Other themes running through the personal constructs which do not appear to have corresponding risk variables concern the client's willingness and capability to handle implementation issues, the degree of freedom of choice of platform/environment available to the developer, and the criticality and degree of "reversibility" of the roll-out of the new system.

Examining Table 3.1 from the other direction, a number of Barki's risk variables do not seem to be **explicitly** reflected in the personal constructs. These variables deal in the main with personal characteristics of the members of the PM's project team, the degree of technical complexity of aspects of the solution, and the adequacy of the resources available to the project. This does not imply that these aspects of a project are unimportant to our PMs. These variables may not have surfaced because of the particular projects which our PMs chose for the construct elicitation process.

How do the personal constructs relate to the items on the SEI risk assessment instrument? Constructs under the following themes have **many** close "equivalents" amongst the SEI questions:

– Level of IT competence/experience in the client organization

– Integration/interfacing needs of the new system with other systems

– Level of scale/co-ordination complexity of the project

- Developer's familiarity with the platform/environment/methods to be used

- Developer's previous experience of the application

- Ease of validation of the solution

- Maturity of the technology to be used (target platform, etc.)

Constructs under the following themes seem to have **some** close equivalents amongst the SEI questions:

- Client's understanding of the requirements/problem to be solved

- Distribution of "control" over the project (developer versus client versus third parties)

- Breadth/Depth of the interface with the client organization

Constructs under the following themes seem to have **no** close equivalents amongst the SEI questions:

- The existence/competence/seniority/commitment of a client project "patron"

- Level of change (to structures, procedures, etc.) to be experienced by the client

- Multiplicity/diversity of users to be satisfied

- Level of enthusiasm/support/"energy" for the project in the client organization

- Logical complexity of the application

- Client's willingness and capability to handle implementation/deployment issues

- Criticality/reversibility of the roll-out of the new system

Conversely, as can be seen from Table 3.1, there are some areas addressed in the SEI instrument which are not reflected in the personal constructs. These seem in the main to relate to technical aspects of the product, and to the management methods and processes to be used in the project.

These differences can probably be at least partially explained by differences in the contexts from which our study and the SEI instrument are drawn. The

PMs are information system "solution-providers", mainly to smaller (<4,000 people) business organizations. The scale, complexity and degree of formality of their projects is limited. The SEI taxonomy seems designed to support risk identification for larger, more formalized, technical (e.g. embedded systems) projects for bigger industrial/defence organizations. Two different worlds?

So what does all of the above add up to? The PMs' personal constructs reflect most of the risk factors identified in the IS/software project management literature. Also, the PMs' constructs include some interesting, additional factors which do not seem to be reflected in the literature. Examples of these additional factors include aspects of "requirements uncertainty" (very much a multi-dimensional notion, to judge by the constructs), the source and nature of control over the project, and aspects of the "interface" between the developer and client organizations. This is all very reassuring! Our PMs seem to be a sane bunch of people!

Here's the final question (for now) . . .

Do different PMs use different sorts of constructs?

Were there any marked "differences" between the constructs elicited by the different project managers? All seemed to express their constructs at much the same level of abstraction, and in much the same emotionally "cool", measured language. In expressing their constructs, they seemed to draw on a shared ontology ("vocabulary") of project management . . . I heard the same terms ("client", "patron", "user", "requirements", and so on) being used repeatedly across the elicitation sessions.

But what of variation in the numbers and content of the constructs? In Appendix 1, I show the numbers of constructs elicited under each theme for each project manager. Two features stand out from this data. The first feature is the obvious variation in the total number of constructs elicited across project managers. The minimum number elicited was ten and the maximum number elicited was nineteen. There are so many plausible explanations for this variation that any attempt at interpretation is probably pointless. Alternative explanations include variation in speech rates, variation in tendency towards digression or other distractions, and so on. Variation in cognitive complexity (the number of dimensions that an individual tends to use in making distinctions between things) is probably one of the factors at work here (see Bieri, 1955). But any effect from this source is inextricably confounded with the effects of other variables.

A second feature in the data in Appendix 1 is the variation from PM to PM in the proportions of their constructs falling under the different themes. Some

PMs seem to "focus" on some combinations of themes to the relative neglect of other themes. I tested the statistical significance of this apparent variation in "focus" across PMs by fitting a linear model to the data in Appendix 1. I used the GLIM statistical package and chose a log link function and a Poisson error term (see Healy, 1988). GLIM converged after four cycles and calculated the residual scaled deviance to be 320 with 273 degrees of freedom. This result is statistically significant at the .025 level. So, there is evidence of significant variation across PMs in the proportions of their constructs which fall under the various themes. In other words, there is evidence that different PMs seem to focus on different combinations of themes.

How are we to interpret this finding? Could this variation in "focus" across PMs be an unintended consequence of the way in which I ran the construct elicitation sessions? For example, did I unwittingly encourage PMs to go down some roads to the exclusion of other roads? Or once a PM had identified a construct falling under a particular theme, did I encourage him/her to stick with that theme to the neglect of other themes? I'm confident that neither of these potential sources of bias was present. If I erred at all, it was to encourage the PMs to take a broad, rather than a narrow perspective of their selected projects.

Could the differences between the PM's constructs simply reflect the fact that different PMs systematically run different sorts of projects? There is no reason to believe that this is the case. All PMs operate in the same business and cultural milieu; all develop mainstream business applications for the same sorts of clients; all use much the same technology; all run projects of much the same scale.

Could the differences between the different PMs' constructs be just a chance consequence of the particular combinations of projects that the PMs happened to select for the elicitation process? For example, a PM who failed to identify any constructs under a particular theme may have done so simply because the projects he/she happened by chance to choose did not vary across that theme. Or, on the other side of the coin, a PM who identified an apparently untypically large number of constructs under a particular theme may have done so because of real, objectively "large" variation across his/her projects under that theme. The fact that the variation across PMs in the proportions of constructs falling under the different themes is statistically significant at the .025 level seems to rule out this explanation.

I showed a number of the PMs the lists of constructs elicited from some other PMs, and asked the question: "How come some of the lists seem to be so different?" A typical response was: "Maybe they have to deal with different situations from me. You asked me for the important differences across the projects I picked. That's what I gave you. By not mentioning these other things, I wasn't saying that they aren't important." This response doesn't get us much further in answering the question!

In summary, there is a lot of overlap across the constructs of the different PMs. It would be surprising if this were not the case. But there is evidence that different PMs tend to focus on different aspects of the situation. This may have implications for the selection and training of PMs. In particular, it points up the need to ensure that multiple perspectives are taken when appraising and planning new projects, if the dangers of "myopia" are to be avoided. It is tempting to propose a taxonomy of PMs on the basis of the pattern of their constructs (the "politician", the "technician", and so on), but there are probably too few PMs in the present study to support this.

. . . finally, an overall impression of the constructs . . .

When one steps back and takes a broad view of the constructs, what overall impression is gained? The constructs strongly suggest that the PMs see themselves as filling the roles of problem diagnoser, problem solver and change agent on behalf of their clients. The constructs seem to capture many of the concerns one would expect to see exercising the mind of an organization development consultant "scouting out" a new intervention. As self-described "solution providers", this is not unexpected.

Maister (1993) proposes a "spectrum of practice" which allows one to place a professional services firm into one of three categories. The "brain" category represents service firms that deal with complex, high-risk, high-expertise, "one-off" problems for their clients. The other extreme, the "procedural" category, represents firms that deal with straightforward, well understood, "programmable" interventions (e.g. accounting firms – his example!). The "grey-hair" firm falls somewhere in the middle. The constructs suggest that the PMs see themselves as being grey-haired! I'll return to this point in the final chapter.

PART 2

"You Want to Know What I'd Do About It?"

Method

4

In Part 1, I identified at least some of the situational factors that IS/IT project managers take into account when shaping up and managing new projects. Particularly factors that can contribute to project risk. I did this using *personal-construct* elicitation. In Part 2, I will start to answer the question: How do PMs respond to these situational factors? In particular, how do they cope with problems like unrealistic customer expectations, disagreement on project goals, lack of client "ownership" of the project, and so on? To do this, I interviewed twenty PMs. The chapters that follow contain their (largely uncensored!) prescriptions for dealing with problems like these . . . their *theories-of-action*. But first, I must describe how I prepared for the interviews, and describe the interview procedure itself.

How I did it in brief . . .

I used the PMs' personal constructs to create five hypothetical project profiles. I randomly chose one of these project profiles for each of the twenty PMs. Then, with each PM, I explored how he/she would handle a project with his/her particular profile. In Argyris and Schön's terms, I defined hypothetical project (**S**)ituations, and I had the PMs describe how they would handle these situations. In other words, to describe the (**A**)ctions they would take.

How I did it in detail . . .

I chose thirty-two constructs from the full set of 113 constructs shown in Table 2.1. I picked these thirty-two constructs with a view to including at least one construct from each of the twenty construct classes, and at least two constructs from the most highly-populated construct classes. In other words, I tried to obtain a good cross-section of the constructs. After pilot-testing my planned interview procedure, I made minor changes to the wording of some constructs, and I added two new constructs. The final set of thirty-four constructs is shown in Table 4.1. The numbers in parentheses are the original construct numbers in Table 2.1. The rightmost column in

Table 4.1 The constructs from which the hypothetical project profiles were constructed

1 (4)	No tricky interfacing with existing applications	Some tricky interfacing with existing applications	Any tricky interfacing?
2 (15)	The customer's PM has the needed time/skill/authority	The customer's PM lacks the needed time/skill/authority	Has their PM time/skill/authority?
3 (18)	We will need only one or two people on the project	We will need three or more people on the project	Need >two people on our team?
4 (20)	The project will take three months or less	The project will take more than three months	Project duration >three months?
5 (57)	We won't need to subcontract anything	We'll have to do significant subcontracting	Must we subcontract?
6 (29)	No major changes to the customer's workflow/procedures	Major change to the customer's workflow/procedures	Major change to customer's procedures?
7 (32)	The new system involves only a single functional area	The new system will span a number of functional areas	Number of different functional areas involved?
8 (84)	We've a good knowledge of the customer's industry	We've little or no knowledge of the customer's industry	Our knowledge of their industry?
9 (68)	We've only to satisfy a single group of similar users	We've to satisfy multiple groups of users with different needs	Must satisfy different groups with different needs?
10 (42)	We're dealing with experienced computer users	We're dealing with inexperienced computer users	Users' computer experience?
11 (44)	The customer has realistic expectations about time, cost and what's "doable"	The customer has unrealistic expectations about time, cost and what's "doable"	Realistic expectations?
12 (45)	The customer is experienced in running computer projects	The customer is not experienced in running computer projects	Their experience in running IT projects?
13 (53)	We'll be able to juggle a bit with timescales	We'll have to work to tight, customer-imposed timescales	Tight, customer-imposed timescales?
14 (11)	Someone on the customer's side has taken clear, committed ownership of the project	Nobody wants to "own" the project	A committed project "owner"?

No.			
15 (63)	The people most affected seem to genuinely want the new system	The people most affected don't seem to really want the new system	People most affected really want the system?
16 (65)	We've experience of this application	The application is new to us	Our knowledge of the application?
17 (72)	The platform/environment is familiar to us	The platform/environment is new to us	Our knowledge of the platform?
18 (73)	We will be using familiar languages/tools	We will be using unfamiliar languages/tools	Our knowledge of the languages/tools?
19 (75)	We'll be dealing directly with the users	We'll be working through their IT department	Who we'll be working with (users or IT)?
20 (77)	The application is straightforward	The application is complex	Application complexity?
21 (87)	We'll be able to show the customer an early prototype	It won't be possible to show the customer an early prototype	Feasible to prototype?
22 (110)	The customer is a very small company	The customer is a larger company	Are they a big versus small company?
23 (105)	The new system isn't mission-critical to the customer	The new system is mission-critical to the customer	Mission-critical application?
24 (104)	It's a transaction processing system	It's an MIS/DSS-type system	TP versus MIS/DSS application?
25 (71)	There seems to be no hidden agenda	The "real" agenda seems to be hidden	Any hidden agendas?
26 (89)	The customer has the willingness and skills to manage implementation issues	We'll have to sort out/drive implementation	Are they able/willing to drive implementation?
27 (3)	We won't have to change other developer's code	We'll have to change other developer's code	Must change other developer's code?
28 (55)	We won't have to share control of the project with a third party	We'll have to share control of the project with a third party (e.g. consultants)	Must share control with a third party?
29 (80)	We can pilot the new system until we get it right	The new system has to go right first time	System must go right first time?
30 (new)	We've no credible competitor for this project	We are up against a credible competitor for this project	Have we a credible competitor?

31 (new)	This is probably a "one-off" project for this customer	This project could lead to other projects for this customer	A 'one-off' project for them or the first of a series?
32 (7)	The new system doesn't have to be particularly adaptable to future needs	The new system must be adaptable enough to cope with unknown future needs	How adaptable must our solution be?
33 (39)	The customer is able to define the problem in IT-addressable terms	We will have to work with them to define the problem	Can they define their problem?
34	They don't disagree amongst themselves about what's needed	They disagree amongst themselves about what's needed	Agree amongst themselves on what's needed?

Table 4.1 contains abbreviated descriptions of the constructs. In the interview transcripts to follow, I have "text-replaced" the full constructs with my abbreviated descriptions. But I must emphasize that the PMs worked with the full constructs, not my abbreviated descriptions.

I next constructed the five hypothetical project profiles. I did this by selecting different combinations of poles from the chosen constructs. A project profile consisted of thirty-four poles, one drawn randomly from each of the thirty-four chosen constructs. To construct a project profile, random numbers were used to decide whether the left-hand pole or the right-hand pole of the construct should appear in the profile. Within any one profile, a fixed probability of selecting the right-hand pole (in the case of most constructs, the "risky" pole) was applied. But this probability was systematically varied across the profiles. In this way, I generated large variation in apparent "riskiness" across the five hypothetical projects.

The five project profiles are shown in Appendix 2.

I interviewed twenty IS/IT project managers. Four of these twenty PMs had participated in the earlier construct-elicitation process. As before, all managed IS/IT development projects for external clients. All twenty had at least six years' experience of running projects. All were in the range thirty to sixty years of age. Almost all were owners or directors of their companies. The numbers of developers employed in their companies ranged from two to twenty persons. The scale of the projects they typically managed fell within the ranges:

Project duration: 3–36 months;
Project effort: 3–250 man-months;
Project team size: 1–9 people.

I spent one to two hours with each PM. I explained that the purpose of the exercise was to learn more about the "recipes" that experienced PMs use to cope with project risk, and that a hypothetical project would be used to help with this task. I asked the PM for permission to tape-record the session. In all cases, this was forthcoming. I then gave the PM a set of thirty-four index cards, one for each of the thirty-four constructs. The top, visible face, of the card showed both poles of the construct. The bottom face, **which I asked the PM not to look at**, showed the pole that belonged to the hypothetical project profile which I had randomly chosen for that particular PM.

I asked the PM to sort the constructs into three piles. The first pile to contain constructs that, depending on which of the two poles applied, could make a VERY BIG DIFFERENCE to the "riskiness" of a project. The other two piles to contain constructs that could make a BIG DIFFERENCE and SOME/ LITTLE/NO DIFFERENCE to "riskiness", respectively.

Then I asked the PM to focus on the VERY BIG DIFFERENCE pile. I asked the PM to choose the construct that could make the biggest difference to project risk. I then explored with the PM why he/she had chosen as he/she had done. I next asked the PM to turn over the card to reveal the pole which applied to the hypothetical project, and to give his/her reaction to this piece of information. I then explored the strategies, tactics, tricks, and so on, that the PM would use to cope with that pole. This procedure was repeated until all of the VERY BIG DIFFERENCE constructs had been turned over. At intervals, I asked the PM to sum up his/her feelings about the unfolding project, and to describe the strategies/tactics/"ploys" she/he would advise a PM faced with managing that project to use. I concluded the session by asking the PM to rate the likely outcome of the project on a set of scales.

The following chapters contain the interview transcripts that I gathered. As before, my interjections are shown in bold type.

5

ALAN

Here's my VERY BIG DIFFERENCE pile . . .

Must share control with a third party?   Realistic expectations?   Our knowledge of the platform?   Any hidden agendas?   Must we subcontract? Our knowledge of the languages/tools?   A committed project "owner"? Mission-critical application?   Tight, customer-imposed timescales?   Must change other developer's code?   Any tricky interfacing?   Our knowledge of the application?

What makes the VERY BIG DIFFERENCE pile different?

It's about the "unknowns". Things like the customer doesn't know what he wants, or they're going to change their minds about what they want. There's stuff around control issues like "will there be more than ourselves involved in the project?" There's the whole area of our experience with the software we're going to work with. It's all about going in and not knowing if we have a level playing field . . . not being able to say "we know everything in advance about this project . . . we can do it". It's about things that are not directly controllable by us. Things that could come back and bite us.

Just work with the most important pile. Which would be the most useful questions to answer?

I'm going for . . .

> *Realistic expectations?* and *A committed project "owner"?*

These are serious ones. Obviously we'd never agree to a project based on what the customer THINKS it will take! We go in and see how big the job is ourselves. we'd try to understand more about the requirements. Then we'd tell them whether they're right or wrong. This would happen in the pre-proposal phase or in the first weeks of the project. Then we can see where the gaps between reality and their expectations are. Often these time and cost expectations are set by someone outside the department you're dealing with, who doesn't understand the application or its complexity, or lack of complexity. Getting the expectations gaps out into the open early on is paramount. Otherwise you're on a hiding to nothing.

I'm looking . . .

> *The customer has unrealistic expectations . . .*

Given this, I'll take . . .

> *A committed project "owner"?*

next. This one ties in with the last one about expectations. We need to be talking to one person, or one group of people, who is controlling the project from the customer's side. Somebody who says "This is OUR project." Someone who can tell us what they really want from us. And if we say "that's not feasible . . . we can never get it done in that time . . . with that budget" will let us examine the scope of the project, and then come back and say what we CAN achieve in that time or with that budget. You can't play simultaneously with variables like time, cost and functionality, and not be pliable on at least one of them.

What would you do if nobody wanted to own it, and they had unrealistic expectations? Would you walk away?

It's a tough call to make. There's a train of thought that says we should walk away. What we would more likely do is to try to define a scope for the project ourselves, and then to tell them what we're proposing to do. If they agree with what we say we're going to do, we'd do it. If no one will sign off on what we say we're going to do, then we'd have to walk away, because things aren't tied down tightly.

Let's see . . .

> *Nobody wants to own the project*

Because no one wants to own it, I'd be suspicious that there's something else going on. Maybe someone has taken us into the company to act as a scapegoat . . . to prove some point . . . which is often the case. Bring in a contractor . . . get him to say no, it can't be done . . . I told you so! . . . blah . . . blah . . . blah. Or maybe just getting a free feasibility study done, or whatever. Or maybe using the project to force change on somebody else. If we can't find an "owner" . . . any way to know what they really want . . . and we smelt a hidden agenda, we wouldn't become involved. It's too risky. We would walk away very quickly.

So,. . .

Any hidden agendas?

is next.

And if you smelt a hidden agenda, you'd really walk away?

Well, I'd say we SHOULD walk away. Of course, it's a public profile thing. It's hard to walk away from something you've just won . . . particularly a prestigious contract with one of the big banks or something. If it's with Joe Bloggs down the street, it's easier to walk away. In this case, if it was a prestigious client, someone I'd been working to get into, as nobody seems to want to own it, you'd have to drive it from your end . . . fix the scope yourself . . . work on the unrealistic expectations . . . tell them what you're going to do, what they're going to get (if there's no owner, you'll get your way anyway), and forget the agenda, hidden or not.

But how would you protect yourself against something going really wrong?

In this kind of scenario, you'd insist on sign-offs on proposals, specifications . . . EVERYTHING . . . before starting to move on the work. We wouldn't do ANYTHING without getting somebody on their side to commit. In this situation, we have found that people are reluctant to sign off . . . to put their name to anything. But you really have to press them to the point where, even if they're not signing off, at least you've some kind of back-up, even a memo or an email that says "I will sign this off, but I can't do it this week." We have a defined development process. It's a big wad of procedures and templates. On some projects, we don't need all this because we have a defined owner . . . we know who we are talking to . . . everybody is happy with what's happening. But in the scenario we're looking at here, you're talking about getting as much coverage of your rear as possible. So everything should be done in triplicate and signed off before you go any further with anything.

Let's see . . .

There seems to be no hidden agenda

OK. These two next . . .

Must share control with a third party? and *Must we subcontract?*

Once we've to subcontract, or to share control with a third party, there's the risk to us that they won't do the job properly, or that they'll walk away halfway through the project, or something like that. I think I'll pick . . .

50

Must share control with a third party?

If there's a third party involved we need to know what role they're going to play . . . where the interdependencies between us are . . . whether they are lateral with us or not . . . basically understand the interfaces between us . . . because we need to know how it will impact us if they fall on their faces. And we need to know all this very quickly.

And if you had to share control?

We'd want to know what kind of processes they have in place. As I said, we have an application development process that we use to control everything we do . . . right down to the format of status reports and that kind of thing. we'd want to know how they control their people and their processes. If we're dependent on them for something they do, we'd need to know more about them. Are they a third party we or the client has worked with before? Or are we jumping into bed with strangers? If the latter, what are their references? What have they done before? Are they facing technology or ideas new to them in the project? Basically, we need to know we can work with them . . . where our dependencies lie.

Let's see . . .

We won't have to share control . . .

Fine. On the contracting one, we contract nearly all the time because we don't want to pigeon-hole ourselves on the sort of work we do . . . mainframe . . . client–server . . . object-oriented . . . the open systems stuff. So, rather than try to carry experts in all these areas, we typically carry experienced project managers or project leaders, and then fatten out the team with contract people. By the way, I assume this is what you mean by subcontracting? Anyway, we don't have an issue with subcontracting as long as we establish what's needed early in the project. The issue comes down to managing the resource. If we're contracting big numbers, we're going to lose some of them during the course of the project, and we need to be able to safeguard against that. We need to have some way of keeping them, and if we can't, to have a replacement process. The key is to have a well-defined development process so that, if someone falls off the manpower list, and we bring in someone else, they can slot in easily. That's basically it.

Turn the card over . . .

We'll have to do significant subcontracting

What do you make of the project so far?

We don't have anyone at the customer end to talk to us. They have unrealistic expectations. The danger here is if we don't define the scope clearly . . . tie it down . . . "This is what we're going to do." No one is going to give us true direction, so we'll have to define our own scope and drive it through . . . we're going to have to pretty much define the project. The danger with significant subcontracting is that you don't own the people. Whereas with employees you can define for them a bit more what they can and cannot do. We'll have to make sure that the contractors don't spin off into genius mode and lose the run of themselves, as has happened.

I'm sticking with the project infrastructure and going for . . .

Tight, customer-imposed timescales?

This one ties in with the kind of resources we're using. If we're working to tight imposed timescales, it's about getting the right people at the right time. It doesn't help that we have to use contractors. But we're lucky in our company in that we have two sides to our business: development projects and IT staff recruitment for other companies. If we can juggle the timescales, we can drive the subcontracting more easily. We can say "We need this fellow now . . . we don't need the other fellow until later."

I'm looking . . .

We'll have to work to tight, customer-imposed timescales

So again this comes back to defining the scope . . . defining as clearly as possible what we're going to do and when. As this must be driven by us, it's less of a risk because we're saying what we are going to do, IF they're prepared to play ball on this basis.

Where the client is trying to impose tight timescales, you need to work with the client to get some degree of flexibility. You need to say "If we ask you for something today and it's not there, we'll be flexible and wait until next week, but you'll have to be flexible too, because it won't be done until then.". . . that kind of deal.

What's next?

We're down now to the actual contents of the project itself. So, I'll go for . . .

Mission-critical application?

If it's mission-critical, it's a big risk to us because we're touching something which, if it breaks, will have a serious impact on the client. In the situation we're looking at on this project, we're getting zero cooperation from them.

This is a really serious issue if the system is mission-critical. It means we're going to develop the system on our own, and then give it to someone who doesn't want to own it . . . who maybe doesn't want to know anything about it. But if it's mission-critical, these are the very people who should be testing it thoroughly. This is real walk-away stuff. You'd have to set the expectation that the users would test it for you. If you can't depend on them to do this, and if, for political or other reasons, you can't walk away, you'd have to plan to beef up your testing effort. This will impact on time and cost . . . beware those unrealistic expectations again!

I'm looking . . .

> *The new system is mission-critical . . .*

So it's mission-critical and we're getting no help from the lads over there. So they're unlikely to help us generate and apply business test cases. This is a serious exposure. We can test the functionality we've developed ourselves, but it should be down to their business people to confirm that the system does what they want it to do. So, we'll have to drive the business testing. This means we must lower the requirements . . . be less ambitious . . . focus on what's reliably "doable". No rocket science!

I see you're building up a little sub-pile of cards there?

> *Our knowledge of the application?   Must change other developer's code? Any tricky interfacing?   Our knowledge of their industry?   Our knowledge of the platform?*

Yes. Most of these are around our familiarity with things like the platform, tools, code involved. They all boil down to the same thing. If we know these . . . have experience of these . . . there's less risk to us. If we don't know the stuff, we're into hiring contract people. If it's all new stuff, our project manager can't really control his people because he doesn't know whether they're doing a good job or a bad job, because he doesn't know the technology. we've had situations like this. Where managers who were mainframe-based were handling C++ projects and couldn't relate to the people they had on board. They'd ask their people, "Were they doing OK?" And they'd answer "We're doing fine. No problem." But the manager couldn't count on this because he didn't have the knowledge.

What's the solution . . . if you're stuck with an unfamiliar platform or tools?

We're back to contracting. It's about getting experienced people that you know know the technology. But also who can relate to people. You don't want techno-heads who know it all, but who can't talk to other people! We want people who can relate to other people in the group . . . relate what's happening . . . what their problems are. If you can't find the right people, you just have to manage it more closely. You need regular weekly meetings with all the people on the team. To say "Tell me what you're going to do next week . . . what's deliverable next week . . . and next week I'll ask you, did you do it? . . . and if you didn't, you'll tell me why." It's those kind of things.

Pick just one or two from that sub-pile.

I'll go for . . .

Any tricky interfacing?

Interfacing across applications affects the complexity of the project. If there is tricky interfacing, it's going to be a more dangerous project. Again, it's related to what's doable and what's not. If there's tricky interfacing and we're using contractors we haven't great experience of, then it's a bigger risk again. it's about getting the people who really understand the interfaces . . . the experts. you'll have to pay more!

Look . . .

Some tricky interfacing . . .

Next?

I'm taking . . .

Must change other developer's code?

We've seen often in projects that other people's codes can be spaghetti. And if there's a lot of functionality to be defined (in a tight timescale as we have on this project), it can take more time to understand and remedy the other code than it would to develop it from scratch. And we have a tight timescale on this project. Anyway, in scoping the project, we'd separate out the new programs to be written from the programs to be changed. For the new programs, we'd use a standard estimating template. So it's easier to do the estimation for these. For the stuff to be changed, we'd have more than one person go through the code to try to understand it. If we couldn't get away with a time-and-materials deal, if we had to quote a fixed price, we'd have to err on the side of extreme caution and bump up our figures.

I'm looking . . .

We'll have to change . . .

It's not looking great. This is going to hit time and cost. Those unrealistic expectations yet again!

Looking at the pattern for this project, advice to your pal?

The first thing to do is to define the scope of the project, what we're going to do, early on and stick with it. If there's any change to this, handle it as a change request. In other words, you say "This is exactly what we're going to do. We want agreement on this now. If you want us to do more, we'll get this piece done first, then move on from there." The next issue is finding the right people to do the job. This has the feel of being a team project. Maybe three or four plus. So, having a team that can work together is critical. Having a project leader on site who isn't involved in actual development is paramount in this case. Someone to keep the team and the customer happy. Especially in a project like this that has a potentially creeping scope. Someone who is on the ground watching the project and saying, this is what we are going to do . . . everyone is on target or not on target . . . handling the issues . . . and the communication, making sure the issues are handled on a weekly basis . . . and guarding against creeping scope.

How do you think this project will turn out?

I "agree" that it's likely to be a positive experience for the customer IF we manage it properly. it's going to take a lot of effort on our part . . . dragging stuff out of them when they don't seem to want to cooperate. But if it's handled right, at the end of the day I agree that it will be a positive experience for them.

And for the developer?

It should be a positive experience once this shield (early definition of the scope, and our man on the ground guarding against creep) is put up. It looks like there could be pressure from the client's side of the fence, but if we have a good man in the middle, to take that pressure, it should be positive for the other people.

Any cards missing?

I can't think of anything off hand. Some of the concerns in this project are around the ownership thing. we've had this problem on a number of occasions. Not only there not being an owner, but there being TOO MANY owners . . . three or four people who say "I'm driving this project". . . demanding different doables and different deliverables . . . all chiefs and no Indians! Maintaining that shield is the key thing here, but even that can be broken.

ANDRE

6

Here's my VERY BIG DIFFERENCE pile . . .

*Agree amongst themselves on what's needed?   A committed project "owner"?
Realistic expectations?   Our knowledge of the languages/tools?   Tight,
customer-imposed timescales?   Has their PM time/skill/authority?   Need
>two people on our team?   People most affected really want the system?
Users' computer experience?   Any hidden agendas?   Must we subcontract?
Must share control with a third party?   Any tricky interfacing?   Major
change to customer's procedures?   Mission-critical application?*

What's different about the VERY BIG DIFFERENCE pile?

One set of big issues for us in the VERY BIG DIFFERENCE pile relates to the
client . . . Do they know what they want? Are they prepared to run with it
. . . have enthusiasm? Do they agree amongst themselves? Is somebody
holding the project together? Are they genuine people with no hidden
agendas? Have they realistic expectations about typical timescales? And so
on. If not, you are beating your head against a brick wall. The second
important set of issues has to do with whether or not we have real control
over the project . . . for example, are we are on our own in the project, or do
we have to work with other people? We just don't subcontract anything in
our company. The BIG DIFFERENCE pile is more about operational things
that are easier to manage.

Concentrate on the VERY BIG DIFFERENCE pile. Pick the single most important one.

A committed project "owner"?

If someone is really committed to the project, this lubricates the flow of
information . . . you have the backing . . . everyone is in it together.
Otherwise you may have to find someone else more junior. At that stage you
would have to be very diplomatic. If Mr A is the person who really SHOULD
be in charge, but doesn't really want it, you may have to find a Mr B who

really wants it. So you work with B without ignoring A . . . just keep A in the picture. When this happens, I have found that Mr A is usually quite pleased to be off the hook. Let me turn this one over.

> *Someone has taken clear committed ownership . . .*

Your next one?

It would have been

> *People most affected really want the system? or Any hidden agendas?*

if nobody had wanted to own the project. So next I'll go for . . .

> *Mission-critical application?*

What difference would this one make to how you'd shape things?

You would have to be extremely careful in delimiting the boundaries of the project . . . be very specific about what the project will do and what it will not do. If it was mission-critical, I'd have to bring in

> *Major change to customer's procedures?*

next. Both mission-criticality and major change to the client's procedures would be a really tough combination to handle.

Let's say both of these did apply?

Then

> *People most affected really want the system?*

would have to come into the picture. You'd have to make sure that people were really behind the new system.

And if they weren't?

You'd really have to be sure you had someone on the client's side who was really committed to the project and you would have to be very careful on all your documentation, all the way up to your project specification . . . everything to be done . . . responsibilities and so on . . . to be pinned down exactly. If it's mission-critical with a lot of change, there will be a lot of ancillary activities to be initiated and managed . . . training, implementation, maybe union negotiations. All of this will have to be spelt-out line by line, saying who is responsible for what. And if you have lower-level managers who are going to resist things, then you will have to do a lot of training . . . a lot of talking to these people to turn them around to your way of thinking. So you will have to be much more diplomatic, as opposed to "Well here's your system . . . now implement it." The people you would have to choose on that project would have to be people who can handle the human side of things.

Let me turn some cards over . . .

> *The new system isn't mission-critical . . . and Major change to the customer's workflow procedures*

So it isn't mission-critical but there's a lot of change for the client. So next I'll go for . . .

> *People most affected really want the system?*

because, although there is a guy who is very committed to the project, he's not going to do it all himself. If the people most affected don't want it, this could have a big impact on the timings and quality of any tasks to be done by users during the project. Things users have to do may take a bit longer. I'm not saying they will tell lies, but they may not volunteer the information you need . . . anyway, you can't be sure what games they will play. You would have to try to bring them onside with you and that could be a very slow process. So in terms of timings, a lot of unforeseen things could happen. So you would need a good contingency figure built into the systems-definition stage of the project. I would expect that it would take longer than a run-of-the-mill project because you will have to run a lot of workshops. Possibly you will have to show them some sort of prototype.

Let's see which applies . . .

> *People most affected don't seem to really want the new system*

What do you make of this project so far?

> I think there is a real risk factor here . . . a medium to high risk of failure. The guy who has taken real ownership of the project . . . he or she may try to bring these guys onside. But this could be a double-edged sword because they could become even more antagonised. You have to be very careful.

The next one?

> *Agree amongst themselves on what's needed?*

Let's say they disagreed?

Then this would be a very high-risk project. It depends on how well qualified the main man is to sort it out. If you are an outsider, you can't go into a user area and tell them what they need . . . those days are gone. Let me see . . .

They disagree amongst themselves . . .

This is looking very bad. It may not be solvable. Project definition . . . stages, deliverables, and so on . . . will take a long, long time because you will have to tie it up in a pink ribbon and build in sign-offs at every step of the way. This is self-protection. Also, it reduces the risk of delivering a duff project. Let me try to clear the air a bit . . . my next is . . .

Any hidden agendas?

We can usually suss that one out in my experience. Personally I would think there is a hidden agenda in this project from what, I've seen so I'll go straight for

Has their PM time/skill/authority? and *Realistic expectations?*

It's very hard to split these two. They come side by side. I'm assuming the client's "main person" is the day-to-day person we would work with . . . not the project patron/owner. If he or she doesn't have the skills or authority, you are going to have a continuous cycle of going back to the "owner". You'd have to put a lot of reliance on him . . . somebody has got to give approval for things. Let's look . . .

The customer's PM has the needed . . .

I'm beginning to smile! He or she can help you out on

People most affected don't really want . . . and *They disagree amongst themselves . . .*

and you could have a good partnership between the two people. I'm going to take these two together . . .

Users' computer experience? and *Realistic expectations?*

What if it was bad news on both of these?

You would have to go into a much greater level of detail in your project plan than if it was the other way around. Make everything very explicit, bureaucratic . . . break it down to a very detailed level . . . pin it down. They could challenge you all the way. Even though the patron and main contact are on your side, you still have this undercurrent going on underneath. I'm going to look . . .

We're dealing with experienced computer users and *The customer has realistic expectations . . .*

How are you feeling now about the project?

Much better. So we don't have to worry about . . .

Tight customer-imposed timescales?

I would worry now about . . .

Any tricky interfacing? and *Major change to customer's procedures?*

I'll come back to *Major change . . .* in a minute. Interfacing with existing applications . . . before I would commit I would need to know a lot more. If I thought there might be some tricky interfacing, I would spend a fair bit of time with whoever is running those existing applications in trying to find out where and how these interface. I would do this at two levels . . . the user level and the technical IT level. You could find non-compatibility of platforms for example. If so you would have to write interfaces. Now the big question is, if you find you have to write interfaces, does that work become part of the main project or is it to be packaged as a separate mini-project? I think I would treat the question "do we have to write an interface?" as an explicit part of the project definition. There would be a fixed charge for answering this question. The contract would be very detailed on this point . . . a separate section dealing with this issue. It would be full of qualifiers about the existing interfaces. Do these conform to the right standards? Do they comply with ISO? Is the documentation up to date? It would be full of "ifs" All the classical questions. The contract would say "Subject to all these 'Ifs' being OK, it will cost you XYZ. If not, we will quote as a separate charge." Because you are going into uncharted territory otherwise. Which applies?

No tricky interfacing . . .

Let me go back to *Major change . . .* If there was to be major change, we'd want to be sure that things like user training, union negotiations, restructuring, etc., which were critical to the project, would all start very early on and would be clearly agreed to be part of the client's responsibility. If the guy wanted to make things like these part of the project . . . then more people . . . these are not things you can put in a fixed-price contract . . . these are time-and-material things. I wouldn't like to do them anyway . . . they're difficult.

Let's see . . .

Major change to the customer's workflow/procedures

Let's make your next one the last one.

OK.

Our knowledge of the languages/tools?

If it's an unfamiliar language, we obviously can't charge the customer for that. The question becomes, is this an opportunity for us to train people or is it something that's deadbeat with no future? If it's an opportunity, it's a cost which we find ourselves . . . it would be an investment. Either we train people or we find subcontractors working to us. That would be a commercial decision.

Let me look . . .

We'll be using familiar languages/tools

We're nearly finished! Looking at the overall pattern for this project, what three or four key bits of advice would you give the guy who has to manage this project?

If it's as bad as it's looking, I would nearly walk away from it. it's a lose–lose situation. They don't really want it. They disagree on what's needed. These are very serious obstacles to overcome. Even given committed ownership by one or two senior people, line managers or supervisors can sink you if they really want to. Fine if you're a big consultancy with organization-development people and so on. You could start by running in-house development courses . . . seminars . . . to sell the benefits of the project. And then get into organizational change things early on. But for a small software house . . . no.

How do you think this project would turn out for both parties?

It could be a positive if you could turn *The people most affected don't seem to really want the new system* around. But I don't think so. I'm afraid it's a no-no.

Which are the two or three real "nasties" in the project?

People most affected don't seem to really want . . ., *They disagree amongst themselves . . .* and *Major change to the customer's procedures . . .*

Is that taking them individually or in combination?

In combination.

Any good news?

Someone has taken clear, committed ownership . . ., The customer's PM has the needed time/skill/authority, we're dealing with experienced computer users and *The customer has realistic expectations . . .*

Any cards missing?

The other side of the coin is not there . . . your developers. Who are they? What are they? How experienced are they?

Here's my VERY BIG DIFFERENCE pile . . .

Major change to customer's procedures?   Our knowledge of the platform? Mission-critical application?   A one-off project for them or the first of a series?   System must go right first time? Must we subcontract?   Our knowledge of their industry?   A committed project "owner"?   Must share control with a third party?   Any tricky interfacing?   Tight, customer-imposed timescales?   Has their PM time/skill/authority?   Must satisfy different groups with different needs?   Who we'll be working with (users or IT)?   People most affected really want the system?   Realistic expectations? Can they define their problem?

What really distinguishes the VERY BIG DIFFERENCE pile from the others?

One theme that runs through this pile relates to the customer . . . the input from the customer . . . the interaction with the customer . . . managing expectations. it's important that you get a good working relationship going. Another theme relates to our understanding of their business. Another one has to do with control . . . having to share control with others or having to rely on third parties in some way. And then there are technical black holes that could open up, like interfacing problems.

Let's just work with this VERY BIG DIFFERENCE pile. Which is the single most important card?

A committed project "owner"?

I think it's crucial to have somebody on the customer's side who will take ownership. If you haven't, you go as high up as possible in their organization and demand that you get somebody who will run with it. Otherwise, you end up running the project the way you think it should be run, and not meeting their requirements. I don't think it's possible to run a successful project without some clear ownership.

Take a look . . .

Nobody wants to "own" the project

What's next?

Has their PM time/skill/authority?

I assume this will be bad news also because it's linked to the last one. If it's bad news, I think I'd walk away . . .

The customer's PM lacks the needed . . .

I'll hang in a bit longer!

I'll go for . . .

People most affected really want the system? and Must satisfy different groups with different needs?

If you decide to stick with the project without real ownership from senior people, the next group to satisfy would be the users.

Let's see . . .

People most affected seem to genuinely want . . . and we've only to satisfy a single group of similar users . . .

That's good news. I'd work in tandem with the users, even though they may not have authority as such, but if you know their industry . . . there's a card somewhere on that . . . it would help, combined with the users . . .

We've a good knowledge of the customer's industry

I'm feeling a bit better!

Any advice for your pal so far?

Assuming he can't escape from the project, and that he has only a single group of users to deal with, I think he should get to know the users well, and select a good, strong person from amongst them . . . someone who has a fair bit of authority and standing in the company, and who is prepared to run with it. So, basically, to try to work around the ownership problem. With a good knowledge of their industry and with users behind the project, your away. Wait though . . . we've pinned our hopes on the users but there's another card here . . .

Who we'll be working with (users or IT)?

From my experience, people from the IT department can be of help. But you do need to get hold of the users as well. The ideal mix is somebody from the IT department and a user. So, if we found ourselves dealing purely with the IT department, we'd try to make sure that users were represented as well on any working group, because at the end of the day it's the users who will either use the system or not.

We'll be dealing directly with the users

Next?

Mission-critical application? and *Tight, customer-imposed timescales?*

If it's mission-critical, there are a couple of things you have to take into account. Firstly, your timescales have to be adequate. There must be a certain amount of flexibility here because it's not just a matter of getting something up-and-running . . . the thing has to really work. If you're in a banking situation or a hospital where the system has to be running twenty-four hours a day, I'd rather be a bit late . . . juggle with my timescales and get it right. Secondly, you'd have to be a lot more careful about putting your team together . . . competent, experienced people. Also beef up your quality control. Being mission-critical is putting a high risk on the project, particularly as we don't have an "owner".

I'm looking . . .

New system is mission-critical . . . and *Tight, customer-imposed timescales* . . .

I want out!!

Take another one anyway.

Major change to customer's workflow/procedures?

If you have to introduce change in the customer's workflow, it can be stressful. In some companies, there are stringent industrial relations aspects, so this takes the project beyond being just about software development. It takes the project into the realms of people management . . . organization development and business process re-engineering. These aspects have to be dealt with before you get stuck into the nitty-gritty of the project. However, in this case the people affected want the new system, so presumably they are aware that things are going to have to change.

How would you prepare the ground for any major change?

I would set up meetings with the users and discuss the changes with them . . . maybe put a prototype together to show them the type of thing envisaged. Where big change is involved nowadays, in bigger projects you'll find they have had consultants in looking at workflow, so the users will be semi-prepared for the change. But I still think that you should sit down with them and prepare the way for it before you get stuck in.

Let's see . . .

> *No major change to customer's . . .*

I'm bringing *We'll have to work to tight, customer-imposed timescales* and *System must go right first time?* together.

Let's say the system had to go right first time and you couldn't just walk away?

Beef up your testing and get the users more involved in this. You need to build up a good relationship between whoever is testing on your side and the users because they will each bring their own perspective to testing. The users testing on their own is not going to achieve it, so I would concentrate on making sure the testing effort is very well planned, executed and managed.

I'm looking . . .

> *The new system has to go right first time*

So it's mission-critical, has to go right first time and we have to keep to tight deadlines!

Next?

> *Realistic expectations?*

This is one we've bypassed. I'm assuming we've got the business, so the cost bits have been dealt with. But sometimes it's unrealistic to do a project to a customer's timescale. I've experienced this in the past. It doesn't work, so it's better to stand firm and say that it can't be done because the quality will suffer. Sure, you can add extra resources, but you get a reducing return from this beyond a certain stage in the project. So I'm quite firm on this one. I'm looking . . .

> *The customer has unrealistic expectations . . .*

Have you definitely decided to walk away?

I decided that a long while back! No ownership, unrealistic expectations, mission-critical. I just wouldn't do it under these conditions.

Maybe one or two more?

I'll take these three together. They've all to do with linking in . . . the fact that you're not on your own . . .

> *Any tricky interfacing?, Must we subcontract? and Must share control with a third party?*

If you're sharing control with someone else, you simply have less say about the overall approach. The interfacing one and the subcontracting are critical as it's a mission-critical application. You'd have to work with other suppliers or their IT department, so you'd need to define your relationships with these other people very well. But it's academic anyway, because I've already walked away.

Let's see . . .

> *Some tricky interfacing . . . , We won't need to subcontract . . .* and *We won't have to share control . . .*

Final bit of advice to your pal who CAN'T walk away?

Make sure you get someone on the client's side who you can relate to, and try to build some form of ownership. Be very careful in building your team . . . that you pick people who can relate to these issues and not the most junior people. Make sure you plan testing carefully. Beef up your quality assurance procedures. Make sure the acceptance criteria are very well defined and agreed in advance. Take a view on how realistic the timescales are and try to come to some acceptable compromise. As you're interfacing to existing applications, make sure the lines of responsibility vis-à-vis the original developer, and so on, are defined as clearly as possible.

If your pal sticks with it, how do you think the project will turn out?

I agree that it is likely to be a positive experience for the client, but I disagree that it will be a positive experience for the developer.

That first one surprises me!

I'm distinguishing the users from the "customer". Sometimes you can build a very good relationship with users, rather than with the customer. But of course the users may not be forking out the money!

Which are the nastiest of the nasties?

Tight, imposed timescales . . . , Nobody wants to "own" the project . . . , Some tricky interfacing . . . and *The new system is mission-critical . . .*

And the best news?

We've only to satisfy a single group . . . , People most affected want the new system . . . and we've a good knowledge of the customer's industry

The best news is that you've got the users on your side, and that you're only dealing with one group of users. The fact that you know your client's industry . . . the nuances of it . . . that you don't have to learn the business . . . particularly as it's a mission-critical system.

And . . . let's see . . .

This project could lead to other projects for this customer

If there's future business with them on the horizon, this could make it worth the pain . . . could be worth investing that bit more.

Any cards missing? For example, there's nothing on maturity of the technology to be used.

I was just going to say that . . . if you're dealing with a new platform, etc., there are ways around that. You buy in consultants, or whatever, with those skills. If these exist! Also, if you're dealing with vendors, say Microsoft or Oracle, it's important to get support from them so you don't go down the wrong road . . . you need somebody to vet your design or whatever.

Things like geographical location are also missing. If you're isolated from the customer . . . long distances . . . lots of travel . . . different culture and language. it's much harder to build relationships with people from a distance.

Here's my VERY BIG DIFFERENCE pile . . .

Realistic expectations?   Must we subcontract?   Any hidden agendas?
Need >two people on our team?   Tight, customer-imposed timescales?
Project duration >three months?   Major change to customer's procedures?
How adaptable must our solution be?   Has their PM time/skill/authority?

My first is . . .

>*Realistic expectations?*

If they have unrealistic expectations, you describe to them previous histories of implementations of similar projects. If no history to draw on, explain you're breaking new ground.

>*The customer has realistic expectations . . .*

Next is . . .

>*Must we subcontract?*

If you don't know the people you're subcontracting to you can have huge problems. It can be a nightmare. You have to be wary of the people . . . are they professional? . . . Have they a good track record of experience? . . . Can you trust them as people? . . . Are they likely to go over your head and to compete with you for the business? Make sure you have penalty clauses in their contract!

>*We'll have to do significant subcontracting*

Given this info so far, I'll take . . .

>*Project duration >three months?*

The answer to this question makes no difference if there are no penalty clauses in your contract. But if this means the project MUST take three months or less, and this is in the contract, and there's a penalty clause around it, it's very nasty if you have to rely heavily on a subcontractor. So make sure to put heavy penalty clauses in HIS contract.

The project will take three months or less

Next is . . .

How adaptable must our solution be?

If the contract explicitly talks about adaptability . . . to some future environment, or to work with some future system, you are buying in to possible hostages to fortune.

Let's see . . .

The new system must be adaptable enough to cope with unknown future needs

Bad news! My next is . . .

Has their PM time/skill/authority?

If their main project person isn't available to you . . . doesn't have the skill or authority to implement change . . . if you have to get the main management involved . . . it could end up in acrimonious relationships and impact on the delivery of the product. It could end up in rows, and the delivered product being not what they expect.

If he or she lacked these things, what would you do?

If the person wasn't willing to change, or to point us in the right direction to someone else, I'd request a meeting with more senior people. I'd try to be as apolitical as possible and I'd say "We need to get a job done, we have a contract to meet . . . we need assistance. We feel this guy isn't giving us enough support, or whatever. Can we change the person?"

I'm looking . . .

The customer's PM has the needed time/skill/authority

My next is . . .

Major change to customer's procedures?

Big change can cause delay in the final delivery of the solution, and to the live-running. If you have to do it in tandem with existing workflows, you may upset the running of the business. If there are major changes, you would have to get the people involved from the different levels . . . who are involved in the workflow . . . and educate them. You would explain that you are not trying to make their jobs harder . . . just easier, and basically get them to accept that there are going to be changes for the benefit of the overall company.

I'm looking . . .

No major changes . . .

Next is . . .

Tight, customer-imposed timescales?

If we're able to juggle timescales, that's grand. If we're not, as long as there are no penalty clauses in our contract, that's OK. If there are penalties, we may have to pull out all the stops to do the work, which could impact on the final quality of the deliverable. There are slippages and teething problems with any project.

Let's see . . .

We'll be able to juggle a bit with timescales

Next is . . .

Any hidden agendas?

If there was a power struggle in the organization, you'd walk away from them, if possible. If you couldn't walk away, you'd make sure people saw exactly what's being contracted for. I don't know . . . you'd tackle hidden agendas on a need-to-know basis.

. . . no hidden agendas . . .

My last one!

Need >two people on our team?

As we can juggle our timescales, we may be able to get away with just one or two people on the project, as opposed to having an army of people. If you need three or more people, you have to make sure that everyone is singing from the same hymn book. With only one or two people, you can manage through informal chats. But with three or more, you need to have formal reviews of progress, etc.

We'll need only one or two people . . .

Good!

Advice to your pal?

You'd carefully choose good subcontractors. As you only need one or two people on the project, these people will have to judge the subcontractor's work. So they need to be the right people. Make sure to liaise well with their main project person.

How do you predict this project will turn out?

They've realistic expectations. it's going to take less than three months. But this is a tough one . . .

> *The new system must be adaptable . . .*

That one is a bit unanswerable . . . hostage to fortune. No major change . . . good. You can juggle timescales. No hidden agenda. Subcontractor . . . a disaster if you don't choose him correctly. You've a good person dealing with you on their side. He'll become a champion for you if you do things right. You don't have need for big management of people on your side . . . a perfect team!

I agree that it will be a good experience for the client. I strongly agree that it'll be a good experience for the developer . . . my only caveat would be the level of subcontracting needed.

Which are the one or two real "nasties"? Are there any?

The new system must be adaptable . . . and *We'll have to do significant subcontracting*

Where's the best news?

The customer's PM has the needed . . . and *The customer has realistic expectations . . .*

What's missing from the cards?

There doesn't seem to be anything about budgeting for the project.

CANICE

9

Here's my VERY BIG DIFFERENCE pile . . .

Any hidden agendas? Must we subcontract? System must go right first time? People most affected really want the system? Our knowledge of the platform? Our knowledge of the languages/tools? Must share control with a third party? Major change to customer's procedures? Any tricky interfacing? Mission-critical application? Must satisfy different groups with different needs? Agree amongst themselves on what's needed? Must change other developer's code? Realistic expectations?

What really distinguishes the VERY BIG DIFFERENCE pile from the other two piles?

There are three areas of big concern in my VERY BIG DIFFERENCE pile. Customer expectations and the whole "needs" thing. If you don't have good customer expectations up front, don't proceed. Our familiarity and experience with the issues around the proposed solution, like the environment to be used. New stuff like a new platform is major. So you multiply your estimates by two or whatever. And our degree of control over the project . . . what we can control versus what we can't control . . . including any involvement of third parties.

Let's work just with this most important pile. Which is the single, most important card?

Fundamentally, there's the area around the customer and their clarity about what they want . . . ideally no hidden agendas and no conflicts of interest. I think that's very important. If you can't get clarity, no matter how successful the execution is, any project could still fail for political reasons or because the proper requirements weren't met. So, I always view this stuff as the first fence of the course. If you don't get these right, no matter how good you are in other areas . . . so my first is . . .

Realistic expectations?

What would you do if expectations seemed to be off-the-wall?

In our company, we are trying to deliver new types of solutions because existing opportunities are being well serviced by other companies. So a lot of our stuff involves proof-of-concept and prototyping. In terms of setting realistic expectations, number one move is to have a workshop at which we drill down into needs . . . into what's really important, and into the real reasons for these needs. Secondly, we'd sell them on the idea that the first revenue-earning phase of the project should deliver a document that tries to capture these needs and the rationale behind each, to their satisfaction. we'd sell them on the idea that the second phase deliverable should be a prototype, or other form of proof-of-concept, that will give further focus and clarity. If someone on their side says "I have this big problem and I want you to solve it", and describes what it should be in very vague terms . . . and when you mention proof-of-concept or prototyping, they say "No – just do it and tell me when it's done", you can pretty well guarantee it won't work. So, if that's their attitude, and they won't accept a more incremental path towards clarification, you just walk away.

Turn it over . . .

> *The customer has unrealistic expectations . . .*

Right now, this is a show-stopper. Until it's sorted out, there's not much point in trying to address other issues.

OK. But let's say you feel you can sort it out. Which card is next?

> *Agree amongst themselves on what's needed?*

is a related one. If different groups within the organization disagree about what the system is to do, we've no chance of pleasing everyone. So, until you can get some sort of consensus view . . . I'd address it much the same way as the expectations one.

I'm looking . . .

> *They don't disagree . . .*

Our knowledge of the platform? and *Our knowledge of the languages/tools?* are related, so I'll go for these two next. These are important because they call into question our ability to execute the project. I'm confident that, given an appropriate time-frame, our organization could develop any competencies required, but it would impact on schedules and delivery . . . and do you multiply by two or five to get the learning-curve "hit" on the project? it's about expectations again. For instance, one of our recent customers uses a proprietary language. They know up front that we don't know this language. So we share the hit with them for our consultants' down time and training. It really depends. For example, if we were learning Java for the first time, and we saw there was a whole spectrum of Java solutions waiting to be done, we wouldn't have a problem taking the hit ourselves. Whereas, if it was an esoteric piece of technology, we would say "We're going to have to learn this stuff in order to do your job . . . and we don't see us getting a great benefit from it, so we'll have to charge you for learning it."

Take a look . . .

The platform/environment is familiar . . . and *The languages/tools are familiar . . .*

Which one next?

People most affected really want the system?

You have a deployment failure if the delivery is successful, but users won't use it. You can find yourself trying to shove technology down people's throats, but you'd prefer to have users on your side, as opposed to fighting you all the way. The politics of it . . . .all sorts of hurdles can be put up.

What would you do if users didn't seem to want it?

We've come across this one before. I'd be very nervous of winning the business if this was the case. I'd want it sorted out before sign-up. I'd dig in a bit to find the reasons. Maybe users don't want it because they perceive it's going to cause them extra work. it's often a matter of ignorance or misperception on someone's part. A perceives it's bad . . . B perceives it's good. Who's right? Who's wrong? there's probably some greater truth that everybody should be able to find. So my first call would be an educational one . . . to try to make sure that everyone has the same facts and to try to straighten out misperceptions about the reasons for the system, and so on.

I'm looking . . .

People most affected seem to genuinely want the new system

What do you make of the project so far?

Users want the system. They are on board. we're on a familiar platform. But there are unrealistic expectations. That's a show-stopper. Basically, you'll have to get them to sign off on the functional spec and the project plan. you'll have to be very clear about what is to be delivered. For a customer like this, the spec really has to be at a fine level of detail . . . no vague "the system will do something like this". . . and the acceptance test must mirror this spec exactly. And customer sign-offs all the way, etc.

My next is . . .

> *Must change other developer's code?*

What would you do if it looked like you'd have to get into someone else's code?

Up front, I'd inspect their code. Look at coding standards, documentation, etc. and try to ascertain how "buggy" or not it has been. Then, as far as possible, I'd try to avoid opening up and touching their code base by trying to "wrap" it instead. Furthermore, I'd get a very clear understanding with the customer on the answer to the question "Who's going to support their code after we've been into it or wrapped it?" we've been here before on this one! The only way to cover yourself when amending or supporting someone else's code is to charge on a time basis. You'd be crazy to take it on on a fixed-price basis. If the code is a mess, you're better off costing it as a total rewrite.

Let's see . . .

> *We'll have to change other developer's code*

That's not so nice!

Next is . . .

> *System must go right first time?*

This one is linked with *Mission-critical application?* If they are both negative, that's very dangerous.

What if they were both negative?

Then you're talking about a non-pilotable, new mission-critical system with other people's code stuck in the middle of it. I'd have to find a way of establishing pilotable components to reduce the risk. If I couldn't or wasn't allowed, I'd have to bail out.

Let me look at both . . .

> *We can pilot the new system until we get it right . . .*

That's much more reassuring.

New system is not mission-critical . . .

That reduces the worry about having to change other people's code.

Another one?

At this stage, probably this one . . .

Any hidden agendas?

If we don't get the real story, we don't have the real requirements. I'll give you an example. There are two different systems out there that do gate allocation at airports, one of which delivers better gate utilization than the other. it's been suggested that at ^&%$£ airport, they deliberately bought the less efficient software because they wanted to use that tool to justify building a new terminal. When you don't actually know the real reasons behind the new system, perhaps someone is setting you up and they want the project to fail for political reasons. You don't have a chance!

How would you protect yourself against a hidden agenda?

Be as rigorous as you can in specifying what the system is to do. Make sure the person who is signing off has lots of clout. Then, at the end of the day, if that person commissions a white elephant, that's their problem. But it doesn't bode well for nice happy, warm feelings in terms of having done something successfully.

So,. . .

The "real" agenda seems to be hidden

One more?

Must share control with a third party?

And if you had to share control?

I guess if you look at that in conjunction with the hidden agenda thing, I'd be very suspicious as to what's really going on there. It could be a situation whereby let's say Andersen's pitch for a piece of work, but they come in too expensive so it goes out to tender, and an organization like ourselves signs up to do it. But we have to share project management with someone internal to the customer who favoured the Andersen solution, who sabotages us and then says "Well guys, I told you we should have gone with Andersen's . . . more expensive, but they DO deliver." And if you have to share control with some sort of consultant, that consultant could very much impede the process, or there may be politics and rivalry brought in.

How would you protect yourself?

I'd be very explicit up front about roles and responsibilities. I'd meet with the third party, look at them, and try to gauge their attitudes and perspective towards the project. I'd look at their background and their experience of having done this sort of stuff before. But as I said, the third party could be someone internal to the customer who you have to share control with, who hasn't got experience, but who still holds a lot of clout, and who'll maybe cave in to a lot of change requests that we wouldn't be prepared to accept ourselves.

Let's see . . .

> We won't have to share control . . .

Looking at the overall profile for the project, any advice?

Our big problems are the hidden agenda, working with existing code and unrealistic expectations. So let's imagine we've gone into, say, a financial institution. Some other software company has already built version one of the system. The software sort of does what they want, but doesn't meet all their needs. They have the unrealistic perspective that the software should be able to do A, B, C, D and E and "surely it's only two man-months work and so can go live in two months, and only cost X?" You also have the suspicion that the real agenda might be coming from some guy in the organization who wants you to fail, or from an IT department waiting in the wings to trip you up.

I think the first thing to do is to invest time in working through with the customer exactly where the project is at the moment, what is realistic, and in what time-frame and at what cost. If you don't get through that exercise to everyone's satisfaction, just walk away. Nine times out of ten, you'll fail on that project. Even if contractually they are obliged to pay you, it will leave a bad taste in their mouth because they thought they were getting one thing, and they "only" got what you gave them. So, the customer's unrealistic expectations are the starting point.

Next, part of the expectation setting is to raise their awareness that there is another developer's code in there, and that this brings risks, and to mutually agree how to manage these risks. If you want the business very badly, you'd probably volunteer to spend a day or two looking at the code at your own expense. But, ideally, you should look for a phase one exercise which analyzes the code and software, and which the customer pays for.

In terms of that real agenda thing, other than frank discussion, there's probably only so much you can do.

How do you think the project will turn out?

I "strongly disagree" that it will be a positive experience for either party.

Which is the nastiest of the nasties?

Unrealistic expectations . . .

And the nicest of the nice ones?

People most affected seem to genuinely want the new system . . ., They don't disagree amongst themselves . . . and *We can pilot the new system until we get it right*

Any cards missing?

In terms of other things to be wary of, it may be that your customer wants you to roll out a solution that gives them some sort of competitive advantage. The compelling reasonis that it's new technology. it's going to enable them to do something that neither they nor their competitors could do before. But to roll out these solutions, you must use new technology. we've encountered lots of problems on projects like these because of new and non-robust tools with poor performance and low integrity. Things like £$Java%^. These problems are always fixed within 18 months or so, but that's no good at the time! These projects were commissioned by our customers on the basis of a belief in all the hype . . . "Give it three months and we'll have native compilers". . . but these never show. So it's not just unfamiliarity with tools that's a risk, it's also their maturity.

COLIN

10

My VERY BIG DIFFERENCE pile:

Tight, customer-imposed timescales?   A committed project "owner"?   Our knowledge of the platform?   Users' computer experience?   Major change to customer's procedures?   Realistic expectations?   Any tricky interfacing? Project duration >three months?   System must go right first time?   Must change other developer's code?   People most affected really want the system? Has their PM time/skill/authority?   Must share control with a third party? Our knowledge of the languages/tools?   Our knowledge of the application? Any hidden agendas?

What really differentiates between the piles?

The VERY BIG DIFFERENCE pile includes things that would be outside your control, or things that, if they go wrong, would be bound to have cost implications. The items in the other piles are more manageable. Whether they are problems or not, you can manage them.

Concentrate on the VERY BIG DIFFERENCE pile. Take these items one by one . . . most important one first.

I think it's . . .

> *Major change to customer's procedures?*

What differences would this make to how you would "shape" and run a project?

If there will not be major changes you will be designing a system to fit in with the known. You can document what they are doing now and it's all relatively controllable. If there are going to be major changes, nobody can predict how things will pan out. There could be a lot of operating difficulties . . . they might not be computer difficulties but they could impact on the project in a major way . . . in a way that you really cannot foresee because it is totally outside your control. The customer comes along and says "This just isn't going to work" after you've built the software . . . so what do you do then? If there's a lot of change involved for the customer, you have to break the implementation into stages. You implement stage one. If it works . . . if it's practical . . . then you can implement stage two. If you don't do it like this, you can paint yourself into a corner. You've gone down an alley that doesn't work . . . then you are in trouble and the whole thing could collapse.

Turn over the card.

> *No major change . . .*

I think this one is a close second . . .

> *Our knowledge of the languages/tools?*

If you don't know your tools you could end up in big trouble. Basically you have no idea what you are doing . . . what technical problems could arise . . . what are sensible timescales . . . the types of exception handling you will need . . . the work arounds you will need. Every platform has bugs in it . . . these are usually manageable, but it takes time and experience to find out what they are.

What would you do if you had to work with unfamiliar tools?

You would have to structure the project so that you had a learning curve built in. You could not take on a major project on a new platform unless you had an unlimited budget. You would try to shape up a small project first as a pilot or test system so you could get the needed experience before you got into the main project. Apart from dealing with bugs and other problems, you have also got to find out the best way to use the platform, not just in a negative way but in a positive way . . . you want to find out how to use that platform to exploit its strengths. The fact is though that you don't really understand until the end of your first project with a new platform how you should have done it. In theory you can study it in books and so on . . . but it's not the same as actually doing it . . . also you would want to adapt it to your own particular development philosophy, which isn't in any book. it's a very tricky one.

Turn over the card . . .

> *We'll be using unfamiliar languages/tools*

What one do you want next?

I think the next one is . . .

A committed project "owner"?

Throughout every project decisions have to be taken on the customer's side, and these have to be made quickly and sensibly. Also you have to make sure that the needed resources are there on the customer's side. Building a system is not like building a house where you are given the plans and you more or less get on with it. They must be involved at every stage and if that involvement is lukewarm you are in trouble because resources are not going to be there, decisions will be delayed or poorly taken . . . guys kicking to touch . . . you could be in big trouble. I would go to the managing director and say "This is not going to work unless someone does want to own the project." You can't impose a system on people that don't really want it . . . that are lukewarm about it. So you would have to go to the top and say, sort this out or forget it.

Would you walk away if it wasn't sorted out?

Assuming you are being asked to do it on a fixed-price basis . . . yes. You'd have to say "I can't do this." If time and money is not a problem then it doesn't matter so much. All of this relates back to one thing . . . time and money. You can get over all these things with time and money.

Turn over the card . . .

Nobody wants to "own" the project

What does this project look like at this point?

Look for some other business quickly! You are using a platform you don't know and the customer doesn't seem to want to take responsibility. But it does depend on the nature of the project. If it's a normal business application where there will be a lot of user involvement, the taking-responsibility thing obviously does matter. If it's a black box sort of project . . . if it's a very technical sort of project . . . if you just have to plug boxes in and the users don't have much to do with it . . . well then it doesn't really matter.

The next card?

It's a choice between a technical one and a management one . . . the technical ones usually can be managed so . . . I'll take . . .

Realistic expectations?

If expectations are looking wrong, you would have to advise them that the project should be broken down into mini-projects, and that if they expect a lot from any one project it will probably go wrong because no one will have understood the complexities of the thing at the outset. Get the first mini-project going then review the situation after its implementation.

Let me turn this one over . . .

The customer has realistic expectations . . .

OK. Reasonably realistic expectations. But unfamiliar languages and tools. So we will have to get some experience of these before we design a major system, no matter what anyone says. So we will have to structure the project in a way that allows us to do this. That's mega . . . number one priority. To deal with *Nobody wants to "own" the project*, I'd sit down with the MD or whoever and try to get that fixed . . . try to make them take responsibility.

I'll take my next one . . .

Tight customer-imposed timescales?

Obviously if you've got a bit of flexibility here that helps. If you find things aren't panning out quite as you had planned . . . if users tell you their requirements but they don't actually know or they get it wrong . . . or you miss something on your side . . . if you didn't appreciate the complexity of something . . . it gives you ability to do a bit of phasing things in. I'm a great believer in that. No matter what anyone says, the "big bang" theory just doesn't work. Things are more likely to go wrong. It ends up being more costly and hard to manage. I like to be able to ask "What do you need next week? What can wait?" So you can tackle the critical bits first. The ancillary or nice-to-have features can be added on later . . . so if there have been other changes in the meantime, you have not wasted money building to a specification which has to be changed.

Let me turn it over . . .

We'll be able to juggle a bit with timescales

Oh, I've just spotted . . .

Our knowledge of the platform?

I should have really taken that along with *Our knowledge of the languages/tools?* No matter, they are effectively both the same anyway.

Now I'm taking . . .

Must change other developer's code?

This could be a nightmare! If it was just a few lines of code, I'd probably just rewrite it. But if it's big, goodness knows what problems you'd face there. Is the other developer available? Is it a matter of "Here's the code . . . you fix it?" Is it documented? How well is it structured? There are a lot of imponderables there. If you are faced with a large piece of strange code which is badly structured, with no documentation and no support, then you are in deep trouble. It would probably be quicker and cheaper to rewrite it. From my experience, it could be a disaster area. You cannot tell by looking at somebody's code what they are thinking. You are seeing the end product of their thinking. You could be looking at a thousand lines of code and asking yourself "What is he trying to do here?" Even if you can execute the code, and observe the system in action, it can be hard to relate the two . . . very time-consuming because you have to understand it before you can change it . . . you could be weeks at it, and still be wrong. You are usually better off to look at what they are trying to do and to rewrite it yourself in your own way.

Let's have a look . . .

We won't have to change . . .

That's a relief!

I'm going to take . . .

Must share control with a third party?

One big cost factor in any project is the personality of the customer, whether corporate or individual. Some customers are literally more expensive to work for than others . . . in the way they do things . . . phoning you up . . . the way they handle everyday things . . . everyone has their own style and expectations about what they are going to do and what you are going to do. If, on top of that, you have a third party with their own "personality" involved . . . depending on their behaviour which might range from very bad to very good . . . all that's going to have a major impact on the project. If there's professional jealousy, lack of cooperation or a bit of obstruction here and there you have obviously got big problems compared to the case of a third party who is prepared to row in and be helpful, and be available when you need them.

Let's see . . .

We'll have to share control . . .

Oh dear!

Next . . .

System must go right first time?

Being able to pilot the new system . . . this is a mega item because from a technical point of view you get the chance to check out your tools . . . your methods . . . plans you have . . . things that you might not have tried before to see how well they really work. But more importantly, the customer gets to see what he asked for, and probably realizes that it is not what he really meant in a lot of cases. So before you have spent too much time and money, he has an opportunity to think through what he wants . . . to see if he has bitten off more than he can chew, to see how it really matches up to the reality of his business, etc. So being able to pilot is very important.

What if the nature of the system meant it had to go right first time?

Well there are two things muddled up on this card. Having to go right first time implies to me that you cannot do a parallel run. This is not the same thing as a pilot. These are not opposite sides of the same coin. Maybe there should be two cards! Obviously in any system you would try to do a parallel run, but that is not a pilot. A pilot is a smaller part of a project, a scaled-down version. I'll assume you mean that a parallel run is not possible. This puts a big strain on things. Obviously you would have to build a simulation model or something that will allow you to test the ideas very thoroughly and rigorously before it goes live. Obviously this is going to put up the cost, and the pressure of getting it to work will be immense. If you can do a parallel run, you have the opportunity to go through another test and correction cycle, maybe even twice. Whereas, if it has to go right the first time, this ups the ante a lot. I would insist on building some sort of simulation model or some sort of lab-based version. Something that would say "This is what it will be."

Turn it over.

The new system has to go right first time

Oh God! I'll take this next . . .

Any tricky interfacing?

Again here you are dealing with something you cannot control. Something you are going to have to dig into . . . something someone else did . . . getting specs from someone else. Basically, it is something outside your immediate control, so time and cost estimates will be difficult to come up with with any accuracy . . . it's a Pandora's box. You don't know what you'll find. You might spend a lot of time testing and figuring it out. Whereas if you had written it yourself, you would know how it works. Because it's outside your control, it could crash the whole system, and then you are in deep trouble.

What would you do if you were faced with some tricky interfacing?

I'd find out what I could from the supplier. Get as much help and cooperation from them as I could. Maybe arrange to have one of their people available all the time, or at critical stages. Do a lot of testing . . . try to "crash" it and find any weaknesses. Again you would have to build all that in . . . make sure you have the money and expertise to do these things. The fact that we can't do a parallel run in this project makes things much worse.

No tricky interfacing . . .

That's a big relief!

Looking at the whole set of cards, what advice would you give your pal?

Firstly, get familiar with those languages and tools in a smaller project, even one which is part of the contract, before you do all your major design so that you get to know their strengths and weaknesses . . . what you can do . . . what you can't do . . . what is actually going to work as opposed to what you think should work.

Would that be a separate, chargeable phase in the project?

If it was a big project, yes. Or I would build it in some other way . . . you might not tell them that. Then I would have to find someone who would want to "own" the project and to motivate that person. I would sit down with the head guy and say "Someone has got to take this project on." I'd keep pestering him until he assigned it to someone suitable. As to sharing control with a third party, I'd have a long, long talk with those people before I got trapped into the project. I would have a very good agreement with them with trigger clauses, so that if they failed to do certain things . . . that if they failed in their obligations to do certain things, something would happen. You would have to build something severe in so that you were not left holding the baby. Unless you knew them of course . . . if you had worked with them before . . . it could be no problem. But if it's someone new . . . or if the relationship is unequal . . . maybe you've a small development team and they are one of the "big six", you might have a problem . . . being sent from department to department . . . whereas if you are dealing with another small company, if it's you and Bill down the street, you can have a pint first . . . he's got the same problems as you anyway, so it could be OK. But you'd still have to work something in to make sure you weren't left holding the baby.

The system has to go right the first time . . . no parallel running . . . it's amazing what you can do by way of simulation with a bit of imagination. People will say "Oh, we can't simulate this, we haven't enough test data." Well you just have to write something, generate some test data, and test it. You must find a way to simulate it to the nth degree so that every feature of the live system which you know about is built in in some way in your test system, and it's reproducible. You have to write whatever utilities are needed to generate it all. It all becomes part of the cost of the project . That's the way to do it. I've done this myself. We had to simulate five years of medical data . . . it took a man-month to come up with the test data . . . but we were able to run this anytime against our test system.

Any major contract is tricky – make sure you have the customer pinned down. If they want any changes to what was agreed, even one comma, they will have to pay, and there will be a delay. Be very, very wary of completely fixed-price contracts. Always try to split it into two phases. In the first phase, do a very detailed spec on a fixed-price basis. Then try to decide if the second phase . . . development, etc. . . . should be fixed price or not. If they don't like it, pull out. Don't let yourself be painted into a corner. we've seen that happen so many times.

How do you think this project is likely to turn out?

Well, provided you are able to do a small project first . . . it's a mixture of good news and bad news. *The customer has realistic expectations . . .* and *We'll be able to juggle a bit with timescales* are good. *The new system has to go right first time* is tricky . . . very tricky. I would try to manage it out of the project. it's unrealistic without massive resources. Software is never finished. there's no such thing as software with no bugs in it . . . and it's never quite what the customer wanted. By the time you catch up with them, they have changed their minds, or the business has changed. I'm very "undecided" on both scales about the outcome, largely because of the need for the system to work first time.

When you look at the cards, which are the really nasty ones?

We'll have to share control with a third party and *The new system has to go right first time*. Obviously *We will be using unfamiliar languages/tools* has to come into it, but it should be manageable if you can run a pilot project that will help you to learn the tools . . . then you have managed that out of the project. You'd have to make it manageable otherwise you better not take the project. Unfamiliar languages/tools and having to get it right first time would be a lethal combination! it's totally off-the-wall that you would take the project without managing one or both of these right out of the picture.

Where's the good news?

The customer has realistic expectations . . ., We'll be able to juggle timescales and *We've experience of this application.*

Are there any cards that you would have expected to see "missing" from the whole set?

None of them mention money . . . constraints on the contract . . . or price. Nor travel required . . . is it just down the road? Or across the country? That's a big factor. Also is the language English? How "accurate" does the system have to be? For example, if you are building a normal, routine application like billing, and if there are errors, it's not the end of the world!

GERRY

11

My VERY BIG DIFFERENCE pile . . .

Must change other developer's code?   Feasible to prototype?   Project duration >three months?   Our knowledge of the platform?   Need >two people on our team?   Tight, customer-imposed timescales?   Our knowledge of the languages/tools?

What really differentiates between the three piles?

Can I answer in terms of how we see things?

Sure.

The reason we would take on a project would be mostly because it involves an environment, languages and tools that we are familiar with, and that we believe we can finish in a reasonable timescale. That's mainly what's common about the items in the VERY BIG DIFFERENCE pile. In the middle pile are things that are not that important to us, like whether the users are up to speed or not, or whether they have experience of project management. Most of the people we deal with don't have experience of project management. We are not too phased by applications that we haven't seen before. We learn quickly. We can very quickly come to grips with a new client's requirements and adapt our solution to meet these. We have done some really weird things over the years, and it doesn't make any difference to us. Obviously, if it's an area that we are familiar with, that's a bonus, but if we have not done it before, it doesn't really matter as long as we believe we can get to understand it. Whether the customer has previous experience with IT, whether we have to subcontract, whether it's a one-off project or not, doesn't really bother us.

We are interested in doing a job that we believe we can do within the timescale we quote, so that at the end of the day we can make some money on it. We have been stung in the past with development projects that overran . . . they became loss-leaders effectively. We want relatively clean projects that we can implement in an environment we know about, in application areas we believe we can come to understand, and all within a relatively short timescale. These are the drivers for us.

Concentrate on the VERY BIG DIFFERENCE pile. Pick the single most important item from your point of view.

I suppose this one has to be it . . .

Project duration >three months?

Why that one?

We have more control over a shorter project, and are more likely to make money out of it than a longer project. This is because there are fewer variables in a short project. The longer the project, the more variables . . . the more difficult it is to decide how to cost it . . . how to spec it . . . the whole thing becomes more and more difficult. Also, we don't have the resources for very large projects, so we have to be careful that what we take on can be achieved in a short space of time.

What would you do if a project was going to take longer than three months?

If we broke our rule by taking on a big project, then we would definitely approach it differently . . . we would probably involve subcontractors as opposed to doing it all ourselves. We would have a much more rigorous review process than we might have with a smaller project, and we would approach the prototyping more seriously.

Let's see which applies . . .

Project will take more than three months

Your next most important one?

Our knowledge of the languages/tools?

We're very keen on using languages and tools we are familiar with. If we have to use unfamiliar languages and tools, I would want to be assured that we could support these in the longer term. In the past, we have found ourselves being forced into projects where we had to use unfamiliar development environments. This left us with a support problem subsequently. Somebody has to maintain the system . . . that's why we choose familiar languages that we know we can deal with on an ongoing basis. But there are situations at the moment, Java is an example, where people are looking for more and more web-based applications. This is not an area we have huge experience of, but we are being forced into it and will have to deal with it eventually. It then becomes a strategic decision: "Yes, we are going to get involved with Java, we are going to employ Java programmers, and we are going to understand Java at the highest levels in the company." We are a small-enough company, so at director level we always like to have our hands on what's going on techni- cally-speaking. it's the only way for us to manage a project. If at director level we don't understand the environment and tools we are using, programmers can spin all sorts of yarns about what's happening on a project.

I'll turn the card over . . .

> *We'll be using familiar languages/tools*

I suppose resourcing would be my next one . . .

> *Need >two people on our team?*

If we needed more than five or six people on a project, we would definitely have to subcontract because we don't have that number of programmers. So I would have to go through my catalogue of subcontractors and rustle some up. We would also have to start thinking about how we should break the project down into chunks that could be distributed to those subcontractors in a meaningful way. Most applications are very difficult to work on in a multi-developer/multi-site mode. Whereas if it's just one or two people from start to finish, it's much more manageable because they are in touch with all the elements of what is going on, and so they can make more seat-of-the- pants type judgements about things. In a bigger application, you need a rigid specification, and everybody needs to know exactly what they are doing, so that the things they do don't impact on other people. Basically, you would need a more controlled project environment.

Let's see what it says . . .

> *We'll need three or more . . .*

What's next?

Being in control of the code is important to us . I don't like mucking around with other people's code. So it's . . .

> *Must change other developer's code?*

If we had to do it . . . at least in this project we are using familiar languages and tools, so it's not such a bad problem provided that the quality of their code is reasonable.

Let's see which applies . . .

We'll have to change . . .

This is beginning to look like a messy sort of project. it's going to be a big project. We are going to need lots of people. We are going to have to modify other people's code. it's going to need a lot of supervision and control. To put that control and effort in, we would need a full-time project manager who does nothing except manage the project. Whereas typically in our company the project manager would do some of the development work . . . a bit like an analyst/programmer role. I'm starting to fancy it less and less as it goes on!

What's next?

Our knowledge of the platform?

We have already said that we are using familiar tools. That implies that we are using a familiar environment. If it's a new platform, let's say it's the same tools in a different environment, that COULD be a cause for concern. Anyway, it doesn't bother me TOO much because at least the tool set is familiar. So most of the development issues that might arise would be ones we had dealt with before. For example, if it's a Sequel-Server database development, at least I'd know that record locking and all that stuff would work.

I'm looking . . .

Platform/environment is familiar . . .

That's good. Only two more . . .

Feasible to prototype?

Prototyping is very important. If we can't show the client a prototype, which is probable in this case because it looks like we are tweaking an existing application in some way, then we will have to go back to old-fashioned printed documentation . . . writing up the details. I guess we would still draft some sample windows that we could show them, even if it could not be within the RAD environment we like to use. We could draw some pictures for the client to show them what it was going to look like, but that would not be typical of how we generally do things. We like to produce a fully-developed prototype front end with all screens painted, but no code behind these, so at least the client can see exactly how everything is going to work. Then we put in the code. Often clients can't understand why putting in the code takes two months!

I'm turning it over . . .

It won't be possible to prototype . . .

As I thought. I'm afraid I really don't like the project at this stage. There are a lot of factors working against us. We are not able to prototype . . . we are using someone else's code . . . it's a big project that's going to take a long time. We would have to have some very good reasons for doing it.

I'm taking the last one and I'm going to turn it over . . .

> *We'll have to work to tight, customer-imposed timescales*

As I said before, three months would be a big project for us. So having to work to a tight timescale imposes even more discipline that we don't like.

At this stage, I've made my mind up – NO! I'd tell my friend in the pub: "Don't take this project on. Get them to talk to someone else!!"

If he was trapped into taking the project on for some reason, what advice would you give him?

OK. Contractually, I would have the contract as open as possible. I'll explain what I mean by this in a minute. it's like being a building contractor. If he has the plan for a brand new house, he can cost it out accurately, and he knows what he is going to make on it. But if he's going into an old Victorian house and has to take down the walls, he doesn't know what he is going to find when he opens it up. it's a bit like this when a developer has to open up other people's code. it's an even bigger disaster if the client doesn't have a clear picture of what he is looking for because the developer is going to have to add new rooms as he goes along. it's a disaster from a costing point of view. If you're the builder who has to take this project on, I would urge you to keep it as open as possible. Get agreement at the outset on a brief that identifies the key elements of what you are going to try to achieve, and get agreement that anything outside that brief will be an extra charge. Most clients are keen to tie us into a fixed-price, all-in contract. If some unanticipated extra arises during development, the customer will then say "But you said you would do X, and surely this includes also doing Y?" Whereas, if we had been able at the start to clearly identify the things that we could clearly achieve, and had drawn a line under these, and said "This is what we are going to do for this amount of money. Anything beyond this will be charged for on a time-and-materials basis", we would at least have some damage-limitation protection. So, don't tie yourself into a fixed-price contract on this one!! That's the first thing I would say.

Secondly, you need to get some good people who understand the tool kit that you are using and manage these people very, very closely. Get a full-time project manager on to it who is almost dedicated to coordinating the development.

Our approach would be to document the minimum requirements for the project in such a way that these can be measured in a month's time, in two months' time, and so on. This would be a very difficult project . . . we have been here a number of times and I know what it's like. In most cases, the things that pop up are so obscure that nobody would have thought about them in the first place, and they end up having major implications for the project. So you really have to protect yourself.

How do you think this project will turn out?

I strongly disagree that this will be a positive experience for the customer or the developer. This is a bad project.

Which are the one or two cards that are the real killers in this one?

We'll have to change other developer's code and *It won't be possible to proto-type*

Any cards that strike you as missing?

I'm sure there was something, but I can't think of it at the moment.

MERVYN

12

My VERY BIG DIFFERENCE pile . . .

System must go right first time? Our knowledge of their industry? Must share control with a third-party? Agree amongst themselves on what's needed? People most affected really want the system? A committed project "owner"? Are they able/willing to drive implementation? Must change other developer's code? Must we subcontract?

What's the big difference between the VERY BIG DIFFERENCE pile and the other two?

The VERY BIG DIFFERENCE pile contains elements that are mainly outside your own control. This is what causes risk. These are the things that can bite you. If it's inside your control, even if it's a big problem, you can probably do something about it.

Focus on the VERY BIG DIFFERENCE pile. Take the single most important card.

There's a cluster here of ones that are a bit similar . . .

> *A committed project "owner"?, People most affected really want the system?* and *Agree amongst themselves on what's needed?*

These are "people" issues. If you're trying to put in a system for people who don't want it, you're hitting your head off a wall.

And these three go together . . .

> *Must share control with a third party?, Must change other developer's code?* and *Must we subcontract?*

These are all to do with third-party issues.

I'll start with . . .

> *A committed project "owner"?*

The reason I'm concerned about this one is simply historical. We have worked in places where somebody senior has said "It would be a good idea to put in a system to do X . . ." and the project gets passed around and actioned onto someone who really doesn't want it, and who just goes through the motions. They don't really own the project. This is very easy to identify. They won't make decisions themselves . . . they are not that clear on exactly what they are trying to do . . . proposals go through a huge number of committees, more so than needed. If anything goes wrong down the line they won't back you up. They will always blame you. They'll say "Don't blame me . . .". If they don't have an owner who is really trying to run with it, you are beating your head off a wall.

What would you do if you spotted this problem?

I'd try to highlight this to whoever asked me to look at the area in the first place. To say, face to face to them, "Do you REALLY want this system? Is what we are proposing what you REALLY want?" If he says "Yes . . . This is REALLY where we want to go", then you are starting to create ownership. If he says "Well, it's not really what we want", he'll probably talk himself out of doing it at all. At that stage you are probably better off walking away, if you can do that. we're an independent software house, so we have the option to walk away. I pity an IT manager who gets handed a project and it's his job to do it . . . he can't escape. This is an issue I would try to identify early in the quoting process. A sign of this problem is in the answer to the question "Who do I send the quote to?" If it's to go straight to a secretary or a purchasing department, it's not looking good. It should be "No . . . no . . . send ME the quote and I will champion it in my organization." Then you're on a winner.

Let's see which applies . . .

Someone has taken clear, committed ownership . . .

Which card next?

If someone has taken ownership, then my next is . . .

Agree amongst themselves on what's needed?

Disagreement is a massive risk for a software company because, assuming that it's a fixed-price job, or even time and materials but within boundaries, when you launch into a project you need to know when you are finished. To know when you're finished, and therefore to get paid, you need to know what you are doing. If the users disagree about what's needed, you will never get a definitive specification signed off because you'll always have someone saying "We want this . . . we don't really want that . . .". What can happen is that you get into an infinite loop of weekly meetings which endlessly review things . . . decide what's in or out or in or out . . . you won't be able to get agreement on exactly what you are trying to do. This causes huge problems. Because until you get agreement, you won't be able to do a quote . . . do a design.

If I had this problem I'd try to summarize the issues from the different camps . . . what they want in . . . what they want out . . . and I would take this to the person who has ownership of the project, and I'd pass the buck back to him. Ultimately, it is their problem . . . it's their concept . . . their baby. Like the chairman of a meeting, he must decide what's in . . . what's out . . . and I'd be guided by him.

Let me turn over . . .

They don't disagree . . .

I'll stick to the thread we are on. My next is . . .

Are they able/willing to drive implementation?

If we have to sort out the implementation, this can become an area that can drag on for a long, long time. This card goes very much hand in hand with . . .

People most affected really want the system?

If we had to drive implementation, we'd be into arranging for people to do parallel runs and trying to arrange for them to do lots of extra work in the evenings and weekends . . . to keep their own work going . . . to keep their existing system and the new system running . . . and if they don't want to or maybe they are not that keen anyway . . . and we are trying to do all the pushing. Ultimately, we are an external organization. We don't have the say-so to make all that happen, and if we are trying to organize meetings and they won't attend these . . . they won't get the impetus going . . . it can cause the implementation phase to drag out by many months, when only weeks are really needed.

Let's say there had been disagreement about what was needed, or the people most affected didn't want the system AND I felt we would have to drive implementation AND I detected all this at the start, I would make sure that the contract stated that implementation costs were to be on a time-and-materials basis. This would be an absolute must. Even if you feel people are keen to put the system in, implementation is the phase where timescales can go absolutely crazy. You can have a piece of software, and it can be working fine in your office in a controlled test environment, but when you hit implementation and you install it on a client's machine . . . maybe they don't have the network ready . . . maybe the client's PCs aren't of the right specification . . . maybe these aren't connected to the network etc. . . . etc. That's when timescales move outside your control. One of your people might go down to do an install, and only after the tenth trip down there they finally get a screen working in front of a user . . . because every time there's some little problem . . . and you ask the client to sort it out if they have their own IT section. Or maybe their hardware vendor has to come in to help with something. it's outside your control. That's why it's such a big issue.

Let's see which applies . . .

We'll have to sort out/drive implementation

OK. In this case, we'll have to get some authority from the client. If we are drawing up the implementation plan, and if we are saying "For this weekend, we need X done, by next weekend we need Y done", we need to make sure that the project leader on the client's side will help us to enforce the implementation decisions we have to make to keep things on track.

My next is . . .

People most affected really want the system?

This could be one to be worked on early on. There might be an inherent reason why they don't want the new system. Systems are replaced for millions of reasons. Maybe they are currently on old hardware which is expensive to maintain, but the users love the application and don't want to lose it. It may be that someone is going to lose their job because the new system is more efficient. You need to track down the reasons why they don't want it. With luck, it's just a cost thing . . . the old hardware is just obsolete . . . therefore no one is losing their jobs, and it's easier to get people onside . . . you can sell them the advantages of the new system. For example, the new system won't be crashing as much, and so on. If the root cause is that half a dozen people are going to lose their jobs, then it's outside your control. there's nothing you can tell these people that will cheer them up, except that it's not your doing . . . it's the bosses who made the decision. This is more an emotional and political thing . . . rather than something you can create an action plan to handle. I'm looking . . .

People most affected seem to genuinely want . . .

Next is . . .

Must change other developer's code?

Changing code becomes a problem in a couple of respects. The immediate problem is to get and understand their code. It may not be written or documented very well. Maybe it's not very robust and won't take change easily.

But usually you can slog your way through it. A huge issue can arise if anything goes wrong in an area of the application that's still being maintained by this other developer. Then immediately ALL problems become your problems because "You broke it!" For this reason, you have to be so careful! You have to get the other developer onside. You have to get him to agree what you are going to change . . . what you are not going to change . . . and make sure he is happy with that, and to get him to sign off on it. We have this situation running at the moment. we're handling it by releasing any changes we make to this other company's software back to them, not directly to the client. This other developer then tests it to satisfy themselves. Then THEY ship it to the client. In this way, all three parties are happy that the software is right. And this other developer is happy because he's getting some chargeable days from our project. Also, the three parties get used to sitting around a table together, sorting out problems. I'm not saying this solves the problem of something going wrong in the future . . . who's at fault . . . but at least there won't be a shouting match. We know one another well enough to be able to work through any problems together.

Let's see . . .

We'll have to change other developer's code

Some bad news. OK. We'll approach it in the way I just highlighted. My next is . . .

Our knowledge of their industry?

The larger the project, the bigger this issue could become. If you're taking on something small like twenty or thirty man-days on a localized departmental system, or an interface, or a small MIS job, not having industry knowledge is not such a problem, because in a short time you will probably learn enough about the specific area you're working in. If you are talking of a large system . . . if your company suddenly decided it was going to write a piece of software for European Airbus to fly their airplane . . . you'd need to know all about the airplane! If you're just writing a system to manage their inventory of aircraft tyres, you could probably have a good crack at that. If something is very big, and you've no knowledge of it, you should simply walk away.

I'm looking . . .

We've little or no knowledge . . .

What do you make of the project so far?

We've got somebody who's leading, so they will have committed to helping us in any way they can. The users are agreed on what's needed, so we can build a good specification of what we are trying to do. we've to try to push the implementation, but that may not be too bad now, because at least we will have a definitive list of what we are trying to implement. If *Are they able/willing to drive implementation?* and *Agree amongst themselves . . . ?* had gone against us, we would have a big problem.

The users want the system, so that enthusiasm will help us to get the implementation through very quickly. We do have to change other people's code. But assuming we have got an agreement on this . . . that they are happy enough for us to do it . . . and that we have a controlled-release mechanism which will make sure they test whether our changes affect any other part of the application, we know whatever changes we make won't cause problems when we go live.

Unfortunately we don't know much about the client's industry and it is maybe a largish project. From the client's side, we have someone who is leading us very strongly and we also have a clear definition of what's wanted . . . so we can get them to document clearly what they want to be done. The more detail we can get from the users in that specification, guided by the main leader, the better. This will document all the knowledge we need to know about the industry. So *Someone has taken clear, committed ownership . . .* and *They don't disagree . . .* help us overcome the industry knowledge question. If the users couldn't agree on what was wanted, and we didn't know the industry, we wouldn't know where we were going.

Next is . . .

Must share control with a third party?

This can be a problem. If the consultants give you a sub-project to do, that's fine. They are your client. If they are in there dabbling and they say "Well, we don't like the way you're suggesting doing it . . . we want it done like this" without good reason, and it's not the way we are used to working . . . maybe it's a different methodology, or not using our own standards, they can impose a huge overhead on your working style. So some consultants you can work with very easily. With others, it's much more difficult.

Let's see . . .

We won't have to share control . . .

My next is . . .

Must we subcontract?

If you are subcontracting because there are one or two small technical interfaces that you don't know how to do, or something like that, that need not be a big problem . . . if you're not getting them to do too much, and you can define it as a black box. If you're subcontracting because of the volume of work . . . if you're taking in a single subcontractor person into your own team of, say, five people, that's OK. But if you are taking in ten subcontractors into your own team of two people, then you are heading for a nightmare because you're going to have contractors changing . . . coming and going . . . they become distracted . . . they all have mobile phones . . . they are all worrying about their next contract . . . they are not as focused and dedicated to your project. That I would see as a big problem. If I had to take in ten subcontractors, rather than do that, I'd try to run the project in conjunction with . . . ideally jointly . . . another software company whereby they would provide maybe five full-time people to you. If you have too many contractors around the place, and it's a longish project, they are on much higher take-home pay . . . they have nicer cars . . . they can afford more drink on a Friday night . . . than your full-time people. So it makes your own full-time people very uneasy. But if you've got a room full of full-time people from two companies, then they are probably on similar terms and conditions. The whole thing is easier to manage.

Let's see . . .

> *We won't need to subcontract . . .*

My last one . . . please!

> *System must go right first time?*

I don't know any software company that managed to get it right first time. All you can do is make sure you've got a clear picture of what you are doing, write your specs in detail, write your code properly, and test the hell out of it before you release it. You have to be as professional as you can. One of the ways to help yourself is to get some of the users onto your test team, to test it at your own site. Get them to provide as much realistic test data as they can . . . get them to give you test cases . . . get somebody who works in that industry to do the testing because they'll know the real pitfalls . . . make the testing as realistic as possible . . . test the hell out of it. That's all you can do.

Let's look . . .

> *We can pilot the new system until we get it right*

Any advice for the guy who has to run this project?

Spend as much time as possible at the start on the client's site, and learn the business. Make sure you keep the client's project leader on your side. Any issue you are unclear about, make sure you discuss it through him and get him to give you clarification and guidance. Make sure you come across as a strong leader. Give them a clear implementation plan showing what you expect from them and showing how you will judge how well things are going. Get the owner of the project to agree the implementation plan. In that way, he will in effect be helping you to push it through. Create as much of a bond as you can with the developer whose code you've to modify. Make things as seamless as possible with him and have them test your code.

How well do you think this project will turn out?

This one should go OK. *We've little or no knowledge of the customer's industry* is a problem, but *Someone has taken clear, committed ownership . . .* should help.

I agree that this project will be a positive experience for the customer. I strongly agree that it will be a positive experience for the developer. He is about to learn a lot about another industry. So it's interesting for the people doing it. So they'll learn a lot. They've someone strong on the client's side who'll help them do the learning. They have only three problems to solve. I think it'll go very well.

Which is the "nastiest" of the nasties?

I think . . . We'll have to sort out/drive implementation

Sorting out the implementation is again a function of size. If it's a single-user system, it's not too hard to implement. If it's a one-thousand-user system and you're talking about a huge budget, and building a new computer room and things like that, then . . . very nasty. Having to change other developer's code is manageable. The lack of knowledge of the industry depends on the size and nature of the project. I think it's between *We'll have to sort out/drive implementation* and *We've little or no knowledge of their industry* as to which is the worst.

And the good news? The biggest risk reducers?

Someone has taken clear, committed ownership . . . is the best news of all. *People most affected seem to genuinely want it . . .* is also great news.

Any cards missing?

There is one missing, I think, about how innovative your project has to be. If you're doing bread-and-butter stuff . . . yet another payroll . . . there's nothing in that that would frighten anyone. Of late, you would see projects come up involving things like intranets, web-based applications, e-commerce systems . . . using new technology. you're up at the bleeding edge of it all. This is scary stuff. you're using Java or something like that. You just won't find people with five years' experience of this stuff. it's just not out there. So, the innovative nature of the project would be a risk element. And the newer the tool sets, the bigger the risk. This one has burnt us.

MICHAEL B

13

My VERY BIG DIFFERENCE pile . . .

*Application complexity?   Any tricky interfacing?   Our knowledge of the
application?   Feasible to prototype?   Realistic expectations?
Agree amongst themselves on what's needed?   Our knowledge of the
languages/tools?   A committed project "owner"?   Has their PM
time/skill/authority?   Must satisfy different groups with different needs?
How adaptable must our solution be?   Are they able/willing to drive
implementation?   People most affected really want the system?   Major
change to customer's procedures?   Our knowledge of their industry?
Our knowledge of the platform?*

What really distinguishes between the three piles?

The ones in the VERY BIG DIFFERENCE pile are the real risk generators in
my view. These are the ones that could cause you to lose control . . . these
generate uncertainty . . . possible black holes.

Let's focus on the VERY BIG DIFFERENCE pile. Which is the single most important of these to project risk?

A committed project "owner"?

We know from experience that we're on a loser if somebody isn't guiding
things from the client's side . . . if there's no real ownership. it's usually been
a disaster in terms of timescales and costs, and the client not really getting
what they wanted. Ideally, I'd pull out. The "owner" should be someone reasonably senior . . . maybe the accountant or the managing director. If we
couldn't pull out, I would get them to encourage somebody less senior, but
very enthusiastic, to take on the project . . . someone who wants to develop
their computer skills. We would home in on that person, say Cecil. I would
say to the MD, or whoever SHOULD be the "owner", "Is it OK with you if we
work with Cecil, because you don't seem to have the time?" Of course, you
lose authority that way. If you ask someone in the organization to do something, they might say "Get lost." But you do get someone working at your side.

I'm turning over . . .

> *Nobody wants to own it . . .*

I'm taking these two together because they are really the same thing . . .

> *Our knowledge of their industry? and Our knowledge of the application?*

If we didn't know the industry, we'd try to get some consultancy or a quick "lesson" from soneone outside the client's organization who did know it. we'd look at any competitors" software products, demo disks and brochures aimed at that industry. If we just didn't know the application, we would work with Cecil on a day-to-day basis and whoever would be running the application . . . we'd gen ourselves up on the application in this way.

Let's see . . .

> *We've a good knowledge of their industry and The application is new to us.*

It's good we know the industry. Getting the application knowledge should be OK.

From our point of view . . . from the developer's point of view . . . in terms of whether things will be a success, my next would be . . .

> *Our knowledge of the platform? and Our knowledge of the languages/ tools?*

These are much the same thing. Though the environment and platform aren't as important to me as the development language. We wouldn't pitch for something if we didn't have the expertise. But if we were forced to, we'd buy in the skills . . . a contractor or whatever . . . to train our people. But we wouldn't write the application and try to learn at the same time.

A lot of guys would just take the business, but it's a disaster area in my experience. We built a hand-held application for salesmen using a palmtop made by ~£%*#. The language we used was called #@*&^%$£. it's a bit like a 4GL. We sourced this language in California . . . got it over here. We committed ourselves to using it. There was no problem doing trivial things with it, but for anything real, it kept falling over . . . memory and configuration problems. Support was by email and telephone with big delays. The application was no problem to us because it was a cut-down version of a laptop application we already had implemented successfully in DBase. Our knowledge of the industry was fine. But we just didn't have a clue about what we were doing with the language and the environment. It turned out to be a nightmare. So today, we'd tell the client up front that we don't know, for example,

Java. I'd say "If you want this written in Java, it's going to take us longer, and it's going to cost." If they say "Fair enough, because the other people we're talking to don't know it either", or if they say "Get lost!", that's fine by me. But I'd be up front with them.

I'm turning . . .

We'll be using unfamiliar languages/tools

Next is . . .

People most affected really want the system?

If they hated the whole thing, if I was stuck in the middle, I'd work really, really hard to get a good relationship with those people . . . by being on site . . . it might be wrong, but by being personal . . . by showing them prototypes . . . by explaining that the system will make things easier for them. We would be very conscious of not trying to be flash computer geniuses. we'd say "Don't worry if you don't know Windows, we'll help train you." As opposed to generating resentment like "Who are you guys anyway, coming in here on huge money . . . ?" We would work really hard to try to win them around.

If this didn't work?

We'd go on with the system regardless and just hope it would turn out OK.

Here we go . . .

People most affected don't seem to really want the new system

What do you make of this project so far?

Very risky. Huge risk actually.

I want . . .

How adaptable must our solution be?

Why is this important?

You can finish the project and do what you set out to do. But if it's not adaptable . . . if it's a very closed system . . . within six months they'll be totally unhappy with what you delivered . . . and after all that effort to get them on your side. The first time they try to expand or adapt it . . . if the whole thing is too tightly written . . . not parameterized . . . then suddenly it can't be done. So you are almost into another project to do it. So adaptability is important to keeping them happy. We always try to have as much of the application parameterized as we can from a design point of view. We avoid the old way of hard-coding things.

Let's see which applies . . .

The new system must be adaptable enough to cope with unknown future needs

This is a project I want to walk away from!

Next is . . .

Are they able/willing to drive implementation?

Implementation is the one part of the project that the client has to manage. While we can help and show people what has to be done, they have to do the implementation. No matter how good the system is, in terms of its development and testing, if the implementation isn't managed it's a disaster. It can drag on for six months or more. It doesn't matter if you're going from a computer system or a manual system. If you don't bring over your balances, your stock figures and so on correctly, and if these aren't checked, the new system won't get a good, clean start. If there's a problem, you're left wondering "Is it the data? Is it our programs?" All this has to be formally managed and signed off. If the client REALLY wanted us to handle implementation, reluctantly we could offer this service. We could put an implementation person in. That person would be a hard-nosed, non-programmer type . . . "I'm here to get things done." But the problem with this is that your person doesn't have the authority to say to accounts staff "I want you to load those balances by Friday, so you'll have to stay back on Thursday night." They'll say "Who are you to tell me what to do?" If we did this, it would be on a time-and-materials basis. If you're not charging the client, and if they don't have the drive to manage it themselves, three days becomes a week then two weeks then three weeks. If you charge the £$%^ a day, they're going to take it a bit seriously.

Let's look . . .

They are willing and able . . .

Nearly there. Next is . . .

Realistic expectations?

If expectations were way out of line, we would document very clearly what is doable, and at what cost, and on what timescale. We would document the limits, what the system will do, what it won't do, where it finishes, where the mainframe or some other system or application takes over. we'd hold regular meetings to make sure everybody was aware of how long things were going to take . . . of the time needed for conversion for example. A lot of this would be self-protection. it's about making sure the users don't think they are going to get some all-singing, all-dancing application when they're not. We always try to deliver more than the client's expectations, so calibrating expectations is critical.

Let's look . . .

The customer has realistic expectations . . .

My next is . . .

Has their PM time/skill/authority?

This is another aspect of their willingness to manage. If their project manager lacked any of these aspects, we might try to fill the vacuum. But it usually backfires. I would very clearly document everything . . . what we've done this week . . . what we're going to do next week. At the end of the day, when the implementation is delayed by a month or two and their directors are kicking up a fuss, at least you can demonstrate exactly what happened . . . "no help from Mr X. Mr X is probably the type of person who will say "I was never asked to do this or that . . .". So, you need everything in black and white. Self-protection.

Which applies?

Their PM has the needed time/skill/authority

What advice would you give a pal who has to run this project?

Get someone on board who is familiar with the language and the tools. Build in extra costs and timescales for this, and tell the client up front. Unless it's a simple little project and you felt you could get away with learning as you went along.

Work really hard to get a relationship going with the people who will actually be using the system. Otherwise it will become a them-and-us battle, as against being a team that is working together to develop the system. If you don't have them on your side, it's very difficult. They'll find fault with every single thing you do. Involvement is the keyword.

The application is new to you, but at least you have a knowledge of the industry, so you are well on the way. Go to exhibitions. Get brochures or demo-disks. Get a feel for competitors' products or systems. it's a bit like spying I suppose.

The new system must be adaptable enough . . . and *The application is new to us* are very nasty taken together. If you don't know the application well, you won't be able to build an adaptable solution. I've no magic bullet for this one.

How do you think the project will turn out?

I'm "undecided" on whether it's likely to be a positive experience for the customer. I disagree that it will be a positive experience for the developer.

The nastiest ones?

We'll be using unfamiliar languages/tools, The application is new to us and *People most affected don't seem to really want the new system.*

The "nicest" ones?

The customer has the willingness/skills to manage implementation . . ., The customer has realistic expectations . . ., The customer's PM has the needed time/skill/authority and *we've a good knowledge of the customer's industry* in that order.

Any issues missing from the cards?

I don't think so.

Oh! Some more advice to my pal. Payment stages are very important in this project. If you don't get paid until it's finished, you'll never be finished! It'll be "Well, do this one more thing, then we'll pay you."

MICHAEL C

14

OK. I've broken the cards up into the three piles. To make sense of the VERY BIG DIFFERENCE pile, I want to talk through all three.

This is my LITTLE/NO DIFFERENCE pile . . .

Need >two people on our team? Tight customer-imposed timescales? TP versus MIS/DSS application? Project duration >three months? Are they a big versus small company? Our knowledge of the languages/tools? Our knowledge of the platform? A one-off project for them or the first of a series? Application complexity? System must go right first time? Feasible to prototype? Our knowledge of the application?

I'll talk through some of them . . .

> *Need >two people on our team?* and *Project duration >three months?*

These two deal with project scale. Unless it's an outrageously big project, scale aspects don't matter.

> *Our knowledge of the application?*, *Our knowledge of the platform?* and *Our knowledge of the languages/tools?*

These are no threat. In fact, being paid to learn about new things is an opportunity! Anyway, with the rapid change in the IT industry, if you can't cope with change, you won't stay in business.

> *A one-off project for them or the first of a series?*

My old engineering professor once said "Treat each project as if it is the only one in the universe. Do the best you can with it. If you get it right, other projects will follow. If you focus your eyes on what could be next, you'll trip over what's under your feet."

> *Tight customer-imposed timescales?*, *Feasible to prototype?* and *System must go right first time?*

I can see you're surprised that I put these three in this pile! As I see it, these are about the "mechanics" of the whole process. You just have to adapt to and live with whatever applies. Sure, it's nice if you can do some realistic prototyping. But if the application doesn't make this feasible, you just have to get on and do the best job you can.

What if anything, are the real underlying differences between the three piles?

When I look over the least important pile, I ask myself what have these items got in common? To me, these are all aspects of a project that are "controllable". Some of them I may not like – but from a self-protection point of view, they wouldn't worry me. The "mechanics" of the project can be tuned to cope with them.

Here's my "middle" pile. This pile mostly includes aspects that MIGHT cause me to lose control of the project and to become vulnerable to some black holes . . .

Must we subcontract? Major change to customer's procedures? Number of different functional areas involved? Users' computer experience? Who'll we be working with (users or IT)? Are they able/willing to drive implementation? Must change other developer's code? Have we a credible competitor? How adaptable must our solution be?

Maybe just a word on *Are they able/willing to drive implementation?*

Many clients will be up front and say "We can't handle implementation by ourselves. Please help." That's fine by me. The real problem arises when they THINK they have the skills, but they haven't. Then when we deliver the system, implementation falls over. We had one case like this recently. We knew that implementation would involve a massive amount of data entry, correction and standardization, and so on right across the organization. At the outset we said "In our view you are not ready for this new system. You don't have the basic procedures in place." But they insisted they could handle implementation. Then, fortunately, I wrote them a letter saying we had grave misgivings on this point, and stating that implementation wasn't in our terms of reference. We modified the new system so that an automatic log of all data entered was kept for the first few months. They got into big data quality problems when they took over the new system, just like we predicted. We looked at the data-entry log and pointed out the problems. They wrote and admitted they weren't coping. Now, if that had been admitted earlier, we could have done something about it.

And on Users' computer experience?

Sometimes we have found that dealing with inexperienced computer users is better. Particularly where we are dealing with experienced users who having been used to mainframe systems. Their whole concept is "mainframe", and you just can't shake them off this way of thinking. They want their modern PC/network system to look like a mainframe system! Most inexperienced computer users will put in a modern system without any thought at all.

Let's move on to the pile that REALLY counts.

Here's my "most important" pile. These are the ones that could leave a PM very exposed to loss of control over events. Lots of potential black holes to fall into here! . . .

Agree amongst themselves on what's needed?   People most affected really want the system?   Realistic expectations?   Can they define their problem?   Must share control with a third party?   Any tricky interfacing?   A committed project "owner"?   Has their PM time/skill/authority?   Any hidden agendas?   Must satisfy different groups with different needs?   Their experience in running IT projects?   Mission-critical application?   Our knowledge of their industry?

Let's go through these cards in order of their importance to you. Most important one first.

Agree amongst themselves on what's needed?

This is the single most important one. Disagreement amongst themselves is an absolute show-stopper as far as I'm concerned. When I see this, I want to walk away. You are in a no-win situation from the beginning.

They disagree amongst themselves . . .

Walk away! In my company, we now have a policy of actually walking out. You cannot make them agree, so you really have no counter measure.

People most affected really want the system?

If users don't want the new system, or if they can't agree amongst themselves about what's needed, one strategy is to think of a price for the contract, then double or treble it! we've done this more than once. It gives you enough of a cushion to cope with these kinds of issues. But it's not a very moral way to do things. Honest guys would walk away.

People most affected don't seem to really want . . .

That's it, walk away pal!

Realistic expectations?

People who have completely unrealistic expectations of what is possible are invariably the people who have no ability in-house to implement the system, amongst other things. If they underestimate what you have to do, they will also totally underestimate what they have to do. These two factors go together. Let's see which applies in this case . . .

The customer has realistic expectations . . .

Fair enough.

Let me turn over my next one . . .

The customer is able to define the problem in IT-addressable terms

Good – that's a very important one.

Must share control with a third party?

We will NOT share control of a project with a third party . . . simply NO! End of story! Any time we have done it, it has caused us trouble. A classic example of this was our work with XYZ [a big computer services company]. They would take prime contractorship and bring us in as a subcontractor. That invariably wound up as a disaster. Why? Their agenda was different from our agenda. Their agenda was to sell more and more hardware, and they were bringing in software as a kind of sop to get the business. They would promise the client anything whatsoever to keep them happy, so no matter what we said we would do, they would promise something else. And because they were in the dominant position, they could force us to do what they had agreed with the client. They were just using us as a pawn. This is an intolerable situation. A definite "walk-away" job.

Let's see . . .

We'll have to share control . . .

Walk away!

Any tricky interfacing?

Interfacing usually causes problems. If you are interfacing into something that is very well and precisely understood it is easy. If you are asked to interface with something that you are only guessing as to what the hell is in there, don't! The only exception to this is if the client accepts that this is a jointly shared risk and if the structure of the contract explicitly says how this risk will be dealt with. Don't put yourself in the position of having to interface with an existing client-developed application unless the client has a very competent computer department. You can run into real trouble when you agree to interface with an existing application that the client's people SAY they understand, but don't. You make a start, and suddenly the ground opens up into big cracks.

Let's see . . .

No tricky interfacing . . .

That's OK then.

I'm going to take these two together and look straight at the "answers". . .

Nobody wants to "own" the project and The customer's PM has the needed time/skill/authority.

Mixed signals. Not looking too good. If both of these had been bad news, my advice would have been to walk away.

I'm going to take the rest of this pile in one go, and look straight at the answers . . .

There seems to be no hidden agenda, we've to satisfy multiple groups . . . , The customer is experienced in running computer projects, The new system is mission-critical . . . and We've a good knowledge of the customer's industry.

A mixture of good and bad news. At least there seem to be no hidden agendas.

What's your overall impression of this project? Key advice to your pal?

Overall, this is really one I would rather walk away from. When you are into a project like this, you are into the self-protection business. The most critical thing is to get the conditions of contract right. If the client insists on a fixed price contract, I WOULD walk away. The contract must define precisely what you will do and what you will not do. You must have proper variations clauses in the contract which enable you to claim for all the various unpredictable problems you could find yourself having to sort out. The big principle is that you don't sort them, or you get paid for sorting them.

The management overhead in this sort of project is huge because you are dealing with multiple users, a lot of uncertainties, and so on. In the past in situations like this we have drawn up two contracts: a project management contract and a software delivery contract, which are quite distinct from each other. The project management contract would be on a time-and-materials basis. It would cover the variable, less-defined aspects of the project like specifying requirements. We would say to the client "If you have not defined exactly and precisely what you want, or if your internal organization structure is not capable of handling this project, we will come in and help you to put it together." We call these "limited-liability" contracts, where we go in,

114

do a study, see what the problems are on a time-and-materials basis, define the next phase and get to the point where we can do a proper contract for the software delivery. If you try to package the two different aspects into one contract, you are dead!

How do you think this particular project is likely to turn out?

If it's not handled well, it's going to turn out to be a very negative result for everybody. The issues we have talked about need to be aired at the beginning with the client, and to be taken care of. This is a very qualified answer I know. I'm very pessimistic.

Were there any issues NOT covered by the cards that you would have expected to see there?

Just one. "How much control have you over the conditions of contract?" At the end of the day, you are doing a job and getting paid X under certain conditions of contract. If these conditions are badly structured, if there are loose ends, you are potentially on a loser. You can get *!# %^£*&'s in organizations who will drive a coach and four through every condition of contract that exists. If you haven't got things nailed down properly, you are defenceless. In this project, the terms of the contract will be critical.

MIKE A

Here's my VERY BIG DIFFERENCE pile . . .

Any tricky interfacing? Agree amongst themselves on what's needed? Any hidden agendas? A committed project "owner"? Has their PM time/skill/authority? Number of different functional areas involved? System must go right first time? Our knowledge of the platform? Must satisfy different groups with different needs? Major change to customer's procedures? Must change other developer's code? Realistic expectations? Who'll we be working with (users or IT)? Tight customer-imposed timescales? Our knowledge of the languages/tools? People most affected really want the system?

What's so special about your VERY BIG DIFFERENCE pile?

It's about things like user ownership, user involvement, the issue of someone wanting to make it work. it's about things that could be significant "unknowns" in the technical area. The area of change . . . upheaval . . . for the customer's organization . . . one can get big trouble from this. It includes some things we just won't get involved in, like changing other developers' code. it's just too risky.

My middle pile includes things that could involve more work, like dealing with inexperienced users, the type of system, the customer's experience with computer projects, and so on. It may cost more money . . . but things like these are not going to collapse the project on you. You can cope with these.

Let's work with the VERY BIG DIFFERENCE pile. Pick the construct that could make the biggest difference.

It has to be . . .

> *People most affected really want the system?*

If people don't want the system, there's a very good chance it won't work. There are so many things that people can do to stop it working. It reduces

CHAPTER FIFTEEN   Mike A

your chances of success hugely. Having committed users is vital. If one was pushed into this situation, then you'd need someone on the client's side with sufficient clout to push things through and to sign off at the completion of each stage of the project. I've seen this situation before. Some guy up in the hierarchy wanted the system badly and he forced it through. it's doable provided the senior guy stays with the project and remains committed. If he or she abandons it, you're dead. You need very active . . . very senior support . . . to deal with this.

Let's see . . .

The people most affected seem to genuinely want the new system

Your next one?

Agree amongst themselves on what's needed?

If they disagree about what's needed, hopefully you can get someone further up the line to steamroller it through. But even if you can, you may find yourself trying to build a system that's very hard to pin down . . . lots of change requests . . . thrashing around. So you would need to be very careful about getting sign-offs at every stage. Even if you get these, you're likely to have a period of instability and conflicting demands for change when the system goes in. Because of the disagreement, whoever wins, someone else will try to get their way later on. Disagreement heightens the need for sign-offs! It can threaten the commercial viability of the project . . . create havoc with timescales.

Let's see which applies . . .

They don't disagree amongst themselves . . .

My next is . . .

Realistic expectations?

This is one I like to tackle very early on. If there are any problems about expectations, I like to get rid of these by telling them very clearly what we think is doable. If they don't buy this, we would bail out. I know lots of our competitors who would take the business anyway, and try to sort it out later. But this is not a route we take. We would try to change the goalposts . . . to make it doable . . . to make it cost-affordable. If you don't do this, you are into constant conflict, and that's not something we want. This is an issue you must deal with at the pre-contract stage. If you can't get it right, tell the client to go elsewhere.

Let's see . . .

The customer has unrealistic expectations . . .

What's it looking like so far?

Not so bad. But we'd have to sort out the expectations problem before signing a contract. Otherwise, the chances of us being offered and taking the business go down rapidly. Mind you, even if you THINK you have sorted out the expectations problem, it can still come back at you during the project . . . it's an ongoing education process.

My next one is . . .

Has their PM time/skill/authority?

If there was a problem here, I'd try to broaden the base of my contact with the company. If it was about lack of authority, I'd look upwards and try to find someone with authority who would support the guy I had to deal with. If it was a lack of skill, I'd broaden my contacts in the direction of the users, and put more reliance on them. I'd try to find someone on that front who had the skills. If it's lack of time, all one can do is highlight this to their management, and carefully monitor what they ACTUALLY do vis-à-vis what they are SUPPOSED to do . . . check if the time is actually being put in. Be very careful to document what they are supposed to do, what's actually done, by whom and when. This is just covering one's $£&. Handling these issues takes time, and diverts attention away from actually developing software . . . into doing a lot of ancillary things for self-protection.

I'm turning over . . .

The customer's PM lacks the needed time/skill/authority

So we have expectations and skills problems. The one probably explains the other. At this stage, I'm becoming very cautious. There is a strong suggestion that one should be broadening one's contact base with the organization, and tying down very, very carefully what one is going to do for the client. If the expectations thing can be sorted out, fine. They either sign the contract for the figure you give them, or they don't. They are either in or out. If you have to walk away, you've done the right thing. It suggests one should be focusing much more on the end-users in this case because they genuinely want the system, and they agree on what's needed. If there is real enthusiasm for the project, one can very often guide things so that they become more doable. It looks like their main project person is going to get left on the sidelines on this project, except for sign-off purposes!

In the light of the "answers" so far, my next card is definitely . . .

Who'll we be working with (users or IT)?

If the answer to this one is wrong, we are definitely in big trouble. Because if you are dealing through the IT department, and not directly with users, their main project person is likely to be in IT. And if he/she is not up to the job, you have a real problem. The chances of anything successful coming out of the project shrink very dramatically.

We'll be dealing directly with the users

This greatly reduces my concern about their PM's lack of time/skill/authority.

My next one is . . . I suppose what I'm doing now is looking for indicators in different areas. I'm checking-out just one of the items in each area . . . the major indicator. The next area that would concern me would be . . .

Our knowledge of the platform? and *Our knowledge of the languages/tools?*

There two are very similar . . . if the answer to either were bad, it makes the problem about unrealistic expectations even worse. If language, tools or environment are not already part of your stock-in-trade, you won't be able to deliver as quickly . . . this would bring in . . .

Tight, customer-imposed timescales?

It would be an excruciating combination if we added having to work under tight, client-imposed deadlines. If we had to use an unfamiliar language, tool or environment, it would lengthen our timescales, rather than actually endanger the project. Before we'd use the language or tool, we would check it out very carefully. We wouldn't adopt something that we hadn't seen proven in practice. But the real danger is that it would take us longer to get it working. It wouldn't be a cost we'd pass on to the customer, it would be a strategic investment for us, and not taken on lightly.

I'm turning over . . .

We'll be using unfamiliar languages/tools

So the next one has to be . . .

Tight customer-imposed timescales?

The unfamiliar bit combined with tight time restrictions is the real danger. So, let's see . . .

We'll have to work to tight, customer-imposed timescales

Unless this is a very strategic project, one should walk away . . . right now. The risks rocket with this combination. Check very, very carefully with people who are already using these tools in the same environment as your own. And check out the back-up available to support these. No matter what you try to do to speed things up, this will involve real delays. Unless I could rescope the project to reduce the risks, I'd definitely walk away.

I'm just going to take one more, and turn it over . . .

> *We've only to satisfy a single group of similar users*

Well at least this helps. If the opposite had applied, given the unfamiliar languages and tools and the tight, customer-imposed timescales, it would definitely be time to leave the party!

What advice would you give a pal who had to manage this project? Who couldn't escape from it?

Document everything carefully . . . every step of the way. Sign-offs . . . the lot. Try to minimise the scope of the project so as to reduce what you have to do . . . in other words, the smallest possible task in the longest possible timescale. Given that the development environment is unfamiliar, if at all possible get hold of someone who IS familiar with it. There will be big delays because of this. So you have to take a strong stand on the needed timescales. Get in tight with the users. They seem to want the system, so establish good relations with them. As the main project person isn't in a position to help you very much, then the users are key. I'd go for a phased contract with a fixed price for specific tasks. But I'd postpone fixing later task costs until the initial study was done. The scope, the definition and the phrasing of the contract should very clearly aim to get an initial, limited functionality working with a number of follow-on phases, because all the indications here suggest that you will want that minimum functionality to go in on time. If the users are then happy . . . wanting to get on with it . . . you have a good chance of success. But if you allow the initial scope to be too broad . . . too challenging . . . the chances are you will be late. Very demoralizing for everybody.

How do you think this project will turn out, assuming the project manager isn't a superman?

I think it's unlikely to be a positive experience for the customer, as they seem to see things. I'm undecided about the developer. It could be quite a positive experience if the scope is contained, and if the new tools turn out to be usable. You could end up getting quite a buzz from the project because you are doing something new . . . you have committed users . . . there is a sporting chance. The downside is the negatives relating to the customer. If the project hits snags, it would be a very nasty experience.

Which are the really nasty factors, or combinations of factors, in this project? The real risk creators?

The combination of *We'll be using unfamiliar languages/tools* and *Tight, customer-imposed timescales*

And the risk reducers? The good news?

We'll be dealing directly with the users, The people most affected seem to genuinely want the new system and *we've only to satisfy a single group of similar users*

... because these are the ones, in combination, that give you a sporting chance of getting somewhere.

Finally, any cards missing? Any big gaps?

There's one area missing. If the company you are working for is likely to be reorganized, or to go through some other upheaval, your project could get dropped or lost in all the change. This need not mean you won't get paid for what you've done, but it's a very unhappy experience for everyone. Government departments are the most troublesome on this point. There is a greater risk due to the movement of key staff, on either side. For example, if you lose your key user . . . maybe promoted . . . the risk level goes up. No cards deal with these aspects.

OWEN

16

My VERY BIG DIFFERENCE pile . . .

Has their PM time/skill/authority?   Realistic expectations?   People most affected really want the system?   Must satisfy different groups with different needs?   Any hidden agendas?   Major change to customer's procedures? How adaptable must our solution be?   A committed project "owner"? Any tricky interfacing?

My VERY BIG DIFFERENCE pile contains items that in my experience are important and over which we have less control. Experience has shown these are the biggest risk generators. My SOME/LITTLE/NO DIFFERENCE pile is about items that we can control. The middle pile just falls between the other two.

We'll work just with the most important pile. Pick the single most important card.

Realistic expectations?

If the client has realistic expectations, then the risk is minimal. If they have unrealistic expectations, you would have to educate them as to what the reality is. Education in our case would be to get them to talk to other clients we know in their industry, so that they could see what is involved, and to generate real commitment to the project. I would certainly try to factor this education into the price of the contract because you can get delays . . . it takes time to tune expectations.

Let's see . . .

The customer has unrealistic expectations . . .

Then my next card is . . .

People most affected really want the system?

If people don't want it, risk increases substantially. You would need to seek leadership and ownership for the project from within the organization . . .

someone with real clout . . . because, from my experience, if they can't create the right environment, we certainly wouldn't be able to.

Let's see . . .

People most affected seem to genuinely want the new system

My next is . . .

Has their PM time/skill/authority?

What if he or she didn't have the needed time, skill or authority?

Go back to top management and educate them as to the requirements and needs of that particular individual. it's hard politically to go back and say "He's not the right guy." I'd only do this if it was a hopeless case. If time can be provided, that's one hurdle overcome. If it's a lack of skill, you can educate him or her. But we cannot give him or her authority. That has to come from within the organization . . . from the top. If this is not sorted out, success of implementation is at high risk.

Let me see . . .

The customer's PM lacks the needed . . .

So far, there is a high degree of risk. However, as people seem to really want the system, it might be possible to turn it around.

I'm taking . . .

Any hidden agendas?

As a supplier, I'd be particularly concerned if there was a different agenda from the one we had been given. It would mean that we were providing a solution that in fact is not the real solution required. we'd certainly try to work to the real objective, but we'd have to do this within the politics of the situation. I'm looking . . .

The "real" agenda seems to be hidden

What do you make of this project so far?

The customer has unrealistic expectations, there's a problem with the main project person, the real agenda seems to be hidden, but people seem to want the system. I would be telling myself to be very, very careful. You are going to have to do a lot of missionary work . . . to prepare the client and the people in his organization for whatever solution you are coming in with.

Another card?

They are all important! . . .

A committed project "owner"?

It's very easy for a supplier to just deliver a "solution". But even if it's the right solution, the risk factor becomes greater if no one wants to take ownership of it. Ownership implies commitment. So if they don't want to own the project, there is a serious lack of commitment. it's coming back to how you relate to your customer . . . how you can develop the right attitudes and environment . . . again, it's up-front missionary work.

That could cost you time and money?

In the short term this could cost money . . . but in the long term . . .

Turn it over . . .

Nobody wants to "own" the project

My God . . . Do I really want this project?

Would you walk away?

Initially, I'd view it as a challenge, and try to figure out what our response should be! But there comes a point in time where, if the risk of failure could affect monetary gain, you'd have to make a hard judgement.

My next is . . .

Must satisfy different groups with different needs?

If it's multiple groups, the question then is have we as developers got the right communication structure in situ for the project? Has the organization got the right communication structure in place for the project? If not, how do we set-up communication structures to meet the situation?

What do you mean by structures . . . user representatives and so on?

Something in that direction. And if you've to talk to multiple groups of users . . . multiple communication channels . . . a time factor comes in, and that's more overhead.

Which applies?

> *We've only to satisfy a single group of similar users*

That's a bit of good news. I'll take the next two together . . .

> *Any tricky interfacing?* and *How adaptable must our solution be?*

I would hope that our own primary design would be capable of satisfying unknown future needs. But it's a bit unanswerable really. On the interfacing one, we'd need the technical expertise to handle it. It certainly would extend time and people estimates . . . and the time needed for testing.

I'm going to look . . .

> *Some tricky interfacing* . . . and *The new system must be adaptable* . . .

Oh dear . . . again! My last one is . . .

> *Major change to customer's procedures?*

The issue here could be, has the client got the capacity to control his industrial-relations situation? And has he got the management skills needed for implementation? If he hasn't, and there's a lot of change involved, it really could put the solution in jeopardy.

I'm looking . . .

> *No major change* . . .

Looking at the overall pattern on this project, what advice have you for the unfortunate project manager?

To immediately start to educate people as to what is entailed in the solution, and the benefits that realistically could be expected. To take the project, we would have to have the confidence that we could resolve these problems, and have the right people to do it. We would make everything very explicit . . . every aspect of the work to be done . . . what we would do . . . what they would have to do . . . so the customer couldn't come back down the line and say he didn't realize or didn't understand . . .

In this case, ideally it would be a time-and-materials contract. If it has to be fixed price, one would be very tempted to load that fixed price . . . this is the way most people in the industry would handle it.

How do you think this project is likely to turn out?

I'm afraid I'll have to tick "undecided" as to whether or not it'll be a positive experience for the customer. I think it MIGHT be a positive experience for the developer.

I'm surprised you say that. Why?

Well, if we didn't feel we could control the situation, we wouldn't be there. We have been there before and survived!

Are there one or two of the "poles" that are really nasty, individually or in combination?

The customer has unrealistic expectations . . . and *The customer's PM lacks the needed time/skill/authority* . . . This is a terrible combination.

What's the good news? Is there any?

The people most affected seem to genuinely want the new system

Any cards missing that should have been there. Any whole areas missing?

Maybe we're not looking at ourselves . . . our capacity. Certainly in examining risk, one has to look at oneself. But at least we are taking a good look at the client.

PADRAIG

17

OK. Here's my VERY BIG DIFFERENCE pile . . .

Our knowledge of the languages/tools? Mission-critical application? Any tricky interfacing? Agree amongst themselves on what's needed? Our knowledge of the platform? Our knowledge of their industry? Major change to customer's procedures? Application complexity? Has their PM time/skill/authority? Must change other developer's code? Our knowledge of the application? A committed project "owner"? Any hidden agendas? Can they define their problem? Realistic expectations?

The VERY BIG DIFFERENCE pile are the key factors, some of which may not be in your direct control . . . like the client not having realistic expectations. You can only manage so many of these factors simultaneously . . . they would add greatly to risk in the project. The SOME/LITTLE/NO DIFFERENCE pile are factors which generally don't affect the risk of the project in terms of estimating or delivery. The BIG DIFFERENCE pile are more important, but generally I would say these are all manageable, but they would need careful monitoring while you are doing the project.

Let's work just with the VERY BIG DIFFERENCE pile. Pick the most important card.

Realistic expectations?

If you're dealing with a company that may not have many other systems in place at the moment and may not have an experienced IT department, they may have unrealistic expectations about what is feasible . . . what can be done for a given budget. The first thing you have to do with any new customer is to ask yourself if they are being realistic in terms of the money they have and what they expect you to do. So one of the first things you do is filter out people to make sure you're not wasting their time and yours.

If they were unrealistic, I would talk to them face to face and explain why their ideas were unrealistic. I might give examples of what might be achievable. Generally, I would come back and say "Look, what you are looking for is this. This isn't feasible in terms of time or cost, but having looked at your requirements carefully, what might be feasible is to take this other approach." So I would come back with something more realistic that would invariably involve narrowing the scope of the project, and would say that we could do something like this within a certain time-frame. I'd say "Let's achieve this over the next three to six months. Then let's review things and go on to a second phase."

I wouldn't go into all this in great detail at this early stage. I would try to come up with some broad estimates of what is achievable, and if the client is interested, then I would put more effort into more detailed scoping. Depending on the size of the work required, I would treat this effort as non-chargeable . . . as part of the pre-sales effort in order to get the work. But obviously there is a cut-off point here . . .

Turn over the card.

The customer has realistic expectations . . .

Your next one?

Agree amongst themselves on what's needed?

Basically, the question is do they know what they want? This is a major risk in any bespoke development. If there are different requirements from different areas of the company and they can't agree amongst themselves, the compromise that's reached may not be optimal from a business point of view. It may have to do with political considerations, and not with functional or business requirements.

If they disagreed . . . there's another card here . . . I would talk to the main project leader on the client's side and put forward suggestions . . . compromises . . . and look to him to provide the necessary decision-making to get the thing done. In this situation, you need to align with whoever is the strongest. But you need to compromise. You may need to emphasize to them that "good enough" is what's required. With bespoke applications, you can really go around in circles trying to get agreement on what's needed, especially on new applications like data warehousing, business intelligence . . . things like that . . . where people don't know what they want, or worse still THINK they know. But you've got to draw a line. A lot of it comes back to scoping . . . to agreeing on what this should be, and to making sure this meets the most important requirements.

Which applies?

They disagree amongst themselves . . .

So you should put forward a compromise that takes something from each of the key players, so that they see their input has been recognised. it's usually possible to do this, without fully meeting any one individual's entire needs. But you've to argue that what you're proposing is "good enough" as a beginning.

My next is . . .

Must change other developer's code?

This could be very much a black box scenario. you're estimating what it would require to provide enhanced functionality . . . to build on an existing system. This is a very risky area because you don't know what's in there until you look. it's a situation in which we would try to avoid giving any estimates before we've had a look at the code. People do want . . . try to force us into giving ballpark estimates . . . but I've never allowed myself to be forced into this. I prefer to have the supplier of the existing system, if they are still available, to keep ownership of their code, and to channel the required changes to them . . . even though it may be preferable from the customer's point of view to have one group of people doing all the work. I'd allocate a fixed number of days in the contract to reviewing and assessing the code . . . the state of the code. Then, based on what I found, I'd come back with estimates as to what changes were required and what was involved.

I'm looking . . .

We won't have to change other developer's code

My next is . . .

Our knowledge of the languages/tools?

The problem in our industry is that every twelve to eighteenth months our tool providers move on to a new version with new features, some of which we want to use . . . others not. But like any supplier, they have a vested interest in your buying the newest version. One of the things they do to squeeze you out of using the old version is to stop providing support for the old tools. The main way we would address unfamiliar tools would be to get the requisite training before undertaking the project. Even with training, if you haven't used the tool in real anger you are going to encounter real-life difficulties that the training just isn't going to help you with. So you need to budget for the learning curve . . . thirty per cent . . . even up to fifty per cent if it's a completely new set of languages and tools. A lot less than this if it's just a slightly newer version of a tool set you are already using. And we'd have to bear that extra cost. The reality is that, in bidding for work one is generally tied to a fixed-price contract and in a competitive situation. So you'd swallow most of that thirty per cent and put it down to training. You can justify this as an investment in moving yourself up the learning curve, if it's an area you want to get into.

I'm looking . . .

We'll be using familiar languages/tools

Next is . . .

Has their PM time/skill/authority?

It makes your life a lot easier if there is a decision maker within the organization who has the requisite understanding of what you are trying to do . . . if you are able to communicate with them and they are able to give and take on the issues that arise during any project . . . to push things through one way or the other. If they don't have the time or authority, things get put on the long finger. This happens a lot in government departments. They don't want to be the person responsible for making a decision and would prefer you to go before committees. If you go to a committee with a twelve-issue list, you'll come out with a twenty-four issue list! So it's a major risk if you can't deal with a competent individual. If the person lacks the necessary skills and decision-making ability, you need to do the decision-making for them, but point out the dangers in doing this, and document your case. This adds to your project management overhead because you will be doing more writing, more documenting, more justifying what you are doing. It takes more effort to get the project done.

If it was pretty hopeless on this score?

You'd have to look at the extra risk you carry if you stick to the original agreed project scope and the initial agreed project plan, and the basis for these. We always put assumptions in the agreed plan about people agreeing designs, for example, by a specific date. If those deadlines are not met because of somebody on the customer's side, at least we've the justification for ensuring we get paid for the work that's been done by us. Obviously this isn't a satisfactory situation. But it needs to be pointed out to the client that any successful project requires effort both from the supplier and the customer.

What is it?

The customer's PM has the needed time/skill/authority

Next is . . .

Mission-critical application?

In our company, the way we're structured, mission-criticality really affects implementation more than development. But the developers would remain on the project right through to hand-over to help ensure that our support people handled the implementation effectively. Mission-criticality means you must plan the roll-out very carefully . . . the details of how the system will go live . . . and you need to ensure that all the necessary testing is done . . . so the risk is minimized when you actually go live.

Let's see . . .

The new system is not mission-critical . . .

My next is . . .

Major change to customer's procedures?

Major change is a risk because, at the end of the day, the people using the system may not be the people who asked for the system. Even if they are, you've got all the issues of change management, be the old system manual or computer based. So, depending on the age profile of the customer's people, whether they are unionised or not and so on, can create varying degrees of difficulty and affect the implementation. Most organizations realize that it is their responsibility to ensure that the organization is ready for the new system. You can only point out what they need to do. The responsibility must be made to rest on the customer's side. It makes a big difference if you've got the right person as project manager on the client's side.

We have one project where the client has been waiting for two years for the unions to agree to changes in procedures and changes in staff grading structures. How does that affect your timescales?! So, it's a real risk, particularly to timescales. But generally customers can't renege on paying you for the work you've actually done.

I'm peeping . . .

There will be major change . . .

Next?

Application complexity?

Complex application logic is a risk. it's one you should be able to identify up front . . . as part of your specification . . . and it should be apparent just how difficult the application is going to be to build. But with the best will in the world, sometimes what people define up front isn't actually what they need. Unfortunately, it may not be until you get into developing the thing, or interfacing with something else, especially in complex systems, that other requirements may surface. So generally there needs to be a bit of give and take along the way as to what's included and what isn't in the scope of the project. One approach is to nail things down by getting agreement on a budget for requirements that are visible up front, and getting agreement that requirements that may surface later will be treated as enhancements, with their own additional budget. But with complex systems, there can be grey areas as to what's involved. This can apply to anything from a two-month project to a project lasting several years.

Which applies?

The application is straightforward

Good! Next is . . .

Our knowledge of their industry?

Knowledge of your client's industry is important in estimating time and cost. it's also important for your credibility . . . ability to use the right jargon, and so on. For example, the terminology and procedures in the retailing industry are very different from those in the shipping industry. The main problem here would arise in the specification phase of the project . . . in deciding on scope . . . understanding the priorities within the client's industry. You'd have to put a bit more into the specification stage. This would be a learning phase, so you would need to budget for that. If you want to get into the client's industry, you would probably take the hit for this extra cost, from a future business point of view. It shouldn't affect down-the-line development much.

I'm looking . . .

We've little or no knowledge of the customer's industry

Next . . .

Any tricky interfacing?

Interfacing with existing applications is something we have to do regularly. There are different ways of interfacing with existing applications, so it depends on the type of interfacing we have to do. Batch-based, say overnight, interfacing is usually straightforward provided they can define what they want to do. If the interface doesn't meet requirements on one side or the other, for example if there will be mapping from one side to the other needed, it's less straightforward and becomes tricky because you could have third parties becoming involved. In other words, the developer or supplier or maintainer of the existing system. You'd have to liaise with them, which adds to your costs. Testing becomes more complex because you have to schedule not only your own resources, but your customer's resources and the third party's resources. So it's an area in which one can easily underestimate the time required.

Then you can have online, seamless interfacing where the applications seem to share the same information immediately in an online manner. This is potentially more complex and risky, particularly when one side or the other is a black box. If both sides are built from the same languages and tools, it makes it a lot easier. If these are different, it could be highly complex and risky. If it wasn't all very straightforward, I'd agree up front what the issues might be . . . an investigation might be needed . . . and budget separately for that.

Let's see . . .

No tricky interfacing . . .

What do you make of the project so far?

I would say it's a manageable project. we've got a few key issues here. We need to hammer down the functional specification of what is required because of the disagreement and the uncertainty about what's needed. But that is going to be the first phase of the project anyway, so we can do all that at the right time. We have little or no knowledge of the client's industry . . . so we have got to ask ourselves, is it a big industry? Is there potential there? And if so, and we are in a competitive bidding situation, do we want to take the hit for the learning ourselves? we're going to have a learning curve to figure out what it is they try to do in this industry. we've to make a call on that one, based on the size of the project. They have realistic expectations. We have a good project leader on the customer's side. No changes to other code. it's not mission-critical. So, even if it's a new industry, we'll have a bit of leeway on roll-out to iron out glitches. There will be major changes for the customer. That's going to affect implementation. So while we are doing the development, we've to make the customer aware prior to roll-out of the changes, and what he needs to do. we've got to put in a formal training plan and allocate the requisite time and resources to ensure that users are on board. We need to budget for more user testing than normal, because there are more changes involved, and we need to lengthen the roll-out of the parallel run.

What key advice for the guy who has to manage this project?

Initially, just bid for the specification of the project. This is because you need to get agreement at the right level as to what is to be built, and because there is potential here for lack of acceptance of the system by some of the key users. Try to stretch the timescale of the specification stage to give yourself time to become familiar with the new industry. Take the hit on some of the cost of this yourself, because you will be trying to get up to speed. Plan the implementation very carefully to address the major changes in workflow and procedures. If possible, prototype and have a long parallel run. If it's a multi-site environment, it's going to be even more complex. Roll out in phases. Ensure you have adequate budget for user testing and assistance for the users in this task. Put lots of budget in there to help users with the new procedures . . . there will be big problems otherwise.

How do you think this project is likely to turn out?

I agree that it is likely to be a positive experience for both the client and the developer. But only if my advice is taken!

Which is the really BAD news on this project?

The combination of *They disagree amongst themselves about what's needed* and *Major change to the customer's workflow/procedures.*

Any cards missing?

I think you've identified most of the main areas.

PATRICK

18

Here's my VERY BIG DIFFERENCE pile . . .

Our knowledge of the languages/tools?   Has their PM time/skill/authority?
Mission-critical application?   System must go right first time?
A committed project "owner"?   Agree amongst themselves on what's needed?
Have we a credible competitor?   Our knowledge of the application?
Our knowledge of the platform?   Any hidden agendas?

What really distinguishes between the three piles?

The VERY BIG DIFFERENCE pile has to do with control and familiarity. These are success versus disaster things. If you're taking on stuff that's unfamiliar to you there's a risk . . . if neither you nor the person paying you is really in control of it . . . if these two things come together you are heading for disaster.

The SOME/LITTLE/NO DIFFERENCE ones, even if there are uncertainties around them, one can acquire the necessary skills and resources . . . these are things one can work around. For example, if the client isn't too familiar with IT and IT projects, we would expect to take on a training role . . . this would just become part of the job.

In the middle pile are those things that are important . . . but not critically so . . . we know we can manage around them.

Concentrate on the VERY BIG DIFFERENCE pile. Take these items in order of importance.

I want to take . . .

> *Has their PM time/skill/authority?* and *A committed project "owner"?*
> *together.*

If nobody wants to own the project, you've no guarantee that anyone will agree that the work has been done or not . . . you probably won't even be paid for the job! I think the PM one is the most important one . . . you have got to get that one out of the way first. You can't take on a project if there is no real authority behind it . . . no guarantee that they are even going to commit to it, or pay you for it.

Turn these two cards over.

> *The customer's PM has the needed . . .* and *Someone on the customer's side has taken ownership . . .*

Looks like the project starts! If either answer had been no, that would be that!

Would you have walked away?

You'd have to. Lack of time, even skill, one could live with, but if he/she doesn't have the authority, there's no real contract.

Which one next?

These three together . . .

> *Mission-critical application?*, *Agree amongst themselves on what's needed?* and *Any hidden agendas?*

If it's mission-critical, if we are going to be involved in a large change in their procedures, in their personnel training, in the way they do business . . . for instance it could be a new product line that needs this kind of system support . . . so for a start they are going to be willing to pay more. Secondly, it's likely to be a high-visibility project, and being late or failing in any aspect of it is likely to cause big problems. So you pay a lot of attention to priorities, to ranking things. Even if the whole project is called "mission-critical", there is probably just a subset of REALLY critical things, so you spend a lot of time finding and defining these.

This is where *Agree amongst themselves . . . ?* comes in. If it's both mission-critical, and they can't make-up their minds about what's needed, the project can't go ahead because you will end up with one side refusing to cooperate. They'll say "That was THEIR specification, not ours." If it isn't mission-critical, you can normally go ahead on the basis that one side is enough to sign a cheque!

Let me peep . . .

> *The new system isn't mission-critical . . .* and *They disagree amongst themselves . . .*

. . . at least they're not both in the same direction.

It's a potential disaster if there's a hidden agenda in the sense that it could all blow up in your face as the real agenda surfaces. Although you do the job and get paid for it, you might never get a job there again because you would be seen to be tainted by supporting one side against another. If there's a hidden agenda, there is usually a political fight in there somewhere. While a hidden agenda is an important thing, you may be able to get away with it by ignoring it and letting it be their problem . . . you just do a job . . . but if it could have any knock-on effects in terms of bad publicity you must ask yourself if you really want the job or not. You'd need to tease it out more and see how important it really is.

Let's see . . .

There seems to be no hidden agenda

No hidden agenda. This is quite a characteristic project for me so far. Let's see if there's anything else not under our own control . . . like a credible competitor . . .

Have we a credible competitor?

This is just a pricing issue. If you are up against a credible competitor, you need to know what they are charging, and how they could possibly get an "in". You might have to stress your own skills in some way . . . make it a non-price issue . . . show that you can bring something unique to the party. If you've no credible competitor, then it's a much easier job. You don't have to work too much around the area of managing the environment . . . for example, someone in the company saying "I've discovered someone down the road who can do the same job at half the price." This is something you MUST find out early on. But it could happen at any time . . . someone could walk in when you've done one phase and grab the rest of the project.

Turn it over . . .

We're up against a credible competitor . . .

The next few I want are all related to our level of experience . . . to our familiarity with the skill-sets needed. I'll go for this first . . .

Our knowledge of the application?

I assume we're talking here about the area in which IT is to be applied . . . it could be a finance application, a production application . . . that kind of thing? If the application is new to us, we'd have to spend more time learning about the business. And we have the problem of being up against a competitor. So unfortunately we can't charge them much for our learning time, so we would have to carry the cost ourselves. If it's an abstruse area it may be that it would cost us too much to educate ourselves . . . it might be beyond us. On the other hand, it depends on the customer. You may find that he is quite proud of doing something abstruse and is happy to explain it to you . . . to teach you . . . at great length. So it very much depends on how quickly we can overcome our unfamiliarity.

Turn it over . . .

We've experience of this application

My next one is . . .

Our knowledge of the platform?

Here you could be caught by environment/platform issues. There could be so many "gotchas" in that you either have to have someone in your company who is fully familiar with the environment and can help you out, or you have to acquire the resources elsewhere. As far as the client is concerned, they're buying a solution from us and it's up to us to understand the environment. If you are used to working in a desktop environment and all of a sudden you are faced with a mainframe application . . . I don't think so . . . maybe a smaller change like moving into a UNIX box would be OK.

Let's see . . .

The platform/environment is familiar . . .

I'm taking . . .

Our knowledge of the languages/tools?

This one is crucial because, if you have to learn a new language, you almost have no hope unless it is very close to what you already know. Given that you are up against a credible competitor, if they have experience in the language and you don't, they have a three-month lead time on you. But there are people out there who would happily take on unfamiliar stuff . . . but you would need at least a three-month lead time to get up to speed on it. I know of one developer who had never used Java before . . . he was told it was like C . . . not a happy story! You have to make a judgement on how unfamiliar it is. If you have been working in Visual Basic up to now and all of a sudden you have to handle Java which is quite different, then you might decide that you want to go into that market anyway and that it's a good thing to do . . . so you chew it over and maybe decide to swallow the extra three-month overhead yourself . . . but you'd need to be up front with the client and give a warning about the extra lead time . . . tricky one!

Let's see . . .

We'll be using familiar languages/tools

Next is . . .

System must go right first time?

Depends on what they really mean by this. They'll always say they want it to go right first time, but they usually can go back to what they had for a month. If "right first time" means absolutely right on the day, like a Y2K project, or if it's related to a new product launch, and if you're late the whole thing gets delayed . . . It isn't mission-critical, we have already established that, but it could still be important to the person who has taken committed ownership of the project. So it has to go right. You would need to be much more conscious of your quality-assurance and project-management procedures, and you'd have to charge extra for this. If you are on a tight schedule and things have to go right, then you have to build a more formal method of controlling things . . . no "seat of the pants! This forms part of your cost. It would need more bureaucracy and explicitness . . . applying more QA than you would normally rely on . . . .this may have staffing implications . . . people may feel that you are checking on them more than they are used to . . . but this is part of the job.

I'm turning over . . .

We can pilot the new system until we get it right

This is a fairly relaxed and normal looking project.

Looking at the whole pattern of the "answers", summarize the advice you'd give your pal . . .

The first thing to be handled is the fact that they disagree amongst themselves about what's needed. So, there will be extra front loading in the contract in terms of specification . . . getting things clear . . . getting agreement. The extra front loading is especially important to you if you are up against a competitor who may or may not know more about that particular application area. You don't know how good they are. If they are naïve and go in with too low a quote after you have put in effort to find out what's really required, the only hope you have is that they will fail and then you get the chance to take it over. Or it could be, this is a timing thing, that the client is still talking to the competitor. So if you spend a lot of time producing a good specification, they could then walk up to the competitor and say "There's the spec . . . give us that." Then you are just giving away the shop . . . doing your competitor's research for him. So, you need to introduce more checkpoints into the contract. You need to say "we will have a formal charge for agreeing things and from what we have seen so far, it will cost $X just to do that stage."

139

The official interface into the company is pretty clear . . . that's good . . . clear, committed ownership, that's great . . . so you don't have to worry too much about the project internals. it's really a case of splitting the contract into project phases and deliverables that begins with clarifying what they want . . . certainly the users are going to have to be involved. You have to be reasonably careful about the budget and the schedule . . . you are up against a competitor. Development shouldn't be a problem because you have all of the experience needed. Implementation shouldn't be a problem. But you need to make sure you don't give away the shop in trying to clarify requirements up front.

How do you think this project is likely to turn out?

I "strongly agree" that it will be a positive experience for both the customer and the developer. Mind you, this depends on how good you feel you are at resolving disagreements amongst customers. But I noticed earlier that there seemed to be no hidden agendas, so I don't think you would be thrown off beam by something totally out of the left field. You would really need to clarify with them first how happy they feel about getting disagreements out of the way first, but if that's done, I don't see why it shouldn't be a strong, positive experience. Our contact has the authority . . . we know how to do it . . . as long as the disagreement is managed, that's grand.

Finally!! Which "answers", or combinations of "answers" would INCREASE in a BIG way any risk in this project?

They disagree amongst themselves about what's needed

And which would REDUCE in a BIG way any risk?

The customer's PM has the needed time/skill/authority and *We can pilot it until we get it right.*

PAUL

19

My VERY BIG DIFFERENCE pile . . .

*Agree amongst themselves on what's needed?   A committed project "owner"?
Any hidden agendas?   Their experience in running IT projects?   People
most affected really want the system?   Must satisfy different groups with
different needs?   Has their PM time/skill/authority?   Realistic expectations?*

What's so special about the VERY BIG DIFFERENCE pile?

These are things that in the main you don't have control over. You can be hit
by them, but there's not a lot you can do about them . . . lack of skill . . . lack
of commitment or interest . . . negative attitudes from users or the customer
. . . people with political agendas wanting it to fail . . . decisions not being
made . . . customers expecting everything to be done by tomorrow. The
project shouldn't start until all this stuff is resolved. it's just a waste of money
otherwise.

Pick one or two cards from your VERY BIG DIFFERENCE pile.

I'll go for . . .

Any hidden agendas? and *People most affected really want the system?*

If people don't want the system, you've to try to find out why not. Are the
reasons to do with politics? Personal advancement? Ignorance? Or are there
genuine business reasons? This is quite hard to resolve because you are an
outsider. The hidden agenda one is hard to get to the bottom of unless
you've a lot of experience dealing with people and figuring out why
someone isn't telling you the truth. You need to conduct interviews with as
many people as you can, without committing yourself on one side or the
other . . . show you're not pushing the system, but just trying to understand
the problem. Easy to say, but hard to do!

Let's see . . .

People most affected seem to genuinely want . . .

OK, so you can work with them and start defining what the system is about. The agenda one is still on the table, but even if there is a hidden agenda, it becomes far less serious when the people you work with closely really want the system. Even if there is another agenda, it doesn't have to be your concern. If the people affected want it, you can work with them and make it a success.

I'm looking . . .

> *There seems to be no hidden agenda*

What's next?

These two seem to go together . . .

> *Has their PM time/skill/authority* and *A committed project "owner"?*

If both of these were negative, my advice would be to escalate these issues up the organization. Find someone who wants to own the project at a higher level before you spend any money. If you can't find a sponsor, someone willing to underwrite the project, then you should start to worry because you won't get paid. You have to find a project owner. Someone on their side has to be able to say "We want this, we have prepared a budget, we can afford it, and it makes sense." You shouldn't get involved in a project that's meaningless, even if eventually you get paid.

Let's see . . .

> *Nobody wants to "own" the project*

You can't move past this one. You have to find someone who'll say "Yes." Otherwise you have to go up-and-up, even to the board. If not resolved, bail out!

Let's assume the ownership thing is sorted out.

OK. You need to have someone on their side looking after the project who has time/skill/authority. I'll put time and skill in one basket, and authority in another. You have to have someone who is given the authority to run the project . . . to control it. It may be that you will have to go up the organization to get the name of someone lower down. Lack of time and skill can be worked around. But he or she must be someone you can go to and say "If you want to proceed, these are the choices you must make." So they must have authority. Otherwise there is the risk of spending time and money and ending up in a cul-de-sac. If the person has NO time, it's unlikely they will acquire the skills at any stage. But if they have SOME time, and are prepared

to work with you, you can try to pass on some of the skills and help them out. But it means that you're going to have to do some of the job that they would otherwise do. If you can do that, fine. If you don't have the time either, then you've a problem! Somebody has to manage the project.

I'm looking . . .

> *The customer's PM lacks the needed time/skill/authority*

I think I'd bail out.

What next?

These make sense taken together . . .

> *Must satisfy different groups with different needs?* and *Agree amongst themselves on what's needed?*

And if both of these are bad news?

Combined with the fact that nobody wants to own the project? I'm out of here! If you have a real owner with authority, these issues can be managed by having a heavy session with the heads of these groups of people. You would explain to these guys that you have a project with a budget, and a group of users who at the end of the day are keen to have a new system, and that they need to resolve their differences. You'd explore why they can't agree. Is it because they have conflicting requirements? Or additional requirements that can't be met by the budget? These are two different problems. If it's about additional requirements, they may need to scale scope down to a manageable size before we start. This can normally be done by consensus . . . compromise. If they have contradictory needs, then it's not a matter of IT functionality . . . it's about business issues. If they have different goals, they need a consultant-type role to work with them to sort it out. But if they have similar goals, this disagreement can usually be resolved by an IT type, but it takes time.

I'm looking at both . . .

> *We've to satisfy multiple groups with different needs* and *They don't disagree amongst themselves* . . .

That's OK, as long as they agree. Just make sure that the scope of your project isn't too open, so you can stay within budget.

Next?

Realistic expectations? and *Their experience of running IT projects?*

If both of these were bad news?

I'd explain why in my view their expectations are unrealistic. I'd keep at this until one of two things happened . . . they changed their expectations, or I'd reckoned I was on a loser and I'd just walked away. People have to understand that everything costs money . . . takes time. You can get nothing straight away. I'd find a way of explaining this to them using non-IT examples, like building a house. Eventually, if through lack of interest or through not relating well together, you can't resolve this one, I'd advise my pal not to get involved. it's going to be a failure.

Let's see . . .

The customer has unrealistic expectations . . . and *The customer is experienced in running computer projects*

These two don't quite add up. One way this can happen is if you're dealing with an IT person who has ten or fifteen years' experience. The unrealistic expectations could just be a façade to put pressure on you. Is it just disguised commercial negotiation? How unrealistic is it? Is it just very tight, or really ridiculous . . . "Write me this new business system in two weeks!" If it's pressure, it's negotiation . . . you have to decide what you can live with. If it's plain unrealism, you have to draw the line. If you give in . . . make promises . . . these won't go away! Some customers don't want to hear the truth. They don't want you to tell them it'll take three months. They want you to tell them it'll take two or three weeks. You must be strong and take a stand as to what you think is the right thing.

Overall advice to your pal?

Don't go further if there's no owner with authority. Walk out. you're going to fail. The users want the system and they don't disagree. And they've no agenda. That's all good news. Someone experienced is running the project on their side, and expectations are unrealistic, this could be a problem. It doesn't make sense. you'll have to find out what's happening. Maybe someone is telling you little lies there, or they're putting pressure on you. Or maybe the "experienced" guy has twenty years' experience, but he's no good! I would ask him to talk about past similar projects he was involved in, and to compare the new project with these old ones in terms of time and cost. Then I'd ask him "How come I'm so wrong now? Why am I so off the mark?" Bring it back to their own experience and they have to get involved.

How do you think the project is likely to turn out?

It's looking pretty good. As long as the ownership thing gets sorted out. You seem to have a group of people who will benefit from what you're doing, so if you put in a good communicator . . . a good listener . . . you should be able to bring them onside. Scope your project very clearly . . . write everything down . . . and work with the users to make it a success at that level. Having said all that, you're going to have difficulty with those customer expectations. If you can withstand that pressure . . . "I don't think it can be done in six months". . . then maybe you don't need to walk away. You have to stick to what you think is right. If this is all OK, and you have reasonable skills, it should be successful. So, I'll tick probably a positive experience for the customer. I'll tick undecided for the developer.

Which are the nastiest of the nasties on this project?

Nobody wants to "own" the project This one really gets to me. I'd walk away from that. The rest can always be worked on.

The best news?

People most affected seem to genuinely want the new system and *The customer is experienced in running computer projects.*

The customer is experienced in running . . . is usually good news. But this and *The customer has unrealistic expectations* . . . don't go together. This means that something is wrong.

Any issues missing from the cards?

Project scale is important. You have different issues in terms of motivation, etc. I think your card *Need >two people on our team?* doesn't reflect scale in our experience. I would say that up to three people is a small project. Three to ten is a manageable project, but for anything over twenty-five to fifty, I think you need different skills.

You have cards dealing with the developer's familiarity with the development environment, and so on. Having no experience with something that is mature is one thing. But you could have a situation where NOBODY has done it before . . . it's leading-edge . . . Y2K for example.

145

20

PHILIP

My VERY BIG DIFFERENCE pile . . .

Need >two people on our team?   Realistic expectations?   Any hidden agendas?   Agree amongst themselves on what's needed?   Must satisfy different groups with different needs?   Number of different functional areas involved?   Project duration >three months?   Application complexity? Must change other developer's code?   Feasible to prototype?   Our knowledge of the languages/tools?   Any tricky interfacing?   Must share control with a third party?   Our knowledge of their industry?   Our knowledge of the application?   Must we subcontract?   Tight, customer-imposed timescales?   A committed project "owner"?   System must go right first time?   Mission-critical application?   Our knowledge of the platform?

What distinguishes the VERY BIG DIFFERENCE pile from the other two?

I think the major theme is control. you'll find topics related to lack of control here, i.e. subcontractors, third party code, people who are unsure of what they want. What you want is control and predictability, so anything that militates against this features in this pile. Some cards I put into the other piles fall into this category as well . . . I made a subjective judgement on importance here.

Which card is the most important one? Would come top of the list?

I find it very hard to rank them, so I'm not sure I could say that any one is the most critical. But I'd pick this lot as core . . .

Our knowledge of the languages/tools?   Our knowledge of the application? A committed project "owner"?   Any tricky interfacing?   Must change other developer's code?   Our knowledge of the platform?   Our knowledge of their industry?   Must we subcontract?   Mission-critical application?   Must share control with a third party?

Make a start somewhere. Pick one.

OK . . .

> *Our knowledge of the languages/tools?*

Using unfamiliar languages or tools . . . it's the unpredictability in terms of your capacity to deliver . . . the timescales to which you are committing yourself. So there's the risk of not meeting deadlines. I'm taking interfacing as well . . .

> *Any tricky interfacing?*

Let's see . . .

> *We'll be using familiar languages/tools* and *Some tricky interfacing . . .*

I'm not necessarily saying that these are my two top critical questions. I just picked them out of this group of critical things.

Sure. Pick what makes sense to you.

Next is . . .

> *Must change other developer's code?*

I suppose I'm picking the ones that are obviously critical.

Let's see . . .

> *We'll have to change other developer's code*

This is the riskiest point so far. You don't know the quality of the code you'll have to deal with.

I'm moving on and looking . . .

> *The application is new to us*

It's time to look for a lot of money! you'd be concerned about the business sense of this project. You can deal with all these things, but you need to be sure you have the risk covered.

How?

One answer would be time and money! Time to learn the application with the people in the business. This one really depends on the volume of the other developer's code . . . making a quick assessment of how well it's written before you commit. You'd look for examples of the code . . . or you'd look through it all to make a quick assessment. But it would have to be a language you're familiar with. Otherwise it's a major problem. Presumably it's not code you've been responsible for in the past?

No. it's third-party code.

So it's new to you . . . that could be a reason for walking away . . . if it's not worth changing you should throw it out and rewrite it. If the client wishes you to do the whole project on a time-and-materials basis, this is the best way of minimising your risk. But if that's not possible, then this third-party code aspect would be a good candidate for time and materials.

Next one?

Our knowledge of their industry?

So, let's see . . .

We've little or no knowledge of their industry

This explains the application being new to us. So there's a learning exercise to be done. Getting to know the industry is very important. So I'd spend time at the client's site.

At his expense?

Of course! Let's assume you've got the project, but you need this knowledge, so you'd spend time there, watching how all the functions that you have to provide within your system are currently carried out . . . plus background reading . . . talking to certain people. You'd include an allowance for this in your project proposal under the first phase to prepare a functional specification. The learning and the functional spec would go hand in hand.

Another one?

I'm looking . . .

The platform/environment is familiar to us

Good news.

What would you do if the answer had been different?

The combination . . . new industry . . . new platform . . . they're strong negatives. It depends, from a business point of view, on whether you would still want to pursue the project and if the client was still keen.

Next?

This one, and I'm looking . . .

The new system is mission-critical . . .

Have you walked away? New application, mission critical, don't know much about the industry, etc.?

You don't necessarily walk away from a project in which you're in a totally new business environment, but it depends on the keenness of the client to deal with you, and your preparedness to see it as a viable business venture. But there's a lot of risk. On the other hand, if you're getting plenty of time and resources to work with, then you can still be comfortable about it.

Advice to your pal?

Time and materials would be the preferred basis for this one. But you may not be able to get agreement to that. If you have to work to very strong time constraints, you may have to walk away. Putting in additional resources to deal with things like the other developer's code is not necessarily an answer to the time constraint issue, because there isn't a linear relationship between level of resources and effectiveness. Maybe you don't want to work on mission-critical applications anyway, so it depends on whether or not you have the stomach for it.

Another card?

A committed project "owner"?

This card should be right up there at the top of the pile. If nobody wants to own this project, then DEFINITELY walk away. If you don't sort this out you are in big trouble. Particularly with the mission-criticality issue. These two issues would be a dreadful combination. It doesn't matter how good you are on the technical things. You've got a user and a client where things are just not right.

Nobody wants to "own" the project

Walk away!

You'd REALLY walk away? No way around it?

Other than confronting the client directly and saying "It doesn't seem to us that this will be a business success for you. Can we talk about the project team on your side? We need a senior manager . . . the board . . . we need the project to be approved . . . underwritten." If that didn't work, then it's goodbye time.

Let's say that one was fixable. Next card?

I'm picking and turning . . .

We'll have to do significant subcontracting

This falls into that third-party category. it's probably manageable. But it's something I'd prefer not to have to do. Someone else might look on this as a plus . . . "we can subcontract the risk to someone else" . . . but you're still carrying the risk because you have to answer to the client. it's about managing them very tightly.

Next one?

We'll need three or more people on the project

This is a management question again. it's indicative of scale. So we're looking at a medium-sized as opposed to a small project. I'd view that as being more risky. It needs to be managed more tightly I think. More formality of reporting. Logging of time and deadlines. there's more management overhead because you've got more people.

Keep moving . . .

OK . . .

Number of different functional areas involved?

Again, this one has to do with scale and complexity. it's just a measure of complexity . . .

The new system involves only a single functional area

That helps.

I'll take this one next and look . . .

It won't be possible to show the customer an early prototype

That's bad news. So for whatever reason, you're lacking in feedback. it's not an overriding issue, but it's a serious issue. Given that it's mission-critical, you'd do your damnedest to find a way of expressing to the client what the system was going to deliver . . . graphically, or in some other form. There would always be some way that you could verbalize or graphically present

150

. . . some written or graphic document to get some confirmation back. You'd need the client's sign-off on something to give you some comfort.

Next?

And I'm taking these two together and turning over . . .

They don't disagree amongst themselves on what's needed and *There seems to be no hidden agenda*

All good news. It can take time to nail down a consensus about what should be delivered. You often find you don't have agreement. it's a real enough issue. Or they're talking different languages and they don't realize it's really the same thing.

I'm taking just one more . . .

The application is complex

So be it.

Advice to your pal?

He'd have to nail down the ownership of the project first. If he couldn't get a satisfactory response on this one, walk away. The other developer's code . . . I don't like this one . . . we talked about it earlier. He'd need to address it to assess the problems it might present. Maybe parcel it up as a separate project. Other than these items, what's unusual here? Users look OK. it's unusual that you can't prototype, so this stands out and needs attention. So focus on these points. Apart from these, you're going to find everything else in projects anyway.

If you had to predict, how do you think this project will turn out?

For a mission-critical application, you'd better have an experienced development team. And as they don't know the client's industry, they'd better learn it . . . and fast! Because of all these points, there is a real danger of an overrun in time, and/or additional resources being unexpectedly required. it's not a run-of-the-mill project.

It depends on the experience of the project team. This could be a very negative experience if the people undertaking it haven't got the wherewithal.

Which are the really nasty features of this project?

We've little or no knowledge of their industry, The new system is mission-critical . . ., Nobody wants to "own" the project and *It won't be possible to show an early prototype*

Any killer combinations?

The new system is mission-critical and *Nobody wants to "own" the project*

Where's the good news?

The new system involves only a single functional area is an obvious one.

The fact that the *platform* and *the languages/tools* are familiar to us is good from a technical point of view. If these answers were not positive, you'd be worried. *There seems to be no hidden agenda* and *They don't disagree about what's needed* are very good.

You made the point about there being no cards dealing with the characteristics of your team. Anything else missing?

There are logistical matters, such as where the client is . . . where you normally reside. The capacity of the people involved is very important because the range of abilities within the IT industry is enormous. Not only in coding but in general systems, ability . . . productivity . . . delivery. That's about it I think.

SUSAN A

My VERY BIG DIFFERENCE pile . . .

*System must go right first time?   Major change to customer's procedures?
Our knowledge of the platform?   Mission-critical application?
Application complexity?   How adaptable must our solution be?   Are they
able/willing to drive implementation?   Our knowledge of the application?
Has their PM time/skill/authority?   Agree amongst themselves on what's
needed?   A committed project "owner"?   Must satisfy different groups with
different needs?   Their experience in running IT projects?   Tight, customer-
imposed timescales?   Users' computer experience?   Any tricky interfacing?
Must share control with a third party?   Must we subcontract?*

Generally, I look at risk in terms of the learning curve involved for us,
complexity, how much we know, how much they know, and how clear the
requirements are.

**Let's work just with your VERY BIG DIFFERENCE pile. If you had
to pick just one of those cards for a starter, which one?**

I suppose . . .

> *Agree amongst themselves on what's needed?*

Basically, there's no way you can deliver something if you don't know what
the goals of the project are. Unless your requirements are clearly laid down
and signed off, no matter what you deliver, it won't meet the requirements.
The project will fail no matter how "good" a job you do.

And if there was disagreement?

You'd have to sit people down and get them to clarify and sign off on the initial
requirements, even if these are expressed at a high level. Then you can go deeper. If you don't do that, you can deliver shining bells and baubles, but you're
going to get disagreement from somebody at the end of it all. So everybody
has to be on board, and to decide on and sign off on the initial requirements.

Have a look at the back of the card and see if it's good or bad news.

Very bad news!

They disagree amongst themselves . . .

In the light of this, I'm taking . . .

A committed project "owner"?

If nobody owns the project, it comes back to the same thing in that you won't get any decisions from the client. You can go forward blindly into the dark, but at the end of the day, no matter what you produce, it's not going to be right because it's your idea of what they want, not theirs.

If you were stuck with this situation . . . if you couldn't walk away?

I suppose the same as before. Basically, it's a meeting with the client to say "We need someone to take ownership and responsibility on your side." Even if they give you a random name because they can't decide on someone better, at least it's a name . . . it's someone you can mail and fax. And if you're not getting feedback and deadlines are expiring, at least you can point the finger . . . "We did all the following with your contact and she never got back to us.". . . Basically, you're putting the ball back in their court.

Let's see . . .

Someone has taken clear, committed ownership . . .

Next is . . .

Tight, customer-imposed timescales?

If you've a timescale to meet, then if you don't meet it, you've failed in some sense of the word no matter what you've delivered. If we're allowed to juggle with timescales, . . . fine . . . you can plan out and do it at your pace. If issues do arise, it can mean that you can get other people on board . . . you can grab some other help. It means it lowers the risk of disappointing people. If timescales are very tight, anything that goes wrong becomes a problem . . . you need to have resources there ready to pull in. You don't have any leeway.

I'm looking . . .

We'll be able to juggle a bit with timescales

OK. So, next is . . .

Must we subcontract?

Preferably, I'd rather not subcontract because it's out of our control once we hand it over. The issues between the subcontractor and us, and between us and the client, are much the same. In both cases, we need to make sure that the communications are right . . . the objectives are clear . . . doing proper requirements documents . . . ensuring everyone knows their role and their task . . . basically to run a tight ship. Subcontracting adds a whole new set of communication problems. I'd rather not do it.

Turn over the card.

We'll have to do significant subcontracting

Your next one?

Has their PM time/skill/authority?

If he or she is a total thicko . . . if he is doing his best . . . going to the correct people . . . feeding back the right information, then it's not an issue if he is clueless himself. But if he is giving us wrong information, or not giving us any feedback, I would have to raise this officially and try to get him ousted because he is jeopardising the project.

Let's see . . .

The customer's PM has the needed . . .

So far, what do you make of the project?

Basically, they have somebody good taking control on the client's side. We can juggle a bit with timescales and we have to do subcontracting. They disagree about what's needed . . . that's an issue they need to sort-out. So the client has a lot of work to do and we need to make sure they're actually doing it before we can move forward. The main client guy looks good, so he can take on the job of sorting them out. The fact that we can juggle with timescales just means that we may still have a couple of weeks that we can get away with. But internally in the project we still need to try to keep to our deadlines. The subcontracting will need someone to sit right on top of it and work it through to a conclusion.

Your next card?

I'm taking these four together . . .

Our knowledge of the application?, Our knowledge of the platform?, Application complexity? and *How adaptable must our solution be?*

Why take these together?

These all have to do with the learning curve involved for us. These are all learning issues.

If you had to pick one?

I think it's the complexity of the application logic. If the logic is straightforward, no problem . . . plough straight ahead. If the logic is complex, we're into a big educational thing for us . . . maybe sending people on courses or some sort of training . . . to do what we can to speed up the learning curve. You need to recognise this one early and act on it.

Let's see . . .

> *The application is straightforward*

I'm going to jump around a bit. My next is . . .

> *Any tricky interfacing?*

This one is similar to the last four. If we have to interface, we need to find out exactly what's involved up front. If we don't have the expertise in-house, we need to buy it in, or maybe go for some training. If it's simple and straightforward, no problem . . . it cuts down that risk.

Look . . .

> *No tricky interfacing . . .*

Good news. Next is . . . and I'm looking . . .

> *The customer is experienced in running computer projects*

That's good too. So let's look at the users . . .

> *Users' computer experience?*

If we don't have experienced computer users, there may be feedback issues. It depends on how we're going to use them. If we're going to use them to help with testing, there may be problems because they won't know how to use the system. If we set aside three weeks for beta testing by the client's people, it could take us the first two weeks of that to get the users up and running. I suppose the initial thing is to find out what type of people they are . . . to decide on how to build them into the project . . . when they are going to get involved. If they weren't experienced, over the course of the project you would have to spend time familiarising them with the operating system to be used, Windows or whatever, and maybe release early versions of the product while on test to them just to play with.

Nearly there. I'm looking . . .

We're dealing with experienced computer users

My last one is . . .

Major change to customer's procedures?

If there are no major changes, then we don't have an issue. If there are, we need to be very careful about how we handle these. The client may not have bargained for changing their internal processes so you need to make sure they're on board . . . you must be very explicit about what has to change. Otherwise there is a risk that you'll implement something that they just won't use . . . that they won't be happy with. So it's actually about getting the client to buy into the advantages of the changes . . . the reasons why and what they are going to get from it.

Turn it over.

There will be major change . . .

Looking at the overall pattern for this project, what advice to your pal?

I think it looks like a very good project. They have somebody good on the client's side taking responsibility for the project. So he can give you a lot of help.

There is the issue that they disagree amongst themselves. You need to take this one head-on to reduce the risk of the goalposts constantly moving. Whether it be by fax, email or whatever, you must get them involved in feedback and sign off on requirements, the functional spec, and on the detailed design if necessary. If they are signing off at all stages, I don't think you can go wrong.

The fact that the application logic is straightforward and that we don't have interfacing to do is great. This reduces the risk of our messing up "codewise."

We're doing significant subcontracting, so the risk is there that we will mismanage this. Basically, we have to act towards them as the client should act towards us . . . to make sure they are delivering exactly what we want . . . that there is regular communication . . . that the right channels are open . . . that we're involved in signing off on what they're doing . . . the same way that we involve the client.

There's going to be big change to the client's processes. So their buy-in on this is very important. You can't just release the product and hope they'll change their internal procedures and workflow. You need to get their involvement on this issue very early on. You need to take them through it all very explicitly so that they can start to think it through and to prepare the ground.

How do you think this project is likely to turn out?

I "agree" that it will be a good experience for both parties!

Which is the "nastiest" of the nasties?

They disagree amongst themselves about what's needed

And the "nicest" of the nice ones?

Someone has taken clear, committed ownership of the project and *The customer's PM has the needed time/skill/authority*

SUSAN B

I'm going to break my VERY BIG DIFFERENCE pile into three sub-piles . . .

*Major change to customer's procedures?   Mission-critical application?
Tight, customer-imposed timescales?   System must go right first time?*

*Realistic expectations?   Agree amongst themselves on what's needed?
Any hidden agendas?   Has their PM time/skill/authority?   A committed
project owner?   Are they a big or small company?*

*Application complexity?   Our knowledge of the application?   How
adaptable must our solution be?   Must we subcontract?   Our knowledge
of the languages/tools?*

Why break this pile into three sub-piles?

My first sub-pile is all about managing the customer. If you're going to
implement something that will make dramatic change to what they're currently doing, this will have a big impact on the scope of the project, and on
the need for flexibility in timescales. Whether or not it's mission-critical
makes a big difference. If it's not mission-critical in some sense, what use is
the system? If it IS mission-critical, or there's a lot of change involved, you
have to insist on prototyping it . . . piloting it, not expecting it to go right first
time . . . and on some flexibility in timescales . . . typically there's no room for
getting it wrong. So that's all about managing the customer's expectations.

Your middle sub-pile . . . what's that all about?

That's all about the management of the project. Client ownership, for
example. If you don't have that, you have a big problem from the very beginning. So that's one of the first things you have to get right. Setting customers'
expectations . . . you may do a fantastic job for the customer, but if they
don't believe it, you haven't! Then there's disagreement amongst themselves
. . . that's a very important one. Hidden agendas can be absolutely critical.
Say you're doing a global-scale project and you're dealing with people from

different countries. They all have different objectives. If you don't consider these, you'll never get off the ground. The time/skill/authority thing for the client project manager ties in with the issue of getting committed ownership for the project.

And your third sub-pile?

The message in this pile is "really know your business". . . do what's familiar to you and don't go off at tangents. For example, if you're not a database development company, accept this up front, and don't try to do it. Your experience of the application . . . the complexity of the application . . . it's about knowing what you're doing. The adaptability of the system to future needs . . . this one could have gone into my first sub-pile. If you're not looking to the future in terms of what you are developing for them, they'll be unhappy in the future. Subcontracting . . . you always get into trouble when you subcontract. it's not under your control. Your familiarity with the languages and tools . . . again, it's all about knowing your business.

If you had to pick one or two cards out of your three VERY BIG DIFFERENCE sub-piles, which ones?

I'd take . . .

Mission-critical application?

The reason I picked this one . . . take *&^% [a prominent international company] who are one of our current customers. In the past, if a customer had a query and phoned them about it, it would take them a week to respond. When we implemented a document management system for them, they could get to documents and answer queries within minutes or seconds. It made a massive difference to their customer service . . . to their competitiveness. Consequently it has been very successful. So I always ask the question "Is the system key to their needs?"

Are you saying that the more mission-critical the system is, the better for the project?

Yes. there's more commitment from the customer's side. they're more realistic in terms of costs and timescales. it's a higher-profile project within your own organization. But you really need to know what you are doing! So you get the commitment from both organizations.

160

If the new system IS mission-critical, what would you do differently?

If it's really mission-critical, you'd tell the client "Don't put in something that's cheap and nasty just to plug the hole. Let's stand back from it . . . do a proper analysis . . . a proper systems spec . . . get users' buy-in . . . set the right budget." That's what you'd say. In fact, there have been occasions when we have walked away from the business because the customer hasn't . . . Let me give you an example. One client said they planned to recruit long-term unemployed people on a casual basis for data entry on the new system. In the same breath, they said they wanted ninety-five per cent keying accuracy. We said you're mad . . . it won't work. We walked away from the business. They were totally unrealistic.

Let's see . . .

> *The new system isn't mission-critical . . .*

Which one next?

If I put my technical hat on, I'd go for . . .

> *Our knowledge of the application?*

If I put my business hat on, I'd say . . .

> *Realistic expectations?*

Interesting! Make a choice.

I see myself as a business person, so I have to go for the expectations one.

If you got a sense that their expectations were unrealistic?

We'd probably walk away from the business to be honest. we've been in that situation a few times. If you can't reset their expectations, you have to walk away.

Is it about educating them in some sense?

Yes. People tend to have no understanding of what's involved in implementing workflow systems. They always underestimate the size of their business processes. You find that something they see as a four-step change in a process ends up as a thirty-four step change. Our rule of thumb is 80 per cent analysis, twenty per cent development on business process change projects. You can reset their expectations by doing a prototype . . . but they will have spent all their money on the prototype, so where do you go next? That's the challenge.

Let's see what's true of this project.

The customer has realistic expectations . . .

So they know what they're about. I think the next important one in terms of risk is . . .

A committed project "owner"?

If that was looking a bit bleak?

If it was, and we've got to take over the whole thing . . . I'm looking . . .

Someone has taken clear, committed ownership . . .

Fine. So they have the budget. They have the person. Now I'd start to look at the application . . .

Our knowledge of the application?

If the application was new to you?

Then *System must go right first time?* comes into play. In fact, what we'd actually do is do an initial requirements spec, and then see if we had the needed skills in-house . . . whether it's our bread and butter or not. Then we'd decide if we wanted the business. Then the piloting.

Let's see . . .

We've experience of this application

What's this project looking like so far?

We've got a budget. we've a client project manager. we've experience of the application. Now we need to look at the timescales. So my next step would be, and I'm looking . . .

We'll be able to juggle a bit with timescales

Good!

If you hadn't been able to juggle?

We'd just have to put more resources on it from our side, and take over the management of it . . . but, thinking again, what we'd ACTUALLY do is to try to reset their expectations about the time needed. we'd suggest a two-phased installation. we'd say "Let's put the infrastructure in place and do the easy things in the time available in phase one, then see where we've got to, and then build on the rest of the functionality in phase two."

What's next?

We know the cost. We know the person. We know the timescale. we've experience of the application. we'd next look at going into the meat of the project. I might start looking at . . .

> *How adaptable must our solution be?*

What difference would that one make?

It would make a difference to the scoping of the project. The customer has specific requirements today. Let's say all he wants now is a document management system which lets him retrieve documents in a Windows environment. But in the future he wants to implement intranet and Internet technology. That means what you're building now must include interfaces that these things can plug into in the future. This is just a simple example. So what you'd have to do now is to scope the project out to multiple phases.

I'm looking . . .

> *It doesn't have to be particularly adaptable . . .*

If all projects were like this, it would be wonderful!

Really, the next thing to start looking at . . . maybe any subcontracting . . . but that really wouldn't make much difference . . . OK, I'll go for . . .

> *Any hidden agendas?*

Maybe there's something to do with a parent company . . . something we don't know about . . . that type of thing which tends to have a big impact.

Let's say you got a sense that there was something behind the scenes that wasn't being revealed to you?

We'd get customer sign-off on everything . . . requirements spec . . . system spec . . . detailed criteria for acceptance testing. we'd mock up screens in advance, so they'd know exactly what they were getting. we'd make sure that the technical specification was something that a technical person could read, but was also something that a management person could read. That's how we have protected ourselves in the past.

Take a peep . . .

The "real" agenda seems to be hidden

You have to find out what that hidden agenda is. Given this, I've to go next for . . .

Agree amongst themselves on what's needed?

And if they disagree?

Then you have to look at the authority aspect of things . . .

Has their PM time/skill/authority?

You'd have to escalate it to their main project guy. Tell him to bang their heads together . . .

Their PM has the needed time/skill/authority

I wonder about that agreement issue . . .

They disagree amongst themselves . . .

We'll have to assume he can sort the disagreement out, and that we now know what the hidden agenda is. So we're now moving into the application. So my next is . . .

Our knowledge of the languages/tools?

And if you didn't know these?

We'd have to bring in subcontractors. there's no other way around it. Or you have a choice of not bidding for the business.

Why not just take a flyer at it?

You can't do that. The business community is far too small for you to take the chance. You've got to walk away from business that's not your core business. If you go down alleyways, it will end up costing you money and maybe reputation.

Let's see . . .

We'll be using unfamiliar languages/tools . . .

Next?

We have to go to the complexity of the application logic. This has to do with whether or not we know what we're trying to do.

Application complexity?

If we didn't know what we are doing, we would walk away from the business. I keep coming back to this point, but we honestly would. There was one occasion where we were working with a database, *&^ %, we were not familiar with. We brought that experience in-house and we trained people on it. The application went in successfully. That's what we do with unfamiliar stuff. We bring the expertise in-house or outsource it. But we never chance doing it on the fly ourselves.

The application is straightforward

Right. My last one will be . . .

System must go right first time?

If we had a customer who was maybe nervous about things not going just right . . . if the application has to be absolutely perfect, we'd set up a test environment here which mimics their environment. We would prototype it . . . bring them in to check it out . . . gain their acceptance of the prototype. we'd do application-acceptance testing and technical-acceptance testing prior to installation. Then we'd install it in a small group of users, bed the system in with them, and then expand it outwards.

Advice for your project manager?

Make sure you know what you're doing . . . stick to the knitting if you possibly can. Set the client's expectations correctly. Make sure the project has been adequately costed. Make sure you have sufficient time for a few things to go wrong. Prototype the solution. Get formal customer acceptance at each stage of the process. Limit your risk by doing a small, controlled installation, and then expand it out.

How do you think the project will turn out?

Probably a positive experience for both. there's nothing too awful here.

What's the worst of the bad news?

The "real" agenda seems to be hidden, They disagree amongst themselves . . . and *We'll be using unfamiliar languages/tools*

I think the unfamiliar languages/tools is the worst bit because we can manage the disagreement and the agenda thing through their strong project manager. The client seems to be committed and has taken ownership, and they have realistic expectations. So the worst news is the unfamiliar languages and tools.

And the best news?

We've experience of this application and *The customer has realistic expectations . . .*

Any cards missing?

Anything I didn't pick out, I felt I could manage . . . inexperienced computer users . . . interfacing to existing applications . . . a transaction-processing system or whatever . . . will take more than three months or not . . . all manageable.

One criticism that's been made is that the things on the cards are mostly customer oriented. What do you think?

I don't think that's a criticism! If you had a technical developer sitting in front of you, you might get a different answer, because he'd be looking at it from a code point of view. They look at it in terms of taking a specification and rolling something out. They tend to be the people who are not with the customer from the very beginning to the very end of the process. They don't see the early parts like winning the business and setting expectations, and so on. Things fail I think because the client doesn't have the money, they don't know what they're doing, or they don't have the commitment. It tends to be the business things that have the real impact, unless you've just made a real mess of what you're doing. I've heard of software houses building things that just don't work. This astounds me! it's incredible! That's why I keep saying "Stick to your knitting. Walk away from business that you're not familiar with."

TOMMY

23

My VERY BIG DIFFERENCE pile . . .

Must we subcontract?   Our knowledge of the languages/tools?   Our knowledge of the platform? Realistic expectations?   A committed project "owner"?   Their experience in running computer projects?   Major change to customer's procedures?   Agree amongst themselves on what's needed? Has their PM time/skill/authority?   Our knowledge of the application?

What really distinguishes between the three piles?

The highest-priority pile contains items that are most likely to affect project success and the items that need the greatest amount of project management skill. These are the ones most likely to cause pitfalls. To handle them you need project management skills and customer management skills. They are a combination of technical issues and customer management issues that normally cause project failure in my experience.

Concentrate on the very big DIFFERENCE pile. Take these items one by one . . . most important one first.

Top one is . . .

Realistic expectations?

If you don't manage your customer's expectations you're on a loser from day one. The customer will have business goals to meet and, particularly for a critical project, it will be part of their business planning to have this project in place at a particular time and for a particular cost. If their expectation about time is unrealistic, and you allow this to persist, it can have a bad knock-on effect on their business plans . . . this dovetails nicely with . . .

Major change to customer's procedures?

I'll bring in this change one again later but most projects result in some changes in the customer's procedures. Often the customer doesn't appreciate this fact. Changes in procedures invariably have to be handled and driven by the customer. An IT supplier can't do it. there's usually a whole cultural thing . . . an ethical thing . . . often industrial relations implications to change. So expectations about the degree of change the customer will have to handle must also be got right.

In terms of customers' expectations about cost, if you don't get this right from the beginning you bring your own credibility into question and could bring the credibility of the project sponsor into question within his organization. In relation to customers' expectations about "what's doable", some customers expect IT solutions to solve all their problems . . . but they never do. In most cases IT solutions just automate SOME elements of the business system. But there are always pieces on the fringes of the IT system that have to be looked at and re-engineered. Some customers don't appreciate this. Computers can't do everything for you, particularly in new applications in the financial area where there's always the need for extra manual controls of some kind.

What would you do if you found the customer had way-out expectations?

All you can do is to meet the customer and reset those expectations. One technique I've used for doing that is to hold workshops involving key people from the customer's side and key people from our side where we learn to speak one another's language. A lot of people don't talk the same language. In a workshop you can get communication flowing . . . you can get debate going . . . people begin to understand what's on the other side of the fence, and when communication begins, the understanding follows. it's often just a lack of appreciation by the client of what's involved. That's why it's so important that, in this situation, good project management relies on sign-offs at different phases in the project. The client should be asked to sign off requirements, to sign off specifications, to do acceptance testing of software. This must not be just a formality. Acceptance and sign-off must be the client saying "Yes. I understand this . . . and I'm happy with it."

Another key thing to improve communication is to get the key users involved in the project at an early stage so that the understanding is not just between the IT company's people and the purchaser on the client's side. It must involve people who understand the business and who appreciate the impact of the system on the business . . . who are part of the thinking . . . who can impart enthusiasm for the project as it goes ahead.

Turn the card over . . .

> *The customer has unrealistic expectations . . .*

So I'm into my workshop, etc.!

I'll take these two next. They go hand in hand.

> *Has their PM time/skill/authority?* and *A committed project "owner"?*

If the project doesn't have an effective sponsor, its chances of being a success are greatly reduced. That sponsor has a responsibility to commit financial budget and people to the project, to get buy-in from all the functions within his organization to changes they may have to make to make the project successful. If that's not there, then the project's success is greatly at risk. Every project needs a champion, and without the champion it won't succeed. That champion has to fight for the funding and to influence people in his own organization to make things happen.

What would you do if both of these items were negative?

Again, this situation, a political one, comes back to communication. it's about establishing with the client that this problem exists. I'd sit the client down and have some hard face-to-face conversations about it. I'd present hard evidence to help the client realize that the problem exists, and that it needs to be tackled. Once the problem is accepted as a problem, it can sometimes be solved by bringing in some third party, be it an additional consultant from your own side, or someone else, to help the client or his representative to either free up the needed time to devote to the project, or else to equip him to be in a better position to argue a case for the project within the organization. Sometimes you can have an individual who can be committed to a project but be without the clout within the organization to influence things. The problem can be not that there isn't someone in place, it can be the wrong person in the wrong place. Anyway, the earlier it's addressed the better.

Turn over the two cards.

> *The customer's PM lacks the needed time/skill/authority* and *Nobody wants to "own" the project*

We're going down the tubes rapidly here!

What do you make of this project so far?

What I would now do is a risk analysis of the project and ask myself "Do I REALLY want this project?" My decision could be influenced by questions like "Is this a strategic project for me? Is this a piece of business that I need to get into because of follow-on business? Because it will give me experience in a technology area that I really want? Because this is a long-time customer that I really need to stay in bed with? What sort of profit margins do I have on the project? If there is a problem, and I have to pour more resources into it, have I got the fat . . . some contingency in my plans that would allow me to soak that up without hurting my bottom line? The timescale on this project is likely to slip. Can I afford to have key people tied up in it for longer than I otherwise intended?" All these sorts of questions would be part of my decision process.

Pick your next card.

We'll turn away from the customer for a while and look at the supplier. There are three that are allied to each other, two of them are technical . . .

> *Our knowledge of the platform?*, *Our knowledge of the languages/tools?* and *Our knowledge of the application?*

These are the sorts of things that impact on the supplier's ability to be confident in what he is proposing. Unfamiliarity with tools . . . working in a new environment . . . means there's a good chance the supplier has never had to produce estimates for a project like this before . . . doesn't appreciate all the pitfalls that can arise in getting the bits and pieces working together. If these items are all new to the supplier, he is probably working with a team that has never worked together before. So there is a lot of risk and a lot of contingency needs to be put into a schedule to cope.

Turn over the cards.

All three bad news!

The platform and the tools I'll put together. The application area can have even wider impact. If you're working in an unfamiliar application area, you're probably trying to work with a client to specify requirements in an area you know little about. At least with tools and environment, if there's a problem you are probably beyond the design stage and into implementation . . . you are further down the road with the project. But if your design is screwed up it's much more difficult to go back and redo it. there's also your uncertainty around how the client is going to use the application . . . the impact it will have on their procedures and so on. So it's kind of important you understand what you are doing out there!

How would you handle this situation?

I think I'd start running now! On the technical side, it's relatively easy to solve technical problems if you are prepared to invest in the right resources, and if you can find these. it's not impossible to find people with the skills and assign these to the project. So if this project was one I wanted to run with, I'd go to the market to look for people with the right skills and experience in the tools and environment, and get them involved in the project at the earliest possible stage so that they begin to do things correctly, rather than us building stuff that won't work.

On the application side, again, the only way you can bolster up the application experience is to get an application consultant who understands the area. He's not necessarily a technocrat, but someone who understands the business aspects of the application. Then I'd try to marry the business knowledge with the technical knowledge.

Do you want to move on?

Just four cards left. I'll pick this next . . .

Must we subcontract?

Subcontracting brings risks with it. Most integration projects now involve some degree of subcontracting. If you subcontract, you need to understand your subcontractors. you're dealing with a different organization with a different business ethos to yours . . . a different approach to doing things . . . different standards. there's the whole business of getting two organizations working together . . . of putting the right mechanics in place to have them work together. there's also the question of the viability of the subcontractor and his ability to finish the project. What if the subcontractor goes bust? What if the subcontractor has other projects that are more important and so doesn't deliver to deadlines? The management of subcontractors is a key skill. With a subcontractor/prime contractor relationship, the prime still carries the can, so the risk is in your court.

Let me see which applies . . .

We won't need to subcontract . . .

The first bit of good news!

The three cards that are left are all customer focused. I'll take this one next . . .

Their experience in running IT projects?

A customer who is experienced in running projects is familiar with the mechanisms that are used to manage and control projects, and will more readily demand that these mechanisms be in place, and will more readily welcome them. They will understand that resources have to be put in place to make it happen, they won't expect the supplier to do everything, and will know that the customer has to make commitments as well. A customer without that experience often expects the supplier to come in, do everything, and walk away with everything done. Not only that, but also that the new system will stay working for evermore with nothing having to be done to it. So it's important, if the customer is inexperienced, that the customer's responsibilities be clearly outlined, up front. That's all you can do.

Let's see . . .

> *The customer is not experienced . . .*

Bad news.

This one next . . .

> *Agree amongst themselves on what's needed?*

One of the key things that a supplier of IT solutions needs to do is to consult. Consulting for me is about influencing people towards a solution. If you continually have disagreement between key players on the customer's side, then it makes the consulting role more difficult. You neglect the process of reaching agreement at your peril because if you do what you deliver is likely to be rejected by someone. So I would put in place a procedure to make sure that everyone reaches agreement. There are various sorts of methodologies out there to help. For instance, I've seen structured groups being formed with opposing parties in each group. Each group then has to identify issues and come up with recommendations. Anyway, there are lots of methods that consultants can use to handle this sort of thing. At the end of the day, it's all about communication and getting acceptance of the common goal that has to be achieved.

I'll turn it over . . .

> *They don't disagree . . .*

That's fine.

My last card . . .

> *Major change to customer's procedures?*

No application gets implemented without changes to how the customer does business, even if it's only a move from one version of a product to another version. Invariably it results in change. it's very often overlooked as a piece of work that needs to be done, and invariably it needs to be done by the client, and driven by them. If it's not factored into the project, the project will

172

flounder immediately on going live and will flounder as they go through user-acceptance testing. you'll hear "Sure this will never work because we'll have to change the way we do this or that . . . and nobody thought of that." So planning and handling change needs to be a key part of the project lifecycle.

Let's see . . .

> *No major changes . . .*

That's good.

Looking at the whole pattern of the answers, what advice would your give you pal?

Engage the cutomer and test if they are really committed to the project. Have they got the budget? Are they willing to put in the resources? Give the customer a detailed project plan, showing what resources they will need to commit and when. Explain to the customer where that project plan has contingencies built into it to cover the major risks that will arise from your unfamiliarity with the languages, tools and environment, the customer's inexperience with IT projects and the lack of application experience on your side.

That's a tricky one. Would you really come up front on these risks?

I think you'd really have to. One way or the other, you've got to plug the resources into the project to cover these off. You could put it more positively by saying that we need two or three months, or however long, from an expert in manufacturing or finance, or whatever. Anyway, I'd use the project plan as the means of communicating the issues to the customer, and getting the customer to buy in to the issues that have to be addressed. Without a project plan, and an agreed list of actions by both parties, this project will fail. Once you've reset the customer's expectations, the customer can decide if he wants the project, and if he doesn't, shake hands and everyone's happy. If he DOES want it, then there's commitment to go for it.

What other advice?

Assuming this is a greenfield situation, and we're developing software from the ground up, I'd start with the functional specification. In this case, this task should be charged for separately on a fixed-price basis, so that it's not open-ended from the client's point of view. When the functional specification is agreed and signed off, then and only then can estimates be given for subsequent phases. Then I'd get into a more detailed design phase, probably including some form of prototyping. Then we're into the coding and development, system test, application test and go-live phases. If we don't fully sign off on a phase before we start the next one, and it happens, we should recognise this and know what new risks we are bringing in.

Assuming that your pal isn't superman, how do you think this project is likely to turn out if he runs with it?

I suppose if you're taking on a project like this, you have to take it on with a positive attitude and with the expectation of success. If the project is successful . . . great for both parties . . . both will have learned new skills in new areas. But if the key things are not managed, in terms of relationships and risks, then it's a disaster waiting to happen.

Which items would be the biggest contributors to risk here?

These three . . . *Customer has unrealistic expectations . . ., . . . unfamiliar languages/tools . . .* and *Nobody wants to "own" the project*

Any cards missing that you'd have expected to see in the deck?

A project team of reasonable size is going to go through lots of grey patches and the project manager has the job of picking the team up after each dismal day. That's an important part of project success . . . keeping up enthusiasm for the project . . . making sure the team are working well together and interfacing properly with the customer. I don't remember any card for this aspect. I can't think of any others that might be missing.

TONY

Ones that could make a VERY BIG DIFFERENCE . . .

A committed project "owner"?   Our knowledge of the application?   Are they able/willing to drive implementation?   Any hidden agendas?   Have we a credible competitor?   Their experience in running IT projects?   Realistic expectations?   Can they define their problem?   People most affected really want the system?   Our knowledge of the languages/tools?   Agree amongst themselves on what's needed?   Our knowledge of their industry?   Mission-critical application?   Has their PM time/skill/authority?

Explain your thinking a bit. What really distinguishes the three piles?

In the VERY BIG DIFFERENCE pile I mostly put things that relate to the ability of the customer to work with us. Like things related to their owner-ship of the project, any hidden agendas and so on. These items look at the more qualitative side of the project. They are mainly things that could get in the way of defining and agreeing what the product is to be.

In the SOME/LITTLE/NO DIFFERENCE pile I've put mainly items that are really just management issues, once you have defined what the product is to be. For example, if it's probably a one-off project for the client, or if on the other hand it could lead to other contracts, that's manageable and it's a pricing decision. If it's a one-off, you've really got to encapsulate the project, to ring-fence it, and get your handover clean and right. If it could lead to other projects, you might look at pricing a bit more competitively, and leave it all a bit more open-ended designwise. The big thing about the items in this pile is that they are manageable . . . handleable.

Let's focus on the VERY BIG DIFFERENCE pile. Take them in order of reducing importance.

I'd put

> *Mission-critical application?*

first.

If it was mission-critical, you'd be looking for a very clear definition of what the project is, what it's supposed to achieve. So you'd be looking for agreement on definite, measurable end results. You'd also be looking for great clarity on the issues and arrangements for handing the product over . . . where responsibilities lie, precisely where does the project start and finish. If it's mission-critical, you'd be trying to ring-fence the project and find out and agree the measures which will demonstrate to everybody that the project has been completed to the customer's satisfaction. Agreeing a precise handover point is also critical.

Turnover the card.

The new system isn't mission-critical . . .

Fine. My next is . . .

Agree amongst themselves on what's needed?

If there's disagreement you have to facilitate reaching an agreement . . . to get a consensus on what the project is about . . . and to define it. If it was a big project, we'd suggest in this situation that they bring in an independent consultant to advise them on their needs. Then we'd pick up from there. In our methodology, we'd be trying at the very start to get a very good functional description of what the project is about. we'd be looking for clarity from the customer on "this is what we require from you".

They don't disagree . . .

That's good.

My next is . . .

A committed project "owner"?

I'm going to cheat . . .

Someone has taken clear, committed ownership . . .

It makes life much easier for us if we have a point of contact who has the authority, the seniority required, to drive the project, and if they take ownership of it. It throws up real warning signals for virtually all aspects of the project if the ownership thing is not there. It could be the deciding factor on whether to proceed or not.

Let me just recap. You'd be looking to see how critical the project is to the client . . . is there reasonable agreement on what it's about . . . and then ownership. These factors are all about equally important.

Next is . . .

Our knowledge of their industry?

If we have a good knowledge of the client's industry, this can shorten project timescales and help us get the project on the road early.

Let me see . . .

We've little or no knowledge . . .

Bad news. Let me pick my next one straightaway . . .

Realistic expectations?

We've no knowledge of the industry, so we need to factor that fact into our timescales and estimates. If they have realistic expectations, you're probably in a position to move forward. If they don't, you are looking for a front-end loading to the contract to learn the business and to establish and pin down the scope of the project.

Let's see which applies . . .

The customer has unrealistic expectations . . .

Bad again! My next is . . .

Their experience of running IT projects?

If they have some experience of computer projects, you can debate the point about what's doable and what's not . . . and the cost. You can have a meaningful discussion about what has to be done . . . and sort out their unrealistic expectations. In our methodology, we first produce the functional specification, which defines the business application. Then we move this into the technical specification, which defines the design and development to be done. Then we establish our timescales out of that. We really have to get these agreed and tied down. there's an educational process to be gone through if the customer hasn't experience of all of this. As I said earlier, in this situation, we would suggest they bring in a consultant to get some objective advice.

Let's see . . .

. . . not experienced . . .

What seems to be emerging in the scenario for this project is that they've taken ownership but they don't have the experience to handle it, we don't know much about their industry, and they have unrealistic expectations. In this scenario, I'd step back and tell them they need some other facilitator to help them, at least to get their needs sorted-out. Then we could put a project together.

Next is . . .

Can they define their problem?

If it's . . . No . . .

And it is!

Now we have a real problem. If the client can't define the problem in IT-addressable terms, there is a very dangerous balance here. If we have to work to define the problem, even if someone has taken "ownership" of the project, the "real" ownership is passed across to me.

What do you reckon this project is beginning to look like?

We've been here before! They feel they have a problem . . . they want a solution . . . but no real thinking or debate has gone into it. They really want someone to outsource the problem to . . . to take responsibility for it. What you would really have to decide in this one is "Is taking responsibility for it doable in the context of the organization?" And, the important point, if you DO take it on, can you escape cleanly at the end, or will you have to live with it in a post-project support role? Here, I'd really encourage them to get some preliminary help in articulating the problem.

What if you decided to take it on anyway?

We'd go for an open-ended time-and-materials contract . . . or nothing.

OK. Pick your next card.

I'm going to cheat again!

Their PM lacks the needed time/skill/authority

We are now on a real hiding to nothing. This project is unmanageable. We would spend all our time trying to substitute skills back into the organization to cover off things that are missing. it's really starting to look like a "bummer"!

Let me take the next card . . . I'm going to cheat from now on . . .

We've experience of this application

This compensates for some of the downsides. If this hadn't been the case, forget it!

Let me look at my next two . . .

We'll be using familiar languages/tools and *We're up against a credible competitor . . .*

If the languages/tools weren't familiar to us, we'd front-load the project because we'd have to bring in training, or contract in new skills for the period of the project . . . it certainly would have an impact on costs. In fact, we wouldn't be able to fix our costs until we got to the point where the technical spec was completed and signed off. So, time and materials up to that point, then you should be able to scope the job fairly well from that point on.

The fact that we are up against a credible competitor . . . .that's when you have to fine-tune your proposal . . . and ask "Can I get value out of this project?"

Stand back a little at this stage, and take an overview. What key advice would you give your pal?

At least the system is not mission-critical. But they aren't applying a senior level of resources to the project, so I'd be very wary. Let me pull in this one again . . .

Agree amongst themselves on what's needed?

You'd be lucky to get a read on that one . . . even though they SEEM not to disagree! They aren't applying a senior level of resources to the project. They have little experience and unrealistic expectations. These are issues that have to be resolved early on because otherwise they will come back to haunt you when you try to get consensus on delivery dates and costs. If you have little or no experience of the industry, there's a learning curve going into the project. Also, they don't have a fairly well-defined understanding of the solution they are looking for. These are all up-front impacts on the project. To get them to the technical design spec stage . . . there'll be a lot of work involved to flush out the functional specification and to make sure it meets the client's needs. The upside is that you have experience of the application and the tools. The big question is, can you get a good, commercial contract out of this one? On the shape of the contract, I'd go for time and materials. I'd insist on a very clear understanding around the contract . . . what it includes and, most importantly, what it excludes, and what the responsibilities of the customer are. The contract will have to define each party's responsibilities very clearly because the scenario suggests there are lots of opportunities for ambiguity. I'd have the contract open-ended time and materials for the first phase . . . until the client gets to the point where he can tie down the project and there can be a fairly clear definition of responsibilities.

I'd be looking to involve the users early on because of the lack of clarity about what the project is to achieve, because whilst the client may initiate the project, at the end of the day it is the users who will judge whether it works or not.

Implementation could be an issue because they don't seem to have a lot of skills to put into the project. So you would need to define the implementation job carefully and put the tasks and responsibilities into the contract.

How do you think this project will turn out, given that your pal is not a superman?

It's shaping up to being a bad one. I think it'll be a bad experience for everyone!

Were there any issues NOT covered by the cards that you would have expected to see there?

If I was PM in this scenario, where they've delegated the job to someone who doesn't even have the skills to handle it, then you are really in the hands of the gods. If there's no referral route back to a steering group or team, or some other person or body who has the seniority to legislate on things, you are out on one big limb! you're highly dependent on the capability of the individual you are presented with, and you are measured on his or her success. Not nice.

PART 3

Distilling Out the Theories-of-Action

Method

In this chapter, I explain how I set about analyzing the interview transcripts shown in Part 2. My goal was to distill out, from this large volume of material, the PMs' core strategies for handling the different situational factors. In the next chapter, I'll give the "spirit" that resulted from this distillation process.

But first, a small diversion. At the start of each interview session, I asked the PM to break the thirty-four constructs into three piles ... the VERY BIG DIFFERENCE (VBD), the BIG DIFFERENCE (BD) and the SOME/LITTLE/NO DIFFERENCE (SLND) piles. Which constructs did the PMs put into which piles? And why?

In characterizing their VERY BIG DIFFERENCE piles, the PMs used phrases such as:

"It's about the unknowns ... it's about things that are not directly controllable by us. Things that could come back and bite us." (Alan)

"These are the real risk generators in my view. These are the ones that could cause you to lose control ... these generate uncertainty ... possible black holes." (Michael B)

"The VBD pile are the key factors, some of which may not be in your direct control ... like the client not having realistic expectations. You can only manage so many of these factors simultaneously ... the items in the BD pile are important, but generally I would say these are all manageable." (Padraig)

"The VBD pile has to do with control and familiarity. These are success versus disaster things." (Patrick)

In Table 25.1 I show the numbers of PMs who assigned each construct to each of the three piles. The constructs are shown in decreasing order of the numbers of PMs placing that construct in the VERY BIG DIFFERENCE pile. it's interesting to see that the top five constructs all relate to customer "people" problems. I'll make a lot of use of this table in later chapters.

Now ... back to the main plot. When all twenty interviews had been completed, the process of analyzing the interview transcripts began. The

Table 25.1   Numbers of PMs putting each construct into each pile[1]

		VBD	BD	SLND
Someone on the customer's side has taken clear, committed ownership of the project	Nobody wants to "own" the project	17	3	0
The customer has realistic expectations about time, cost and what's "doable"	The customer has unrealistic expectations about time, cost and what's "doable"	16	4	0
The customer's PM has the needed time/skill/authority	The customer's PM lacks the needed time/skill/authority	15	5	0
There seems to be no hidden agenda	The "real" agenda seems to be hidden	14	6	0
They don't disagree amongst themselves about what's needed	They disagree amongst themselves about what's needed	14	6	0
We will be using familiar languages/tools	We will be using unfamiliar languages/tools	13	3	4
No major changes to the customer's workflow/ procedures	Major change to the customer's workflow/procedures	12	6	2
No tricky interfacing with existing applications	Some tricky interfacing with existing applications	12	5	3
The platform/environment is familiar to us	The platform/environment is new to us	12	5	3
The people most affected seem to genuinely want the new system	The people most affected don't seem to really want the new system	11	7	2
The new system isn't mission-critical to the customer	The new system is mission-critical to the customer	11	7	2
We'll be able to juggle a bit with timescales	We'll have to work to tight, customer-imposed timescales	10	8	2
We've experience of this application	The application is new to us	10	8	2
We won't need to subcontract anything	We'll have to do significant sub contracting	10	7	3
We can pilot the new system until we get it right	The new system has to go right first time	9	9	2
We've only to satisfy a single group of similar users	We've to satisfy multiple groups of users with different needs	9	5	6
We won't have to change other developer's code	We'll have to change other developer's code	8	9	3

		VBD	BD	SLND
We won't have to share control of the project with a third party	We'll have to share control of the project with a third party (e.g. consultants)	8	8	4
We've a good knowledge of the customer's industry	We've little or no knowledge of the customer's industry	7	12	1
The new system doesn't have to be particularly adaptable to future needs	The new system must be adaptable enough to cope with unknown future needs	5	13	2
The customer is experienced in running computer projects	The customer is not experienced in running computer projects	5	11	4
The application is straightforward	The application is complex	5	9	6
The customer has the willingness and skills to manage implementation issues	We'll have to sort out/drive implementation	4	14	2
We will need only one or two people on the project	We will need three or more people on the project	4	8	8
The project will take three months or less	The project will take more than three months	4	8	8
The customer is able to define the problem in IT-addressable terms	We will have to work with them to define the problem	4	8	8
We'll be able to show the customer an early prototype	It won't be possible to show the customer an early prototype	3	12	5
We're dealing with experienced computer users	We're dealing with inexperienced computer users	3	10	7
We've no credible competitor for this project	We are up against a credible competitor for this project	3	4	13
We'll be dealing directly with the users	We'll be working through their IT department	2	12	6
The new system involves only a single functional area	The new system will span a number of functional areas	2	10	8
This is probably a "one-off" project for this customer	This project could lead to other projects for this customer	1	8	11
The customer is a very small company	The customer is a larger company	1	5	14
It's a transaction processing system	It's an MIS/DSS type system	0	7	13

[1] Reprinted from Journal of Systems and Software, Vol 53, Moynihan, T., "Coping with requirements uncertainty", 99–109, Copyright (2000), with permission from Elsevier Science.

fragments of the interview transcripts in which the PMs described the strategies they recommended for coping with the risky poles were extracted from the interview transcripts. A total of 289 fragments were obtained. I sorted these fragments into piles. To each pile, I assigned those fragments that seemed, in their essence, to be referring to the same, underlying strategy. Then, for each pile, I tried to capture that common strategy by creating a textual synthesis of the fragments the pile contained (the "label"). A number of iterations of this sorting and labelling process were required. The goal was to achieve piles and labels which, in a semantic sense, maximized "variation" across the piles, and which minimized "variation" within the piles. By the conclusion of this process, the 289 fragments had been broken into thirty-seven piles, and I had synthesized a label for each pile. In the next chapter, I show the thirty-seven labels (the strategies) I composed. For each strategy, I show the numbers of PMs who seemed to allude to that strategy, and the frequency with which each construct pole elicited that strategy. I also show one or two of the interview fragments which I "assigned" to that strategy. In Appendix 3, I show, for each strategy, the complete set of interview fragments which I assigned to that strategy, and the identity of the PM who uttered each fragment. So, I hope I've provided full traceability between the strategies and the support I found for each in the interview transcripts.

One further point. Despite my best efforts to tease the strategies apart in the sorting and labelling process, the descriptions of the various strategies may not all appear to the reader to be logically "disjoint". For example, it may be argued that some of the "strategies" are merely special cases of other, more generic strategies. Also, it is easy to argue that some of the strategies overlap. In my defence, I have tried to stay as close as possible to the PMs' own words and phrases, and I have tried to avoid the temptation of imposing a tidy, but possibly spurious, structure on the strategies. Anyway, I did my best.

Some "Strategies", "Recipes", Call These What You Will . . . 26

26.1 On Project Ownership and Leadership Problems . . .

> **#1**
>
> **If there is no committed/enthusiastic project "owner", ask or search for one (maybe an influential, enthusiastic user). Go up the line if necessary. If this fails, confront the client organization with the problem. If not resolved satisfactorily, walk away. Don't proceed until the problem is sorted out.**
>
> *Number of PMs mentioning: 10*
>
> *Elicited by:*
>
> *No real owner (10)*
>
> *Their PM lacks time/skill/authority (1)*
>
> *Mission-critical application (1)*

"I think it's crucial to have somebody on the customer's side who will take ownership. If you haven't, you go as high up as possible in their organization and demand that you get someone who'll run with it. Otherwise, you end up running the project the way you think it should be run, and not meeting their requirements . . . without real ownership from senior people, work in tandem with the users . . . get to know the users well and select a good strong person from amongst them . . . someone who has a fair bit of authority and standing, and who is prepared to run with it." (**ANNE**)

#2
If the client project manager hasn't the needed authority, find/demand an alternative who has. Bring issue up the line if necessary. If not resolved, walk away.
Number of PMs mentioning: 5   *Elicited by:*   *Their PM lacks time/skill/authority (6)*   *No real owner (1)*   *Unattributable (1)*

"Go back to top management and educate them as to the requirements and needs of that particular individual . . . If time can be provided, that's one hurdle overcome. If it's a lack of skill, you can educate him or her. But we cannot give him or her authority. That has to come from within the organization . . . from the top." (**OWEN**)

#3
If the client project manager hasn't the needed time or skill (but has the needed authority), try to get him/her support/training. If this doesn't work, ask for a suitable alternative person, or try to work around him/her.
Number of PMs mentioning: 5   *Elicited by:*   *Their PM lacks time/skill/authority (5)*   *No real owner (1)*

"If their main project person isn't available to you . . . doesn't have the skill . . . to implement change . . . It could end up in rows, and the delivered product being not what they expect . . . I'd request a meeting with more senior people. I'd try to be as apolitical as possible and I'd say 'We feel this guy isn't giving us the needed support or whatever. Can we change the person?' "(**BOB**)

#4
Put more reliance on key users and other key managers and less reliance on the client project manager or official project "owner".
No. of PMs mentioning: 3
Elicited by:
Their PM lacks time/skill/authority (2)
No real owner (1)
Unrealistic expectations (1)
Real agenda hidden (1)

"Get in tight with the users. They seem to want the system, so establish good relations with them. As [their] main project person isn't in a position to help you very much, then the users are key." (**MIKE A**)

26.2 On Being an Agent of Organizational Change . . .

On managing expectations . . .

#5
Recalibrate unrealistic expectations about cost, timescales, or what's "doable" upfront. Try an educational strategy . . . show them what their competitors are doing . . . run workshops on the state of the art, etc. Give examples of what might be achievable. Maybe have them bring in an independent consultant to give objective advice. Walk away if all this doesn't work.
Number of PMs mentioning: 8
Elicited by:
Unrealistic expectations (8)
They're inexperienced in running computer projects (2)

"If unrealistic expectations . . . have a workshop to drill down into needs . . . into what's really important and the real reasons for these . . . this is a show-stopper. Until it's sorted out, there's not much point in trying to address other issues . . . I think the first thing is to invest time in working through with the customer exactly where the project is at the moment, what is realistic, and in what time-frame and at what cost. If you don't get through that exercise to everyone's satisfaction, just walk away." (**CANICE**)

#6

Get early feedback on your ideas for the solution. Make your ideas for the solution as concrete as possible for the client and users. Help people see what your solution entails for them. Ideally, build a working prototype. If this is not feasible, build some form of mock-up/simulation to test proof of concept.

Number of PMs mentioning: 9

Elicited by:

Major change for the customer (4)

People most affected don't want it (2)

System must go right first time (2)

Mission-critical application (2)

Unrealistic expectations (1)

Project duration >three Months (1)

Real agenda hidden (1)

Unattributable (1)

"Prototyping is very important. If we can't show the client a prototype . . . then we will have to go back to old-fashioned printed documentation . . . draft some sample windows . . . draw some pictures for the client to show them what it was going to look like . . . so at least the client can see exactly how everything is going to work." (**GERRY**)

Make sure any "people problems" are addressed at an early stage . . .

#7
Ensure that organizational-development issues (re-structuring, IR, etc.) and people-centred issues/obstacles (disagreement, resistance to change, etc.) are addressed before getting into the "nitty-gritty" of the project. Sit down with the people who'll be impacted and prepare the way ahead before getting stuck in.
Number of PMs mentioning: 6   *Elicited by:*   *Major change for the customer (3)*   *People most affected don't really want it (2)*   *They disagree amongst themselves (1)*

". . . we'd want to be sure that things like user training, union negotiations, restructuring, etc. which were critical to the project, would all start very early on and would be clearly agreed to be part of the client's responsibility." (**ANDRE**)

#8

Ensure careful, early and detailed implementation planning. Be very clear about implementation tasks and responsibilities. Strengthen user training/user preparation. Plan details of roll-out very carefully. Resource roll-out very well. Roll out in controllable phases. Agree a precise handover point.

Number of PMs mentioning: 6

Elicited by:

Mission-critical application (3)

Major change for the customer (2)

They disagree amongst themselves (1)

People most affected don't want it (1)

Client unable/unwilling to drive implementation (1)

Inexperienced computer users (1)

System must go right first time (1)

Unattributable (1)

"If major change for the customer . . . Put in a formal training plan and allow the requisite time and resources to get the users on board . . . Lengthen the roll-out of the parallel run . . . Plan the implementation very carefully . . . Roll-out in phases." **(PADRAIG)**

Be an educator/facilitator, but don't try to play a "heavy" change agent role . . .

> **#9**
>
> **Where there is disagreement, unwilling users or negative politics, try to resolve it through an educational/facilitating strategy. If there have to be winners and losers, pass the problem to the client's power structure for resolution. Don't get sucked into the problem yourself. Tell them to get expert consultancy help if needed.**
>
> *Number of PMs mentioning: 12*
>
> *Elicited by:*
>
> *They disagree amongst themselves (8)*
>
> *People most affected don't want it (6)*
>
> *Real agenda hidden (2)*
>
> *Major change for the customer (1)*
>
> *We must satisfy multiple groups with different needs (1)*

"Maybe users don't want it because they perceive it's going to cause them extra work. it's often a matter of ignorance or misperception on someone's part. A perceives it's bad . . . B perceives it's good. Who's right? Who's wrong? So my first call would be an educational one . . . to try to make sure that everyone has the same facts and to try to straighten out misperceptions." (**CANICE**)

"If they disagree amongst themselves . . . I'd summarize the issues from the different camps . . . what they want in . . . what they want out . . . and I'd take this to the person who has ownership. I'd pass the buck to him. He must decide. I'd be guided by him." (**MERVYN**)

But despite all of the foregoing . . . the client is ultimately responsible for managing organizational change . . . not you!

#10
Ensure the client accepts overall responsibility for managing organizational change . . . for preparing the organization for the new system. Be very explicit with the client about any changes to internal processes, etc. entailed by the new system. Ensure preparations for change (restructuring, IR, user training) start at an early stage in the project.
Number of PMs mentioning: 3   *Elicited by:*   *Major change for the customer (3)*

"Most organizations realize that it is their responsibility to ensure that the organization is ready for the new system. You can only point out what they need to do. The responsibility must be made to rest on the customer's side." (PADRAIG)

Don't bite off more change/challenge than you . . . or the client . . . can chew . . .

#11
Restrict project scope to match the client's capacity for absorbing change.
Number of PMs mentioning: 2   *Elicited by:*   *Major change for the customer (1)*   *Client unwilling/unable to drive implementation (1)*

"We had one case like this recently. We knew that implementation would involve a massive amount of data entry, correction and standardization, and so on right across the organization. At the outset we said 'In our view, you are not ready for this new system. You don't have the basic procedures in place'." (MICHAEL C)

#12
Restrict project scope/content to what's reliably "doable" by you in time, cost and technical sense.
Number of PMs mentioning: 3
Elicited by:
Unrealistic expectations (2)
Mission-critical application (1)
Unfamiliar platform/environment (1)
Unfamiliar languages/tools (1)
Tight, imposed timescales (1)
Unattributable (1)

"If it's mission-critical it's a big risk to us because we're touching something which, if it breaks, will have a serious impact on the client . . . [so] lower requirements . . . be less ambitious . . . focus on what's reliably 'doable'. No rocket science!" (ALAN)

. . . and still on not biting off too much . . .

#13
Use an incremental/evolutionary life cycle. Scope the project into multiple phases, each with a mini-implementation. Roll out the least risky or most urgent infrastructure/functionality first. Then review progress and decide where to go next.
Number of PMs mentioning: 4
Elicited by:
Unrealistic expectations (2)
Tight, imposed timescales (2)
Major change for the customer (1)
Unattributable (1)

"If there will not be major changes, you will be designing a system to fit in with the known . . . it's all relatively controllable. If there are going to be major changes, nobody can predict how things will pan out . . . it is totally outside of your control . . . you have to break the implementation into stages. You implement stage one. If it works . . . if it's practical . . . then you can implement stage two, etc. If you don't do it like this, you can paint yourself into a corner." (COLIN)

. . . and on the need for some flexibility . . .

#14
Negotiate the flexibility to juggle timescales and deadlines.
Number of PMs mentioning: 2
Elicited by:
Mission-critical application (2)
Major change for the customer (2)

"Mission-critical application . . . need flexibility to juggle with timescales . . . rather be right and be late." (ANNE)

And put the right sort of people on your team . . .

#15
When there's a lot of change for the client, or when there are client people-related issues to be handled (e.g. disagreement, politics, etc.), put people-oriented people on your team (good listeners, communicators, etc.)
Number of PMs mentioning: 2
Elicited by:
Major change for the customer (1)
People most affected don't want it (1)
We must satisfy multiple groups with different needs (1)
Unrealistic expectations (1)

". . . if you have lower level managers who are going to resist things, then you will have to do a lot of training . . . a lot of talking . . . to turn them around to your way of thinking . . . the people you would have to choose on that project would have to be people who can handle the human side of things." (ANDRE)

26.3 On Learning and Learning Curves . . .

View the decision to learn as an investment decision . . .

#16

If a project involves a big learning curve for you, view the choice of whether or not to get involved as a strategic decision. In particular, only take the financial "hit" yourself if the learning is of future strategic benefit.

Number of PMs mentioning: 6

Elicited by:

Unfamiliar languages/tools (5)

Unfamiliar platform/environment (3)

We've little/no knowledge of their industry (2)

The application is new to us (1)

"If the application is new to us, we'd have to spend more time learning about the business . . . being up against a competitor . . . we would have to carry the cost ourselves. If it's an abstruse area, it [might] cost us too much to educate ourselves . . . You have to make a judgement on how familiar it all is . . . .you might decide you wanted to go into that market anyway . . . maybe decide to swallow that overhead yourself . . . [if unfamiliar language/tools] it's three-month overhead. Strategic decision to swallow it yourself." **(PATRICK)**

Don't try to learn and do at the same time . . .

#17
If there is a critical learning curve for the developer around some aspect of the project, structure the project to build this learning in early on. Get up to speed before embarking on the "main" project. Don't risk learning on-the-fly.
Number of PMs mentioning: 5
Elicited by:
Unfamiliar languages/tools (3)
We've little/no knowledge of their industry (3)
Unfamiliar platform/environment (2)
The application is new to us (1)
Unrealistic expectations (1)

"We wouldn't pitch for something if we didn't have the expertise. But if we were forced to, we'd buy in the skills . . . to train our people. But we wouldn't write the application and try to learn at the same time." **(MICHAEL B)**

Don't make premature commitments around risky items . . .

#18
If there is a lot of technical risk around some aspect of the project, resolve this up front with a separate investigation task/phase with its own budget. Don't make any commitments around this aspect of the project until the risk is quantified or resolved.
Number of PMs mentioning: 6
Elicited by:
We must change another developer's code (3)
Some tricky interfacing (2)
Unfamiliar languages/tools (1)

"If some tricky interfacing . . . find out exactly what's involved up front. If we don't have the expertise in-house, buy it in or maybe go for training. If it's simple and straightforward, no problem . . . it [up-front investigation] cuts down that risk." (SUSAN A)

A caution on plugging skills gaps with contract staff . . .

#19
Plug any skills gaps on your side with imported training, consultancy, contract staff, etc. But don't disrupt/unsettle your team by importing too many "outsiders". If this is a risk, subcontract out or structure the project as a joint venture with another developer.
Number of PMs mentioning: 8   *Elicited by:*   *Unfamiliar languages/tools (6)*   *Unfamiliar platform/environment (3)*   *Some tricky interfacing (3)*   *Complex application (2)*   *Application is new to us (1)*

"If you are [contracting] because there are one or two small technical inter-faces that you don't know how to do, or something like that, that need not be a big problem . . . if you're taking in a single [contractor] into your own team of, say, five people, that's OK. But if you're taking in ten . . . then you're heading for a nightmare because you'll have them changing . . . coming and going . . . they all have mobile phones . . . they're all worrying about their next contract . . . they're not as focused and dedicated . . . they have nicer cars . . . they can afford more drink on a Friday night . . . so it makes your own full-time people very uneasy . . . if lots of people are required, run the project jointly with another software house."

(MERVYN)

Learn from Nellie . . .

#20
Learn the client's industry/business/application by spending time on-site with the client's people, including the key users, and observing how they currently do things. Learn by getting them to document what they want the new system to do. Also look at other developers' solutions to the same problems in similar companies.
Number of PMs mentioning: 3 *Elicited by:* *We've little/no knowledge of their industry (3)* *The application is new to us (3)*

"We've little/no knowledge of their industry AND the application is new to us . . . there's a learning exercise to be done. So I'd spend time at the client's site. At his expense. Watching how all the functions that you have to provide within your system are currently carried out . . . plus background reading . . . talking to certain people. You'd include an allowance for this in your project proposal under the first phase to do the functional spec. The learning and the functional spec would go hand in hand." **(PHILIP)**

Where there's a lot of learning involved, or other technical or "human" uncertainty, insist on a time-and-materials deal . . .

#21

Agree a time-and-materials deal (or, at least, variation clauses) for aspects of the project which involve a lot of learning, aspects over which you don't have full control, or where there is disagreement, unfavourable politics, or other big "human" or technical uncertainties. "Package up" such aspects separately in the contract. Only accept a fixed price if you can add a big contingency figure, or if the project is of key strategic importance to you.

Number of PMs mentioning: 8

Elicited by:

People most affected don't want it (3)

We must change another developer's code (2)

They disagree amongst themselves (2)

Client unable/unwilling to drive implementation (2)

Major change for the customer (1)

Some tricky interfacing . . . (1)

Unfamiliar languages/tools (1)

Unattributable (2)

"If the client is unable/unwilling to drive implementation . . . put in a hard-nosed non-programmer type as implementation person . . . 'I'm here to get things done.'. . . If we did this, it would be on a time-and-materials basis. If you're not charging the client, and if they don't have the drive to manage it themselves, three days becomes a week then two weeks then three weeks. If you charge them £$%^ a day, they're going to take it a bit seriously." **(MICHAEL B)**

26.4 On the Merits of Bureaucracy and Explicitness . . .

When things could get nasty, cover your rear . . .

#22

Behave bureaucratically/Put everything in "black and white"/Make everything explicit/Break everything down to a detailed level/Pin it down!/Tie it up with a pink ribbon.

Number of PMs mentioning: 8

Elicited by:

Unrealistic expectations (4)

They disagree amongst themselves (3)

No real owner (2)

Mission-critical application (2)

People most affected don't want it (1)

Real agenda hidden (1)

Major change for the customer (1)

Their PM lacks time/skill/authority (1)

They are inexperienced in running computer projects (1)

Unattributable (3)

This theme is also reflected in many of the other strategies. Here, I'm bringing together instances of explicit, generic expressions of this sentiment.

"Real agenda hidden AND no real owner . . . you're talking about getting as much coverage of your rear as possible . . . everything should be done in triplicate and signed off before you go any further with anything." (**ALAN**)

"Unrealistic expectations . . . make everything very explicit, bureaucratic . . . break it down to a very detailed level . . . pin it down." (**ANDRE**)

. . . bureaucracy and explicitness as applied to project scope . . .

> **#23**
>
> **Document and agree project scope/boundaries with precision. . . . what the project includes . . . what it excludes, where it starts . . . where it finishes. All "extras" to be treated as change requests with their own additional budget. "Ring-fence the project" by erecting barriers against creeping scope.**
>
> *Number of PMs mentioning: 11*
>
> *Elicited by:*
>
> *Unrealistic expectations (3)*
>
> *Mission-critical application (2)*
>
> *Tight, imposed timescales (1)*
>
> *Real agenda hidden (1)*
>
> *They disagree amongst themselves (1)*
>
> *Complex application (1)*
>
> *We've little or no knowledge of their industry (1)*
>
> *Unattributable (6)*

"[Where things could go wrong] Get agreement at the outset on a brief that identifies the key elements of what you are going to try to achieve, and get agreement that anything outside that brief will be an extra charge . . . draw a line under these and say 'This is what we are going to do for this amount of money. Anything beyond this will be charged for on a time and materials basis.' We would have at least some damage limitation protection . . . document the minimum requirements for the project in such a way that these can be measured in a month's time, two month's time, etc. . . . you really have to protect yourself." **(GERRY)**

. . . and . . .

#24
Negotiate a separate contract for a first phase to agree project scope, requirements and functional specification.
Number of PMs mentioning: 8
Elicited by:
Unrealistic expectations (2)
They disagree amongst themselves (2)
They are inexperienced in running computer projects (1)
Unattributable (4)

"If they disagree amongst themselves . . . extra front-loading in the contract in terms of specification . . . getting things clear . . . getting agreement. Need to say 'We'll have a formal charge for agreeing things and from what we've seen so far this phase will cost X.' It's really a case of splitting the contract into project phases and deliverables that begins with clarifying what they want." (**PATRICK**)

. . . bureaucracy and explicitness as applied to requirements and specifications . . .

#25
The requirements analysis, functional specification and system specification must be particularly rigorous and detailed.
Number of PMs mentioning: 7
Elicited by:
They disagree amongst themselves (3)
Unrealistic expectations (1)
Real agenda hidden (1)
System must go right first time (1)
Mission-critical application (1)
We'll have to subcontract (1)
Need >two people on our team (1)

"If unrealistic expectations OR they disagree amongst themselves . . . be very clear about what is to be delivered . . . spec really has to be at a fine level of detail . . . nothing vague." (**CANICE**)

. . . the need for an explicit and detailed definition of BOTH the client's AND your responsibilities and commitments to the project . . .

#26
Make both the developer's AND client's responsibilities/commitments explicit. Get agreement and clarity on where responsibilities lie . . . "what, and by whom, and by when". . . and on the resources the client will need to commit, and by when.
Number of PMs mentioning: 7
Elicited by:
Mission-critical application (2)
Major change for the customer (2)
Their PM lacks time/skill/authority (2)
People most affected don't want it (1)
Unrealistic expectations (1)
They are inexperienced in running computer projects (1)
Unattributable (4)

"Mission-critical application . . . You'd also be looking for great clarity on . . . where responsibilities lie . . . I'd insist on a very clear understanding around the contract, what it includes, and most importantly, what it excludes, and what the responsibilities of the customer are . . . define each party's responsibilities very clearly." (**TONY**)

. . . and keep a list of the client's failures in this regard . . .

> **#27**
>
> **Keep a record of all failures on the client's part to meet agreed responsibilities, commitments, deadlines, etc. and of any other "problems" for the project which originate in the client organization.**
>
> *Number of PMs mentioning: 3*
>
> *Elicited by:*
>
> *Their PM lacks time/skill/authority (3)*
>
> *Unrealistic expectations (1)*

"Unrealistic expectations AND their PM lacks time/skill/authority . . . carefully monitor what they actually do vis-à-vis what they are supposed to do . . . check if the time is actually being put in. Be very careful to document what they are supposed to do, what's actually done, by whom and when. This is just covering one's $£&." (**MIKE A**)

. . . and be explicit about how project success will be judged . . .

> **#28**
>
> **Ensure that project "success" measures, including acceptance-testing criteria, are well defined and agreed in advance.**
>
> *Number of PMs mentioning: 3*
>
> *Elicited by:*
>
> *Unrealistic expectations (1)*
>
> *They disagree amongst themselves (1)*
>
> *Mission-critical application (1)*
>
> *Unattributable (1)*

"Mission-critical application . . . you'd be looking for agreement on definite, measurable end results . . . you'd be trying to ring-fence the project and find out and agree the measures which will demonstrate to everybody that the project has been completed to the customer's satisfaction." (**TONY**)

. . . and for that extra bit of protection . . .

#29
Get customer sign-offs on every deliverable and on each stage of the project. Don't proceed without sign-offs.
Number of PMs mentioning: 8
Elicited by:
They disagree amongst themselves (4)
Unrealistic expectations (3)
Real agenda hidden (3)
No real owner (1)
People most affected don't want it (1)
Mission-critical application (1)
Can't show a prototype (1)
Unattributable (2)

"Real agenda hidden AND no real owner . . . You'd insist on sign-offs on proposals, specifications . . . EVERYTHING . . . you're talking about getting as much coverage of your rear as possible . . . everything should be done in triplicate and signed off before you go any further with anything." **(ALAN)**

26.5 On Dealing with Subcontractors, Third Parties, and Their Artefacts . . .

#30
Manage your subcontractors at least as tightly as the client is managing you. Include non-performance penalty clauses in their contract. Insist on sign-offs on all their deliverables. Make sure communications/interface with them is right. Get clarity on respective roles/responsibilities. Research their background, experience, and compatibility with the way you do things.
Number of PMs mentioning: 4 *Elicited by:* *We'll have to subcontract (4)*

"Preferably, I'd rather not subcontract because it's out of our control once we hand it over. The issues between the subcontractor and us, and between us and the client, are much the same. In both cases, . . . make sure the communications are right . . . the objectives clear . . . doing proper requirements documents . . . ensuring everyone knows their role and their task . . . basically to run a tight ship . . . regular communication . . . the right [communication channels] are open . . . that we're involved in signing-off on what they're doing . . . the same way that we involve the client." (**SUSAN A**)

. . . and any third parties . . .

#31

If there are third parties involved in the project, e.g. other consultants, ensure their roles, their responsibilities, and their relationships with you are very clearly defined. Research their background, experience, and compatibility with the way you do things.

Number of PMs mentioning: 5

Elicited by:

Must share control with a third party (5)

We'll have to subcontract (1)

"If you have a third party with their own personality involved . . . depending on their behaviour which might range from very bad to very good . . . all that's going to have a major impact on the project . . . If there's professional jealousy, lack of cooperation . . . a bit of obstruction here and there, you have obviously got big problems . . . I'd have a long, long talk with these people before I got trapped into the project . . . I would have a very good agreement with them with trigger clauses, so if they failed in their obligations, something [nasty] would happen." **(COLIN)**

. . . and their artefacts . . .

#32

Don't open up another developer's or supplier's artefact (code, interface, etc.) if you can avoid it. Treat it as a potential "Pandora's box". If you can't "wrap it", and must open it up and rework it, try if possible to have the original developer/supplier/maintainer take responsibility for the work, or to sign off on the changes you'll make. If this is not possible, unless a very straightforward change, rewrite or redevelop from scratch. Do a lot of testing . . . trying to crash it. Get clear agreement on "Who's going to support it after we've been into it or wrapped it."

Number of PMs mentioning: 6

Elicited by:

We must change another developer's code (5)

Some tricky interfacing (3)

"We must change another developer's code . . . This could be a nightmare! If it was just a few lines of code, I'd probably just rewrite it . . . goodness knows what problems you'd face there . . . is the other developer available? . . . is it documented? . . . how well is it structured? . . . you are usually better off to look at what they are trying to do and to rewrite it yourself in your own way." **(COLIN)**

"You have to get the other developer on side. Get him to agree what you're going to change . . . what you're not going to change. Make sure he is happy with that and get him to sign off on it . . . release any changes we make back to this other company's software back to them, not directly to the client. This other developer then tests it to satisfy themselves. Then THEY ship to the client." **(MERVYN)**

26.6 And Some Extra Ones for When It's Mission-critical or Must Go Right First Time . . .

#33
Strengthen quality assurance/increase the level of formality of the development process.
Number of PMs mentioning: 9
Elicited by:
System must go right first time (4)
Mission-critical application (3)
We'll have to subcontract (2)
Some tricky interfacing . . . (2)
Project duration >three months (1)

"If the system must go right first time . . . You would need to be much more conscious about your quality assurance and project-management procedures, and you'd have to charge extra for this . . . you have to build a more formal method of controlling things . . . no seat of the pants! . . . need more bureaucracy and explicitness . . . more QA than you would normally rely on." **(PATRICK)**

#34

Intensify the level of user input into business test-case generation and testing.

Number of PMs mentioning: 4

Elicited by:

System must go right first time (2)

Mission-critical application (1)

Major change for the customer (1)

"If the system must go right first time . . . build a good relationship between whoever is testing on your side and the users, because each will bring their own perspective to testing. Beef up testing and get users more involved in this." (**ANNE**)

#35

If the application is mission-critical for the client, ensure there is a high level of technical competence and application experience on your team.

Number of PMs mentioning: 2

Elicited by:

Mission-critical application (2)

". . . you'd better have an experienced development team." (**PHILIP**)

And if the project is that bit bigger/longer . . .

#36
Increase the formality and rigour of project management. Manage the project more formally, more tightly. Control by deadlines and deliverables. Lots of supervision and control.
Number of PMs mentioning: 5
Elicited by:
Need >two people on our team (4)
Project duration >three months (1)
Unfamiliar platform/environment (1)
Unfamiliar languages/tools (1)
Must to right first time (1)
Must change other developer's code (1)

"If you need three or more people, you have to make sure that everyone is singing from the same hymn book. With only one or two people, you can manage through informal chats. But with three or more, you need to have formal reviews of progress, etc." (**BOB**)

26.7 And the Doomsday Strategy . . .
"Walk Away" . . .

At the risk of boring the reader, I show below all of the circumstances in which the PMs said they would "walk away" rather than pursue the project.

#37
Unless it's a very strategic project for you, walk away if . . .
Number of PMs mentioning: 14
Elicited by:
Defies easy analysis! . . . see full listing of PMs' comments below.

ALAN

Unrealistic expectations AND No real owner: "What we would more likely do is to try to define the scope for the project ourselves . . . if they agree with what we say we're going to do, we'd do it. If no one will sign off on [this], then we'd have to walk away, because things aren't tied down tightly."

Real agenda hidden AND No real owner: "I'd be suspicious that there's something else going on . . . maybe someone has taken us into the company to act as a scapegoat . . . or maybe getting a free feasibility study . . . or maybe using the project to force change on somebody else . . . it's too risky. We would walk away very quickly . . . Of course, it's a public profile thing . . . it's hard to walk away from a prestigious contract with one of the big banks or something . . . so [maybe] you'd have to drive it from your end . . . fix the scope yourself . . . work on the unrealistic expectations . . . forget the agenda, hidden or not."

ANNE

Their PM lacks time/skill/authority AND No real owner AND People most affected don't want it: "[You could] stick with the project without real ownership from senior people [by] working around the ownership problem . . . I'd work in tandem with the users [if they really wanted the new system]. Otherwise I'd walk away."

Mission critical application AND Tight, imposed timescales: "I want out!"

No real owner AND Unrealistic expectations AND Mission-critical application: "I just wouldn't do it under these conditions."

BOB

Real agenda hidden: "If there was a power struggle in the organization, you'd walk away from them if possible. If you couldn't walk away, you'd make sure that people saw exactly what's being contracted for."

CANICE

Unrealistic expectations: "If they won't accept an incremental path towards clarification [of their requirements], walk away!"

COLIN

No real owner: ". . . go to the top and say, sort this out or forget it."

Unfamiliar languages/tools AND No real owner: "Look for some other business quickly!"

Unfamiliar languages/tools AND System must go right first time: ". . . totally off-the-wall!"

MERVYN

No real owner: "I'd try to highlight this to whoever asked me to look at the area in the first place. To say, face to face to them, 'Do you REALLY want this system? Is what we're proposing what you REALLY want?' If he says 'Yes. This is REALLY where we want to go', then you're starting to create ownership. If he says 'Well, it's not really what we want', he'll probably talk himself out of doing it at all. At that stage, you're probably better off walking away, if you can do that."

We've little/no knowledge of their industry AND ["if [the project] is very big"]: "If something is very big, and you've no knowledge of it, you should simply walk away."

MIKE A

Unfamiliar platform/environment OR Unfamiliar languages tools AND Tight, imposed timescales: "[this] would be an excruciating combination . . . Unless this is a very strategic project, one should walk away."

Unfamiliar languages/tools AND Tight, imposed timescales AND Must satisfy different groups with different needs: ". . . it would definitely be time to leave the party!"

MICHAEL B

No real owner: ". . . we're on a loser if someone isn't guiding things from the client's side . . . if there's no real ownership . . . it's usually been a disaster in terms of timescales and costs, and the client not really getting what they wanted. Ideally, I'd pull out . . . If we couldn't pull out, I would get them to encourage someone less senior but very enthusiastic to take it on . . . someone who wants to develop their computer skills."

MICHAEL C

They disagree amongst themselves: "This is the single most important one. Disagreement is an absolute show-stopper as far as I'm concerned . . . We now have a policy of actually walking out. You cannot make them agree, so you've no countermeasure."

They disagree amongst themselves OR People most affected don't want it: ". . . one strategy is to think of a price for the contract, then double or treble it! . . . it gives you enough of a cushion to deal with these kinds of issues. But it's not a very moral way to do things. Honest guys would walk away."

Must share control with a third party: "We will NOT share control of a project with a third party . . . simply NO! Any time we have done it, it has caused us trouble . . . their agenda was different from our agenda . . . they would promise the client anything to keep them happy . . . a definite 'walk-away' job."

No real owner AND Their PM lacks time/skill/authority: ". . . my advice would [be] to walk away."

PATRICK

Their PM lacks time/skill/authority: "You'd have to [walk out]. Lack of time, even skill, one could live with, but if he/she doesn't have the authority, there's no real contract."

No real owner: ". . . that would be that! [i.e. walk away]"

Mission-critical application AND *They disagree amongst themselves:* ". . . the project can't go ahead because you will end up with one side refusing to cooperate. They'll say 'That was THEIR specification, not ours.' If it isn't mission-critical, you can normally go ahead on the basis that one side is enough to sign a cheque!"

PAUL

No real owner: "You have to find someone who'll say 'Yes' [to your proposals, ideas, etc.]. Otherwise you have to go up and up, even to the board. If not resolved, bail out!"

Their PM lacks time/skill/authority: ". . . lack of time and skill can be worked around . . . but they must have authority. It may be that you will have to go up the organization to get the name of someone lower down . . . who can decide/is given authority. [If not resolved] I think I'd bail out."

Must satisfy different groups with different needs AND They disagree amongst themselves AND No real owner: "I'm out of here!"

Unrealistic expectations AND They are inexperienced in running computer projects: "I'd explain why, in my view, their expectations were unrealistic. I'd keep at this until one of two things happened . . . they changed their expectations, or I'd reckoned I was on a loser and I'd just walked away."

PHILIP

We must change another developer's code: ". . . make a quick assessment of how well it's written before you commit. This third-party code aspect would be a good candidate for time and materials. Maybe parcel it up as a separate project. If it's not worth changing, throw it out and rewrite it. But it would have to be a language you're familiar with . . . That could be reason for walking away."

We've little/no knowledge of their industry AND Unfamiliar platform/ environment: "The combination . . . new industry . . . new platform . . .

219

they're strong negatives. It depends, from a business point of view, on whether you still want to pursue the project."

Tight, imposed time scales AND We must change another developer's code: ". . . you may have to walk away."

No real owner AND Mission critical application: ". . . confront the client directly and say 'We need a senior manager . . . the board . . . to approve . . . underwrite this project.' If that didn't work, then it's goodbye time."

SUSAN B

Unrealistic expectations: ". . . We'd probably walk away from the business to be honest . . . if you can't reset their expectations, you have to walk away."

The application is new to us AND System must go right first time: ". . . do an initial requirements spec, check if we had the needed skills in-house . . . whether it's really our bread and butter or not. Then we'd decide if we wanted the business."

Unfamiliar languages/tools: "We'd have to bring in subcontractors. there's no other way around it. Or you have a choice of not bidding for the business . . . You've to walk away from business that's not your core business."

TOMMY

Their PM lacks time/skill/authority AND No real owner: "We're going down the tubes rapidly here! . . . I'd ask myself do I REALLY want this project? . . . Is this a strategic project for me?"

The application is new to us AND Unfamiliar platform/environment AND Unfamiliar languages/tools: "I'd start running now!"

PART 4

"So, It Works in Practice . . . But Will It Work in Theory?"

Through the "Looking-glasses" of Trust, Agency, Change, Capability, Action, Rationality and Control . . . 27

In Chapter 26, I led the reader on a whirlwind tour through the PMs' action strategies for handling "risky" situations. Now I want to slow down a little, and take a more reflective view of at least some of the strategies. One way I could do this is to take each strategy in turn, and to say some wise things about it. But this might become repetitive, and boring. Instead, I've organized this chapter, and the next, around a small number of perspectives (looking-glasses) which I have selected from the literature on organization theory and IS project management. This approach allows me to deal in a more integrated way with whole groups of strategies, rather than with individual strategies.

But I first want to make two preliminary points. When reading Chapter 26, and what follows below, you may be tempted to say to yourself "I'm really surprised that the project managers didn't recommend strategy X for dealing with situation Y. I wonder why not?" I think the answer is in part in the following. If a PM failed to recommend a particular strategy in a particular context, it cannot be automatically concluded that the PM considered that strategy to be inappropriate in that context. It could simply mean that, in the course of the interview, it didn't occur to the PM to mention that strategy in that context. And that, had I explicitly prompted the PM to consider that strategy, the PM might well have supported its use. I'll return to this point in the final chapter.

My second point relates to the counts shown in the tables and figures that follow. In a number of places in the interview transcripts, one can find PMs making oblique, less direct, references to the strategies they would use. I've included a small number (only three or four) of these weaker "mentions" in this chapter. I did NOT include these weaker mentions in the counts shown in Chapter 26. So, the accountants amongst my readers will find some small discrepancies between the counts in the tables and figures that follow, and the frequencies shown in Chapter 26.

. . . Through the Looking-glass of Interorganizational Trust . . .

In Table 25.1 in Chapter 25, I showed the numbers of PMs who put each of the thirty-four constructs into the VBD, BD and SLND piles. It's interesting to see that the most frequently VBDed constructs relate to client-based "people-problems": unrealistic expectations; lack of real customer ownership of the project; disagreement amongst the customer's people on project goals; personal deficiencies on the part of the customer's project manager; user resistance; the presence of hidden agendas or "nasty" politics on the customer's side. In Table 27.1 below I reproduce these "people-problem" constructs.

Which of the strategies were most frequently recommended as being "antidotes" to the "risky" poles in these constructs? In Table 27.2, I show all of the strategies which were referred to by at least three different PMs in the context of one or more of these "risky" poles. I have broken the construct related to the client project manager's time/skill/authority into two parts, one concerned with time availability and skill, and the other with authority, because the PMs made this distinction during the interviews. The counts in the table are the numbers of PMs who alluded to each strategy in the context of each of the "risky" poles. The "Unattributable" column shows the frequency with which each strategy was alluded to in an unspecific way, but

Table 27.1 Numbers of PMs putting each "people-problem" construct into each pile

		VBD	BD	SLND
Someone on the customer's side has taken clear, committed ownership of the project	Nobody wants to "own" the project	17	3	0
The customer has realistic expectations about time, cost and what's "doable"	The customer has unrealistic expectations about time, cost and what's "doable"	16	4	0
The customer's PM has the needed time/skill/authority	The customer's PM lacks the time/skill/authority	15	5	0
There seems to be no hidden agenda	The "real" agenda seems to be hidden	14	6	0
They don't disagree amongst themselves about what's needed	They disagree amongst themselves about what's needed	14	6	0
The people most affected seem to genuinely want the new system	The people most affected don't seem to really want the new system	11	7	2

Table 27.2 Number of PMs espousing each strategy for coping with "people-problems"

	Number of PMs mentioning strategy (ex 20)	Unrealistic expectations	No real owner	They disagree amongst themselves	Their PM lacks authority	Their PM lacks time/skill	The people most affected don't want it	Real agenda hidden	Un-attributable
#9 Where there is disagreement, unwilling users or negative politics, try to resolve this through an educational/facilitating strategy. If there have to be winners and losers, pass the problem to the client's power structure for resolution. Don't get sucked into the problem yourself. Tell them to get expert consultancy help if needed.	12			8			6	2	
#1 If there is no committed/enthusiastic project "owner", find/demand one (maybe an influential, enthusiastic user). Escalate the issue up the organization if necessary. If not resolved, walk away.	10		10		1	1			
#23 Document and agree project scope with precision . . . what it includes . . . what it excludes, where it starts . . . where it finishes.	9	3		1				1	5

225

	Number of PMs mentioning strategy (ex 20)	Unrealistic expectations	No real owner	They disagree amongst themselves	Their PM lacks authority	Their PM lacks time/skill	The people most affected don't want it	Real agenda hidden	Un-attributable
#5 Recalibrate unrealistic expectations up-front with an educational strategy . . . show them what their competitors are doing . . . run workshops on the state of the art, etc. Walk away if all this doesn't work.	8	8							
#22 Put it in writing/Everything in triplicate/Pin everything down exactly/Bureaucracy/Tie it up with a pink ribbon.	8	4	1	3	1	1	1	1	3
#24 Negotiate a separate contract for a first phase to agree project scope, requirements and functional specification.	8	2		2					4
#29 Get customer sign-offs on every deliverable and on each stage of the project. Don't proceed without sign-offs.	7	3	1	4			1	3	
#26 Make both the developer's AND client's responsibilities/commitments explicit . . . "what, and by whom, and by when". . .	6	1			2	2	1		4

	Number of PMs mention-ing strategy (ex 20)	Unreal-istic expec-tations	No real owner	They disagree amongst themselves	Their PM lacks authority	Their PM lacks time/skill	The people most affected don't want it	Real agenda hidden	Un-attrib-utable
#2	If the client project manager hasn't the needed authority, find/demand an alternative who has. Bring issue up the line if necessary. If not resolved, walk away.	5		1		5				
#3	If the client project manager hasn't the needed time or skill (but has the needed authority), get him/her support/training. If this doesn't work, ask for a suitable alternative, or try to work around him/her.	5		1			5			
#6	Get early feedback on your ideas for the solution. Make your ideas as concrete as possible for the client and users. Ideally, build a working prototype. If this is not feasible, build some form of mock-up/simulation.	4	1					2	1	
#21	Agree a time-and-materials deal for aspects of the project over which you don't have full control, e.g. where there is disagreement, unfavourable politics, or other big "human" or technical uncertainties.	4			2			3		2

	Number of PMs mentioning strategy (ex 20)	Unrealistic expectations	No real owner	They disagree amongst themselves	Their PM lacks authority	Their PM lacks time/skill	The people most affected don't want it	Real agenda hidden	Un-attributable
#4	Put more reliance on key users and other key managers and less reliance on the client project manager or official "owner".	3	1	1		1	1		1	
#7	Ensure that organizational-development issues (restructuring, IR, etc.) and people-centred issues/obstacles (disagreement, resistance to change, etc.) are addressed before getting into the "nitty-gritty" of the project. Sit down with the people who'll be impacted and prepare the way ahead before getting stuck in.	3			1			2		
#25	The requirements analysis, functional specification and system specification must be particularly rigorous and detailed.	3	1		3				1	
#27	Keep a record of all failures on the client's part to meet agreed commitments, deadlines, etc. and of any other "problems" for the project which originate in the client organization.	3	1			3	3			
#28	Ensure that project "success" measures, including acceptance-testing criteria, are well defined and agreed in advance.	3	1		1					1

still in the presence of one or more of these "risky" poles. In other words, in which the strategy was referred to by such phrases as "Overall, I think I'd . . ." or "In this case, one should . . .".

In many cases, the PMs identified combinations of poles, rather than individual poles, as triggers for the use of some particular strategy. In Table 27.2 I have "credited" all of the poles involved in such combinations.

To repeat a point I made earlier, despite my best efforts to tease the strategies apart in the sorting and labelling process, the descriptions of the various strategies do not appear to be logically disjoint. For example, one might argue that strategy #23 ("Document and agree the project's scope with precision . . .") is a special case of the more generic strategy #22 ("Put it in writing"/"Pin everything down exactly"/etc.). In my defence, I have tried to stay as close as possible to the PMs' own words.

The most frequently mentioned strategy (#9) in Table 27.2 relates to the personal position that the PM should take when he/she encounters disagreement, reluctant users, hidden agendas, and the like. In essence, the strategy urges the PM to be cautious in exercising the role of "change agent" in the client organization. I will take this point up later.

Three strategies constitute direct "fixes" to project ownership problems and to any inadequacies on the part of the client project manager (#1, #2, #3). Strategy #4 is an attempt to manage around any such problems. In essence, it says "Don't put all your eggs into a one-relationship basket, e.g. the relationship with the client project manager. Reduce your dependency on him/her by building strong relationships with the users and with other key players in the client organization."

The need to carefully manage the client's expectations from the outset of the transaction is reflected across a number of the strategies. The interview transcripts show that, rather than tailoring the project to meet the client's (probably unrealistic) initial expectations, the PM scopes the project to reflect what he/she feels to be achievable, and then tries to recalibrate the client's expectations accordingly. This he/she attempts to do primarily through a process of education (strategy #5). Where the client's expectations are unrealistic, the PMs also advocated the need for an increased level of formality and explicitness in the transaction [e.g. #22, #23, #29].

Most of the individual counts shown in the body of Table 27.2 are low. So, one must be wary of over-interpreting the data. This said, however, two strategies in particular were mentioned by PMs in the context of practically all of the seven "nasty" poles. These two "broad-spectrum" antidotes are the introduction of formality/explicitness/bureaucracy into all aspects of the project (#22), and obtaining client "sign-off" at every stage, and on each deliverable (#29). The clear intent of these two strategies is to provide self-protection for the PM.

Many of the strategies in Table 27.2 seem to be based on a common principle: "self-protection by means of explicitness, clarity and formality". The literature on trust in organizations lends support to this principle. In the context of interorganizational relations, trust has been defined as:

> The expectation that an actor (1) can be relied on to fulfil obligations, (2) will behave in a predictable manner, and (3) will act and negotiate fairly when the possibility for opportunism is present.
>
> Zaheer et al., 1998: 143.

Zaheer states:

> Under conditions of low trust, lengthy and difficult negotiations over unforeseen contingencies are likely to take place between exchange partners because of the possibility of both ex ante and ex post opportunism. In addition, contractual and structural safeguards are put in place to protect investments in the relationship. Under high trust conditions, in contrast, firms are less inclined to rely on elaborate safeguards for specifying, monitoring and enforcing agreements.
>
> ibid.: 144

Where a project is subject to the sorts of "people-problems" in Table 27.1, it seems likely that the level of trust the PM would invest in the client organization would be low. Thus one would expect the PM's theories-of-action to reflect the above generalization. This seems to be the case.

. . . Through the Looking-glass of Agency Theory . . .

At least two of the strategies (#21 and #24) in Table 27.2 have a direct resonance in agency theory (Eisenhardt, 1989). Agency theory is concerned with the transactions between two parties: the principal and the agent. The principal is an individual or organization that has a need which it wants to satisfy. The principal delegates the task of satisfying the need to the agent. The agent attempts to satisfy the principal's need, usually in return for a reward.

Agency theory focuses on the nature of the exchange between the two parties. In particular, it focuses on the contractual, or other mechanisms, that the principal can use to protect himself/herself against opportunistic behaviour on the part of the agent. The possibility that the agent will behave "badly" is seen, in agency theory, to be especially high when there is an information asymmetry which favours the agent (Sharma, 1997). In other words, in situations when the agent possesses (or is believed by the principal to possess) the specialist knowledge and skills needed to satisfy the delegated need. The risk of opportunistic behaviour by the agent is seen to be high in this situation because, not possessing the necessary knowledge and skills himself/herself, the principal would find it difficult to assess the quality and quantity of the agent's work.

Where there is information asymmetry, agency theory proposes means by which the principal might limit the possibility of opportunistic behaviour by the agent. Examples of these means are:

- Employment by the principal of a third party who has the expertise to monitor the work of the agent.

- Insistence on an outcome-based, as opposed to a behaviour-based, contract. In other words, "payment by pre-defined results" rather than payment on the basis of the level of effort expended by the agent (Sharma, 1997).

- Attempt by the principal to assure the agent's "good behaviour" by compelling him/her to expend his/her own resources in the creation of transaction-specific assets (e.g. intermediate "deliverables") which have a deferred value to the agent, and then only in the context of the "successful" completion of the transaction (Williamson, 1985).

Strategy #21 ("Insist on a time-and-materials deal . . .") seems to be a direct countermove to the second of the above control mechanisms. Strategy #24 ("Negotiate a separate contract for a first phase . . .") seems to be a counter-move to the third control mechanism. It seeks to avoid the early investment by the PM of his/her own resources to create an asset (the requirements/functional specification) which may subsequently have no value to the PM in the event, for example, of project termination, or some other negative outcome. As one PM put it, in the context of disagreement amongst the client's people: ". . . if you spend a lot of time producing a good specification, they could then walk up to [a] competitor and say 'There's the spec . . . give us that.' Then you are just giving away the shop . . . doing your competitor's research for him . . . so, you need to say 'we will have a formal charge for agreeing things . . .' "

. . . Through the Looking-glass of "Planned Organizational Change". . .

All of the PMs alluded to their role as agents for change in their client organizations. Of the twenty PMs I interviewed, twelve PMs put . . .

No major changes to the customer's workflow/ procedures	Major change to the customer's workflow/procedures

. . . into their VERY BIG DIFFERENCE pile. In other words, they saw this distinction to be a very important one to them when managing an IS project.

In Table 27.3, I show all the strategies that the PMs alluded to when their project scenarios included major change for the customer. I've abbreviated some of the strategy descriptions. I apologise once again for apparent overlaps across the strategies . . . I did the best job I could to disentangle them.

Table 27.3 *Strategies which are salient when there is major change for the customer*

#6	Get early feedback on your ideas for the solution. Make your ideas for the solution as concrete as possible for the client and users. Help people see what your solution entails for them. Ideally, build a working prototype.
#7	Ensure that organizational-development issues (restructuring, IR, etc.) and people-centred issues/obstacles (disagreement, resistance to change, etc.) are addressed before getting into the "nitty-gritty" of the project.
#8	Ensure careful, early and detailed implementation planning. Be very clear about implementation tasks and responsibilities. Strengthen user training/user preparation. Plan details of roll-out very carefully. Resource roll out very well. Roll-out in controllable phases. Agree a precise hand over point.
#9	Where there is disagreement, unwilling users or negative politics, try to resolve this through an educational/facilitating strategy. If there have to be winners and losers, pass the problem to the client's power structure for resolution. Don't get sucked into the problem yourself. Tell them to get expert consultancy help if needed.
#10	Ensure the client accepts overall responsibility for managing organizational change . . . for preparing the organization for the new system. Be very explicit with the client about any changes to internal processes, etc. entailed by the new system.
#11	Restrict project scope to match the client's capacity for absorbing change.
#13	Scope the project into multiple phases, each with a mini-implementation. Roll out the least risky or most urgent infrastructure/functionality first. Then review progress and decide where to go next.
#14	Negotiate the flexibility to juggle timescales and deadlines.
#15	Put people-oriented people on your team (good listeners, communicators etc.)
#26	Make both the developer's AND client's responsibilities/commitments explicit . . . "what, and by whom, and by when". . . and on the resources the client will need to commit, and by when.

On the surface at least, strategy #6 might seem to be just a recapitulation of the well-worn advice . . . "Get feedback by prototyping." But the conversations with the PMs show that strategy #6 goes much deeper than this. Beckhard and Harris (1987) write about the problems of managing change in organizations. They emphasize the need for managers, and others helping to lead change, to articulate and communicate their "vision" of the desired future state. The advantages of doing so could include:

- Optimism replacing pessimism as the prevailing mood amongst those involved in the change.

- The existence of the "vision", even if only "hazy", allows those affected by the change to begin to visualize their own role in the change process, and in the envisaged future state. This can reduce resistance to change, and can increase the energy that people are prepared to commit to the change.

- The description of the planned future state helps people to see what must change, and so offers a transparent rationale for managerial action.

(adapted from Beckhard and Harris, 1987: 48)

Strategy #6 seems to embody this spirit.

Strategy #11 relates to the capability and willingness of the client organization to implement the envisaged changes. In this connection, Harrison advises any external consultant to ask questions such as:

- Does the organization have the resources–people, funds, skill, knowledge – to implement the proposed changes? Can it obtain or develop the resources it lacks?

- Is there a good "fit" between the envisaged solution and the organization's dominant ways of thinking, behaving, and generally "doing things"?

- Even if the organization has the capabilities needed to implement and absorb the change, is there the **willingness** to do so?

(adapted from Harrison, 1994: 51–52)

But what if the client's people have no shared "vision" of the future state? Or what if there is a shared vision, but the consultant judges the vision to be unrealistic in time, cost or technical terms? Or there is a shared vision, but the consultant doubts the client's ability to manage the transition from here to there, or to "absorb" the change? In these circumstances, the writers on organizational change say, in effect, "Take a first, achievable, step in what seems to be the right direction. Then see where you've got to. Then decide

233

where to go next." Expressed in IS/software engineering terms, this approach to change corresponds to evolutionary or incremental development. This seems to be what strategy #13 is all about.

Getting from "here" to "there" has been called the *transition state* (Beckhard and Harris, 1987) . . .

> The critical question is: How should this time of transition be managed? Should the person involved in the old bookkeeping operation supervise the change in terms of allocating work, rewarding people, and determining timetables for going on the electronic system, or should the person who will run the new system be in charge during the transition period? Or should both people be in charge, or their common supervisor? . . . There is no cut-and-dried answer. The most appropriate management system and structure for the ambiguous transition state is the one that creates the least tension with the ongoing system and the most opportunity to facilitate and develop the new system . . .
>
> (ibid.: 75).

Strategies #7, #8, #10, #14, and #26 all relate to the transition state. In particular, to the need for a high degree of clarity on how the transition is to be managed.

Strategy #9 seems to include both pragmatic and ethical considerations. It urges PMs to be very wary of becoming embroiled in the client's "people-problems" (disagreement, reluctant users, and so on). Where there are such problems, the great majority of the PMs believed they should act as unaligned (neutral) educators and facilitators, as opposed to acting as unquestioning tools of the client's management. In terms of the change-agent models proposed in the IS literature, the PMs seem to see themselves as filling a combination of the facilitator and advocator roles (Markus and Benjamin, 1996). It must be said, however, that a small minority take a more "Rambo-ish" view of their role. ("If users don't want it, get someone further up the line to steam-roller things through.") This latter group seem to espouse values which are close to those of what Markus and Benjamin term the traditional IS change-agent model. In this model, the IS specialist sees himself or herself as serving primarily as the client's unquestioning "pair of hands".

. . . Through the Looking-glass of Capability . . .

. . . I keep saying "Stick to your knitting. Walk away from business that you're not familiar with." (SUSAN B)

. . . with the rapid change in the IT industry, if you can't cope with change, you won't stay in business (MICHAEL C)

In the interview transcripts, one can sense the tension between, on the one hand, the PM's desire to reduce immediate project risk by working only within the limits of his/her organization's current capabilities and, on the other hand, the ongoing need for the PM's organization to gain experience of, and to exploit, developments in technology.

A lot has been written in recent years about the relationship between capability and business strategy. This literature makes the point that a firm's current capabilities can act both as enablers of and as constraints on the firm's business strategy. Strategies that are far removed from the firm's capabilities are inherently risky. Strategies that underexploit current, potentially valuable, capabilities may reflect missed opportunities.

So, capabilities need to be managed, like any other resource. Hence the following questions:

● Which of our current capabilities are likely to become obsolete or irrelevant?

● Which should be sustained and improved upon?

● How can we better leverage our existing capabilities?

● What new capabilities should be developed?

(adapted from Javidan, 1998: 68)

On mechanisms for acquiring new competencies, Javidan observes:

> Companies can take a variety of approaches in acquiring new competencies; they can develop them in-house by making the necessary investments in technology and manpower/training, or they can acquire them through partnerships, alliances, mergers or acquisitions. The choice of the appropriate alternative depends on the required speed and timing of acquiring the competency, the appropriate level of control and the required financial resources.
>
> (Javidan, 1998: 69)

The notion of capability (or rather, the lack of capability) seems to be most explicitly reflected in four of the PMs' personal constructs. In Figure 27.1, I show the right-hand poles of these four constructs, and the strategies elicited by each.

As can be seen from Figure 27.1, three strategies (#16, #17 and #19) were triggered both by the lack of application/industry experience, and by the lack of platform/methods/tools experience. To use the jargon, the advice seems to be "treat capabilities as you would any other strategic asset . . . and put these in place before you really need to draw on them."

The application is new to us **OR** We've little or no knowledge of the client's industry (Note: many PMs seemed to view these two poles synonymously. Hence, I've combined the two)	• Get early/continuous feed back on your ideas, e.g. prototype (#6) • Where there is a big learning curve for you, treat the decision to get involved as a strategic decision (#16) • Where there is a critical learning curve for you, build this learning in early on. Don't risk learning on-the-fly (#17) • Plug any skills/knowledge gaps you have with training and/or contractors. But don't disrupt/unsettle your team by importing too many 'outsiders'. If this is a risk, subcontract out or structure the project as a joint venture with another developer (#19) • Learn about the client's industry/business/application by spending time on-site with the client's people and seeing how they currently do things. Learn by getting them to document what they want the new system to do. Learn by looking at other developers' solutions to the same problem in other companies (#20) • Agree a time-and-materials contract (#21) • Document and agree project scope with precision (#23)
Unfamiliar platform/environment **OR** Unfamiliar development methods and tools (Note: many PMs seemed to view these two poles synonymously. Hence, I've combined the two)	• Restrict project scope to what's reliably 'doable' by you in time, cost and technical terms (#12) • Where there is a big learning curve for you, treat the decision to get involved as a strategic decision (#16) • Where there is a critical learning curve for you, build this learning in early on. Don't risk learning on-the-fly (#17) • If there is a lot of technical risk around some aspect of the project, resolve this up front with a separate investigation task/phase with its own budget. Don't make any commitments around this aspect of the project until the risk is quantified or resolved (#18) • Plug any skills/knowledge gaps you have with training and/or contractors. But don't disrupt/unsettle your team by importing too many 'outsiders'. If this is a risk, subcontract out or structure the project as a joint venture with another developer (#19) • Agree a time-and-materials contract (#21) • Increase the formality and rigour of project management (#36)

Figure 27.1 Strategies for coping with lack of capability

. . . and Through the Looking-glass of Action, Rationality and Control . . .

In Chapter 25, I described how I had each PM break the set of thirty-four personal constructs into three piles: The VERY BIG DIFFERENCE pile, the BIG DIFFERENCE pile and the SOME/LITTLE/NO DIFFERENCE pile. I then asked the PM to explain his/her rationale for assigning the constructs to piles as he/she had done. Almost without exception, the PMs said they built their VBD piles from constructs whose "nasty" poles could lead to their "losing control" over the project. I asked the PMs to focus on these VBD constructs, and on the strategies they would use for coping with these. So, it's not surprising that many of the PMs' strategies have the flavour of "buttoning things down", "ring-fencing" aspects of the project, avoiding or filling in "black holes", and so forth.

Thompson writes about the notion of *action, rationality* and *control* in organizations:

> Instrumental action is rooted on the one hand in **desired outcomes** and on the other hand in **beliefs** about **cause/effect relationships**. Given a desire, the state of man's knowledge at any point in time dictates the kinds of variables required and the manner of their manipulation to bring that desire to fruition. To the extent that the activities thus dictated by man's beliefs are judged to produce the desired outcomes, we can speak of technology, or technical rationality.
>
> (Thompson, 1967: 14)

> This does not mean, however, that technologies operated by complex organisations are always instrumentally perfect. The instrumentally perfect technology would produce the desired outcome inevitably, and this perfection is approached in the case of continuous processing of chemicals or in mass manufacturing – for example, of automobiles. A less perfect technology will produce the desired outcome only part of the time.
>
> (ibid.: 15)

> When a technology is put to use, however, there must not only be desired outcomes, and knowledge of cause/effect relationships, but also **power** to control the empirical resources which correspond to the variables in the logical system.
>
> (ibid.: 18)

So, to the extent that the actor (in our terms, the PM) cannot exercise control over relevant variables, the outcome he/she desires cannot be guaranteed. And human beings (particularly PMs it seems!) don't like a lack of control. This is almost certainly why so many of the PMs' strategies seem to represent attempts to gain or to retain control over variables which could influence project outcomes. In Thompson's terms, this is a totally rational way for a PM to behave.

Through the Looking-glass of "Requirements-uncertainty"... **28**

"Requirements-uncertainty" (I'll call it RU from now on) is one of the "big" ideas in the information systems and software engineering literature, so I think it deserves a chapter of its own. The advice to project managers in the RU literature is that, as the level of uncertainty around user requirements increases, one should move away from the traditional waterfall life cycle model and towards a more "experimental" model, based on prototyping and evolutionary or incremental development. How does this advice square with the strategies advocated by our PMs? To answer this question, we must first pin down the notion of "requirements-uncertainty".

Davis (1982) introduced the concept of *overall requirements process uncertainty*. This concept is operationalized as the "sum" of three variables: *the existence/stability of a set of usable requirements, the level of ability of users to specify requirements* and *the level of ability of analysts to elicit and evaluate requirements*. In turn, these latter three variables are described as being the "sum" of:

- *Uncertainty deriving from the utilizing system* (e.g. the stability of the environment into which the new system is to be embedded and whether the activity the system is to support is structured or unstructured).

- *Uncertainty deriving from the application* (e.g. its complexity, the number of users and extent of change to structures/tasks).

- *Uncertainty deriving from the users* (e.g. extent of experience in using computers, level of understanding of the application and politics).

- *Uncertainty deriving from the systems analysts* (e.g. extent of experience with similar systems and knowledge of the business).

With increasing levels of *overall requirements process uncertainty*, Davis advocates that one moves from a primary strategy of asking users what they want, through basing the solution on an existing system, through deriving requirements from an analysis of the user tasks to be supported, to an experimental approach (e.g. prototyping).

Building on Davis, Burns and Dennis (1985) introduced a distinction between *requirements-uncertainty* and *requirements-complexity.* They define *requirements-uncertainty* in terms of:

- *degree of "structuredness" of the user tasks to be supported*
- *degree of understanding the users have about their tasks*
- *degree of experience and training of the system developers*

They defined *requirements-complexity* in terms of:

- *relative project size*
- *number of users*
- *volume of new information required from the system*
- *complexity of this new information*

They suggest the choice of basic project approach (i.e. traditional waterfall model versus prototyping versus a mixed model) be as shown in Figure 28.1.

Stork and Sapienza (1995) distinguish between RU and "equivocality". They define RU in much the same terms as other authors. They define equivocality as being the difference between the level of agreement and understanding between the people involved which is needed to accomplish the goals of the project, and the existing level of agreement and understanding. Equivocality, in their view, is a function of aspects of the project, such as the degree of innovativeness of the task, and aspects of the people involved, such as how diverse people are in terms of training and background. To reduce equivocality, these authors recommend that people must interact to communicate their different perspectives (not just factual data) and to resolve their conflicting views.

	Uncertainty Low	*Uncertainty High*
Com plexity High	Waterfall life cycle model	Mixed model
Complexity Low	Prototyping	Prototyping

Figure 28.1 Selection of approach based on complexity and uncertainty (Burns and Dennis, 1985)

Nidumolu (1996) identifies three dimensions of RU:

Requirements Instability: *The extent of changes in user requirements over the course of the project.*

Requirements Diversity: *The extent to which users differ among themselves in their requirements.*

Requirements Analyzability: *The extent to which the process for converting user needs to a set of requirements specifications can be reduced to mechanical steps or objective procedures.*

Nidumolu found evidence to suggest that total project RU, defined as being the sum of the project's scores on these three dimensions, is negatively associated with ultimate project and "product" performance. He also found that the use of appropriate software development standards reduced the negative effects of RU on both these outcome variables.

In summary of the literature, there appear to be common features across the different definitions of RU. All definitions treat RU as a multi-dimensional construct. Specifically, requirements-uncertainty is defined to be the aggregation of a number of requirements-uncertainty-generating "sources". The level of requirements-uncertainty for a project is measured by rating the project separately on each of these "uncertainty sources", and by then combining (e.g. adding) the individual "uncertainty" ratings to yield an overall requirements-uncertainty rating.

Also, there seems to be a fairly strong consensus amongst researchers on what constitute the main "uncertainty-sources". "Sources" common to many definitions of RU include:

● Attributes of the application (e.g. complexity, stability, novelty).

● Attributes of the users (e.g. number, previous computer experience, diversity of their needs, their understanding of the application).

● Attributes of the analysts/developers (e.g. knowledge of the application, knowledge of the business).

● Wider aspects of the organization (e.g. any unhelpful "politics").

The notion of RU seems to be reflected across a number of the PMs' constructs. In Table 28.1, I show the personal constructs which seem to most closely correspond to the various components of "requirements-uncertainty" as this notion has been described above.

If one compares Table 28.1 with the complete listing of constructs shown back in Table 25.1, it seems that the RU constructs do not "top the poll" in

Table 28.1 Numbers of PMs putting each "requirements-uncertainty" construct into each pile

		VBD	BD	SLND
There seems to be no hidden agenda	The "real" agenda seems to be hidden	14	6	0
They don't disagree amongst themselves about what's needed	They disagree amongst themselves about what's needed	14	6	0
We've experience of this application	The application is new to us	10	8	2
We've only to satisfy a single group of similar users	We've to satisfy multiple groups of users with different needs	9	5	6
We've a good knowledge of the customer's industry	We've little or no knowledge of the customer's industry	7	12	1
The customer is experienced in running computer projects	The customer is not experienced in running computer projects	5	11	4
The application logic is straightforward	The application logic is complex	5	9	6
The customer is able to define the problem in IT-addressable terms	We will have to work with them to define the problem	4	8	8
We're dealing with experienced computer users	We're dealing with inexperienced computer users	3	10	7

terms of risk generation. Of the RU related constructs above, the presence of hidden agendas and disagreement are seen by PMs to be by far the biggest risk generators. The other, "non-political", aspects of RU such as application complexity, the developer's knowledge of the application, or the client's ability to define their "problem", are seen by PMs to be relatively low risk generators. What principles or strategies do the PMs advocate for handling these issues? Do these strategies include prototyping and evolutionary/ incremental development, as the theory predicts?

In Figure 28.2, I show, for each of the "nasty" RU poles, all of the strategies that were advocated by at least one PM. For brevity, I've shortened the descriptions of some strategies.

The use of prototyping is well represented in Figure 28.2. But, as was seen in Chapter 26, prototyping is **also** recommended in a number of non-RU related situations, e.g. when there is major change for the customer, there are reluctant users, the system must go right first time, the application is mission critical, etc.

241

The 'real' agenda seems to be hidden	• Rely more on key users and other key managers … and less on the official 'owner'/project manager (#4) • **Get early/continuous feedback on your ideas, e.g. prototype (#6)** • Be an educator/facilitator … but don't take on a 'heavy' OD role (#9) • Protect yourself with bureaucracy (#22) • Document and agree project scope with precision (#23) • Requirements analysis and the functional specification must be regorous and detailed (#25) • Get sign-offs on EVERYTHING (#29)
They disagree amongst themselves about what's needed/We've to satisfy multiple groups with different needs (Note: many PMs seemed to view these two poles synonymously. Hence, I've combined the two)	• Ensure 'people-problems' are sorted out before getting into the 'nitty-gritty' of the project (#7) • Be an educator/facilitator … but don't take on a 'heavy' OD role (#9) • Put 'people-oriented' people on your team (good communicators etc.) (#15) • Agree a time-and-materials contract (#12) • Protect yourself with bureaucracy (#22) • Document and agree project scope with precision (#23) • Negotiate a separate first phase to agree scope and requirements (#24) • Requirements analysis and the functional specification must be rigorous and detailed (#25) • Ensure that project success measures are well defined and agree in advance (#28) • Get sign-offs on EVERYTHING (#29)
The application is new to us/We've little or no knowledge of the client's industry (Note: many PMs seemed to view these two poles synonymously. Hence, I've combined the two)	• **Get early/continuous feedback on your ideas, e.g. prototype (#6)** • Where there is a big learning curve for you, treat the decision to get involved as a strategic decision (#6) • Where there is a critical learning curve for you, build this learning in early on. Don't risk learning on-the-fly (#17) • Plug any skills/knowledge gaps you have with training and/or contractors. But don't disrupt/unsettle your team by importing too many 'outsiders' (#19) • Learn about the client's industry/business/application by spending time on-site with the client's people and seeing how they currently do things. Learn by getting them to document what they want the new system to do. Learn by looking at other developers' solutions to the same problem in other companies (#20) • Agree a time-and-materials contract (#21) • Document and agree project scope with precision (#23)
The customer is not experienced in running computer projects/We're dealing with inexperienced computer users (Note: many PMs seemed to view these two poles synonymously. Hence, I've combined the two)	• Recalibrate any unrealistic expectations up front with an educational strategy (#5) • **Get early/continuous feedback on your ideas, e.g. prototype (#6)** • Ensure early and careful implementation planning … roll out in controllable phases (#8) • Protect yourself with bureaucracy (#22) • Negotiate a separate first phase to agree scope and requirements (#24) • Make both yours and the client's responsibilities and commitments to the project explicit (#26)
The application logic is complex	• Where there is a critical learning curve for you, build this learning in early on. Don't risk learning on-the-fly (#17) • Plug any skills/knowledge gaps you have with training and/or contractors. But don't disrupt/unsettle your team by importing too many 'outsiders' (#19) • Document and agree project scope with precision (#23)
We'll have to work with them to define the problem	• Only four PMs put this one into their 'Very Big Difference' pile. No PMs discussed this pole explicitly.

Figure 28.2 Strategies espoused for addressing the components of requirements-uncertainty

In Figure 28.2, there are no **direct** references to incremental/evolutionary development. But the PMs **did** explicitly recommend an incremental or evolutionary project life cycle in a number of non-RU related situations, e.g. unrealistic expectations, major change for the customer, etc.

So, what can we conclude from all of this? Requirements-uncertainty does not "top the poll" of IS project managers' concerns. Things like lack of real project "ownership" and unrealistic client expectations are seen to be bigger risk generators. The data suggest that project managers use a rich mixture of strategies to address "requirements-uncertainty". The data also suggest that project managers use very different strategies, or combinations of strategies, to address different components of requirements-uncertainty. It also seems that project managers see prototyping and incremental/evolutionary development as being useful for addressing a wide variety of concerns, in addition to requirements-uncertainty. So, maybe "requirements-uncertainty" is not all that useful an idea in practice?

Conclusion

29

What's the Book Really Been About?

In cognitive science terms, this book has been an exercise in *knowledge elicitation* . . . which is the process of finding out what's in people's heads in relation to some matter of interest. So, what's *knowledge*? This question has exercised the minds of philosophers for millennia. One definition that I like is:

> *Knowledge is a justified belief that increases an entity's capacity for effective action*
> (Nonaka, 1994)

A *justified belief* is one which, in a utilitarian sense, has stood the test of time . . . it has worked in the past. So, unfounded conjectures or mere musings are not knowledge!

Alavi and Leidner (2001) propose a *Knowledge Taxonomy*, based on this definition. My Figure 29.1 is a slightly simplified version of their taxonomy.

The distinction between tacit knowledge and explicit knowledge is a key one. Tacit knowledge is knowledge that has not been articulated in verbal or written form. The "owner" may not even be aware that he/she "possesses" it. And even if aware of having it, he/she may find it difficult or even impossible to verbalize it to others. Take the "how to" of riding a bicycle for example. Tacit knowledge is usually accumulated through practical experience . . . not through "book learning".

In contrast to tacit knowledge, explicit knowledge is knowledge that has been articulated, codified, and communicated in symbolic form and/or natural language. It can be passed on through "book learning".

In Alavi's terms, my aim in this book has been to make explicit at least some of the cognitive, tacit knowledge about handling risk that sits in the heads of experienced IS/IT project managers . . . their Know-about, Know-how, Know-why, Know-when and Know-with.

Knowledge type	Definition	Example
Tacit	Not articulated (i.e. in one's head) or not 'articulatable'. Based on involvement and experience in a specific context	Best means of dealing with a specific customer Surgery skills
Explicit	Articulated, generalized knowledge	Knowledge of major customers in a region
Individual	Created by and located in the individual	Insights gained from a completed project
Social	Created by and inherent in the collective actions of a group	Norms for inter-group communication
Declarative	Know-about	What drug is appropriate for an illness
Procedural	Know-how	How to administer a particular drug
Causal	Know-why	Undcerstanding why the drug works
Conditional	Know-when	Understanding when to prescribe the drug
Relational	Know-with	Understanding how the drug interacts with other drugs
Pragmatic	Useful knowledge	Best practices, projects experiences

Figure 29.1 A taxonomy of knowledge (based on Alavi and Leidner, 2001)

How Generalizable Is the PMs' Knowledge and Advice?

The project managers in this study were all located in Ireland. This raises the obvious question: "Would IS/software project managers in other countries espouse much the same recipes and strategies as Irish-based project managers?" There is empirical evidence to suggest that IS/software project managers working in developed economies, but in different countries and in different cultures, share their thinking on IS /software project risk and its management. For example, Schmidt et al. (2001) conducted a delphi study with software project managers in the USA, Hong Kong and Finland. All converged on much the same project risk drivers, and all ranked these in roughly the same order of importance. Moynihan (1996) describes a number of studies which support the proposition that Irish IS/software project managers think about project risk in much the same way as do project managers in the USA, Canada and a range of European countries. So, it is probably safe to assume that project managers in other countries would espouse much the same theories as Irish project managers.

The "sizes" of the projects typically managed by the PMs in the present study were in the range:

Project duration: 2–36 months;

Project effort: 2–250 man-months;

Project team size: 1–9 people.

Many PMs would consider these to be small projects. Would the theories-of-action held by our PMs be held by PMs of larger projects? Analysis of the interview transcripts suggest that the PMs' theories-of-action are driven by such motivations as the desire to do a good job for the client, the necessity to provide self-protection against potentially damaging or arbitrary client behaviour, the desire to deal fairly and ethically with the client's people, the need to turn a profit, and so on. Aims such as these are shared by managers of projects of all sizes. The PMs' espoused strategies for achieving these aims (sign-offs, prototyping, incrementalism, user involvement, etc.), appear to be quite generic, and to be based on management principles of wide efficacy. Also, it's hard to construct a convincing argument to the effect that the PMs' strategies would **not** be applicable to larger projects. So, it is likely that the theories-of-action identified in this study would be shared by PMs of projects of all sizes.

Now for a tough question. Is all the stuff in this book of relevance only to managers of IS/software projects? Or could it also be of relevance to managers of other sorts of projects? One way to answer this question would be to find a validated and widely-accepted classification of project types. One could then locate IS projects in that classification, and maybe argue that the findings of our study on IS/software projects apply also to other project types in the same class. But which classification to use?

> Not many authors have attempted to classify projects according to any specific scheme, and those who have tried rarely offered extensive empirical evidence.
>
> (Shenhar, 2001: 394)

Shenhar reviewed previous attempts to build classifications of projects. He found that most proposed classifications are based on variants of the same two generic dimensions: project complexity and project uncertainty. What distinguishes between different classifications is the way in which these two dimensions have been operationalized. In other words, how uncertainty and complexity are defined. He observed that virtually all project classification-

DIMENSIONS	Maintenance interactive	Task interactive	Personal interactive
Information:			
Information quantity to be exchanged with the client	Low	Moderate	High
Precision (detail, formality, etc.) of information to be exchanged	High	Moderate	Low
Decision:			
Complexity of employee decisions/judgements	Simple	Complex	Complex
Feedback from client to employee	Immediate	Slow	Slow
Time:			
Interface duration (time spent face to face with client)	Brief	Moderate	High
Problem awareness:			
Client understanding of the 'problem'	High	Moderate	Low
The client's ability to evaluate the service being provided	High	Moderate	Low
Transferability:			
Substitutability of the employee (e.g. someone else taking over the transaction)	High	Moderate	Low
Power:			
Employee's perception of his/her power with respect to the client	Low	Moderate	High
Attachment:			
Need for employee empathy/identification with the client	Low	Moderate	High
Conflict potential in the transaction	Low	Moderate	High

Figure 29.2 *A typology of service (based on Mills and Margulies, 1980: 262)*

building efforts have been focused on R&D projects, particularly on new product development projects. So, the taxonomy we are looking for is probably not to be found in this literature.

One place where we might find a suitable taxonomy is in the literature on service and service organizations. One long-established taxonomy of service is that proposed by Mills and Margulies (1980). They identify three basic types of service: *maintenance-interactive*, *task-interactive* and *personal-interactive*. They give as examples of these three kinds of service: a routine transaction with a bank (*maintenance-interactive*); an advertising company working on a new campaign with a client (*task-interactive*); and a counsellor working with a client who has an emotional problem (*personal-interactive*). Their typology is based on seven underlying dimensions of the interface between the client/customer and the service organization.

In Figure 29.2, I show a somewhat simplified version of their taxonomy. The term *employee* refers to the employee of the organization providing the service.

Maister (1993) proposed a somewhat similar taxonomy. He identified three types of service project: *Brains, Grey Hair* and *Procedure* projects.

> In the first type (Brains), the client's problem is at the forefront of professional or technical knowledge, or at least is of extreme complexity. The key elements of this type of professional service are creativity, innovation, and the pioneering of new approaches. In effect, new solutions to new problems. The firm that targets this market will be attempting to sell its services on the basis of the high professional craft of its staff . . . "hire us because we're smart". Brains projects usually involve highly skilled and highly paid professionals. Few procedures are routinizable. Each project is a "one-off".
>
> (Maister, 1993: 4)
>
> Grey Hair projects, while they may require a highly customized "output" in meeting the client's needs, involve a lesser degree of innovation and creativity . . . The general nature of the problem to be addressed is not unfamiliar, and the activities to be performed may be similar to those performed on other projects . . . the firm sells itself by saying "Hire us because we have been through this before; we have practice at solving this type of problem." At least some of the tasks to be performed (particularly the early ones) are known in advance and can be specified and delegated.
>
> (ibid.: 4–5)
>
> The Procedure project usually involves a well-recognised and familiar type of problem . . . The steps necessary to accomplish this are somewhat programmatic . . . "Hire us because we know how to do this and can deliver it effectively."
>
> (ibid.: 5)

It's tempting to speculate that most IS/software projects for external clients would fall into Mills and Margulies' *Task-Interactive* class and into Maister's *Grey Hair* class. It's also tempting to speculate that the advice offered by our PMs would be of relevance, at least in broad terms, to managers of Non-IS/software projects that fall into these classes. But this is conjecture!

Some Comments on the Research Method I Used

This book is about project managers' **espoused** theories-of-action. In other words, about what project managers **say they would do** in this or that set of circumstances. But, obviously, what project managers **actually do,** their theories-in-use, could differ from what they say they do. Perhaps the PMs mentioned some "strategies", not because they really did use these, but because they felt that they would look foolish if they **didn't** mention them. Or perhaps they deliberately **didn't** mention some of the strategies they actually used, because to mention these might make them look bad in some light. Ajzen(1988) makes the point that, in reporting on their own behaviour, people tend to overestimate the extent of their "socially-desirable" behaviour, and to underestimate the extent of their "socially-undesirable" behaviour. For behaviour which is "socially neutral", self-reports tend to be unbiased. Given the nature of the topic, there seems to be no reason to suspect the presence of either bias in the results.

For this study, I used a grounded research approach; the study was not theory driven, and I used very open-ended, non-directive, data collection techniques. For these reasons, the study may have understated the range of strategies which PMs would espouse. For example, had I prepared lengthy checklists of situational factors and possible strategies for coping with these, and prompted the PMs from these lists, I might have elicited more factors and more strategies. But I think the price paid for going down a more structured route would have been a loss of spontaneity and vigour in the PMs' accounts of how they said they do things.

Finally . . . Was It Not All Obvious Anyway? Why Go to the Bother?

> Critics have argued that organization theories which "work" are obvious to practicioners; that is, the theories simply confirm relationships that are already well understood by experienced managers.
>
> (Priem and Rosenstein, 2000: 509).

If you search the text books on project management, I can practically guarantee that you'll find there all of the advice offered by the PMs in this study, and more besides. There's very little that's truly new under the sun! Concerning *obviousness*, Weick has said "the reaction *that's interesting* essentially signifies that an assumption has been falsified" (1989: 529). Likewise, the reaction *that's obvious* signifies confirmation of one's experience-based expectations. I hope that, at least in places, the reader's reaction has been *that's interesting!*

249

APPENDICES

Appendix 1

Numbers of Constructs under Each Theme by Manager

Theme#	1	2	3	4	5	6	7	8	9	10	11	12	13	14	Total
1	1	1		2		1	1	1	1	1	2	1	1	1	14
2		2		1	1	1	4		1		3	3	1		17
3	1		1	1		2		2		3	1	1	2		14
4	4		2			1	1	2	3	1		2		3	19
5	2	4		3	1	1			3	1		1			16
6	1		2			1	2		2	2		2		2	14
7		3	2		3	3	1		1			1	2		15
8			1	1		1	1	1	1		1		1		7
9	1		1	1			1		1	1	1		1		7
10	1			1							1		1		7
11	1	1	2	1	1							1		2	8
12		2	3		4						2				12
13		1			2	1						1		1	6
14					1	1						1	1		4
15											1	1	2		4
16		1								1				1	3
17					2	3									5
18										2			2		4
19		1										1			2
20	1	1													2
21		2		2											4
22			2		2	2	4	2			2	1	2		17
Totals	13	19	16	13	18	19	13	10	13	10	16	14	15	12	201

Appendix 2

The Five Hypothetical Project Profiles

The numbers in each profile refer to the constructs shown in Table 4.1. L/R indicates whether the left-hand pole or the right-hand pole of the construct was selected for the hypothetical profile.

Scenario 1 was built using a .5 probability of choosing the right-hand pole.

The make-up of this scenario is:

1L, 2L, 3L, 4L, 5R, 6L, 7R, 8L, 9R, 10L, 11L, 12L, 13L, 14R, 15R, 16R, 17R 18R, 19L, 20R, 21L, 22R, 23R, 24L, 25L, 26L, 27L, 28R, 29R, 30L, 31R 32R, 33L, 34R.

Scenario 2 is the 'opposite' of Scenario 1:

1R, 2R, 3R, 4R, 5L, 6R, 7L, 8R, 9L, 10R, 11R, 12R, 13R, 14L, 15L, 16L, 17L, 18L, 19R, 20L, 21R, 22L, 23L, 24R, 25R, 26R, 27R, 28L, 29L, 30R, 31L, 32L, 33R, 34L.

Scenario 3 was built using a .3 probability of choosing the right-hand pole.

The make-up of this scenario is:

1L, 2L, 3L, 4L, 5R, 6R, 7L, 8R, 9R, 10L, 11L, 12L, 13L, 14L, 15R, 16L, 17L, 18L, 19R, 20L, 21L, 22R, 23L, 24L, 25L, 26R, 27L, 28R, 29L, 30R, 31L, 32L, 33L, 34R.

Scenario 4 is the 'reverse' of scenario 3.

Scenario 5 was built using a 0.5 probability of choosing the right-hand pole.

The make-up is:

1R, 2R, 3R, 4L, 5R, 6L, 7L, 8R, 9R, 10R, 11R, 12L, 13R, 14R, 15L, 16R, 17L, 18L, 19R, 20R, 21R, 22L, 23R, 24R, 25L, 26R, 27R, 28L, 29L, 30L, 31R, 32R, 33R, 34L.

APPENDIX 3

The "Strategies"/"Recipes"

#1
If there is no committed/enthusiastic project "owner", ask or search for one (maybe an influential, enthusiastic user). Go up the line if necessary. If this fails, confront the client organization with the problem. If not resolved satisfactorily, walk away. Don't proceed until the problem is sorted out.
Number of PMs mentioning: 10
Elicited by:
No real owner (10)
Their PM lacks time/skill/authority (1)
Mission-critical application (1)

The Evidence

ANDRE

No real owner: If someone is really committed to the project, this lubricates the flow of information . . . everyone is in it together. Otherwise you may have to find someone else more junior. At that stage, you would have to be very diplomatic. If Mr A is the person who really SHOULD be in charge, but doesn't really want it, you may have to find a Mr B who really wants it. So, you work with B without ignoring A . . . just keep A in the picture.

ANNE

No real owner: . . . I think it's crucial to have somebody on the customer's side who will take ownership. If you haven't, you go as high up as possible in their organization and demand that you get someone who'll run with it. Otherwise, you end up running the project the way you think it should be run, and not meeting their requirements . . . without real ownership from senior people, work in tandem with the users . . . get to know the users well and select a good strong person from amongst them . . . someone who has a fair bit of authority and standing, and who is prepared to run with it.

COLIN

No real owner: I would go to the managing director and say "This is not going to work unless someone does want to own the project"... So you would have to go to the top and say sort this out or forget it.

MERVYN

No real owner: I'd try to highlight this to whoever asked me to look at the area in the first place. To say, face to face to them, "Do you REALLY want this system? Is what we're proposing what you REALLY want?" If he says "Yes. This is REALLY where we want to go", then you're starting to create ownership. If he says "Well, it's not really what we want", he'll probably talk himself out of doing it at all. At that stage, you're probably better off walking away, if you can do that.

MICHAEL B

No real owner: ... we're on a loser if someone isn't guiding things from the client's side ... if there's no real ownership ... it's usually been a disaster in terms of timescales and costs, and the client not really getting what they wanted. Ideally, I'd pull out ... If we couldn't pull out, I would get them to encourage someone less senior but very enthusiastic to take it on ... Someone who wants to develop their computer skills.

PATRICK

No real owner: If nobody wants to own the project, you've no guarantee that anyone will agree that the works been done or not ... you probably won't even be paid for the job! ... you've got to get [this] one out of the way first. [If not], that would be that! [i.e. walk away].

PAUL

No real owner: ... escalate [this issue] up the organization. Find someone who wants to own the project at a higher level before you spend any money ... You shouldn't get involved in a project that's meaningless, even if eventually you get paid ... You can't move past this one. You have to find someone who'll say "Yes" [to your proposals, ideas, etc.]. Otherwise you have to go up and up, even to the board. If not resolved, bail out!

PHILIP

No real owner AND Mission-critical application: These two issues would be a dreadful combination . . . [confront] the client directly and [say] "It doesn't seem to us that this will be a business success for you . . . We need a senior manager . . . the board . . . to approve . . . underwrite this project." If that didn't work, then it's goodbye time.

SUSAN A

No real owner: Basically, it's a meeting with the client to say "We need someone to take ownership and responsibility on your side." Even if they give you a random name, because they can't decide on someone better, at least it's a name . . . it's someone you can mail and fax. [So] if you're not getting feedback and deadlines are expiring, at least you can point the finger . . .

TOMMY

Their PM lacks time/skill/authority AND No real owner: . . . I'd sit the client down and have some hard face-to-face conversations about it . . . Once the problem is accepted as a problem, it can sometimes be solved by bringing in some third party, someone from your own side, or someone else, . . . to free up some time for the client or his rep . . . or to equip him to be in a better position to argue the case for the project within the organization . . . Anyway, the earlier it's addressed the better . . . I'd ask myself "Do I REALLY want this project?" . . . . Is this a strategic project for me?

> ### #2
>
> **If the client project manager hasn't the needed authority, find/demand an alternative who has. Bring issue up the line if necessary. If not resolved, walk away.**
>
> *Number of PMs Mentioning: 5*
>
> *Elicited by:*
>
> *Their PM lacks time/skill/authority (6)*
>
> *No real owner (1)*
>
> *Unattributable (1)*

The Evidence

BOB

Their PM lacks time/skill/authority: ... If their main project person isn't available to you ... doesn't have the skill or authority to implement change ... It could end up in rows, and the delivered product being not what they expect ... I'd request a meeting with more senior people. I'd try to be as apolitical as possible and I'd say "... We feel this guy isn't giving us the needed support or whatever. Can we change the person?"

MIKE A

Their PM lacks time /skill/authority: If it was about lack of authority, I'd look upwards to find someone with authority to support the guy I had to deal with.

OWEN

Their PM lacks time/skill/authority: ... Go back to top management and educate them as to the requirements and needs of that particular individual ... If time can be provided, that's one hurdle overcome. If it's a lack of skill, you can educate him or her. But we cannot give him or her authority. That has to come from within the organization ... from the top.

PATRICK

Their PM lacks time/skill/authority: you'd have to [walk out]. Lack of time, even skill, one could live with, but if he/she doesn't have the authority, there's no real contract.

PAUL

Their PM lacks time/skill/authority AND No real owner: Escalate these issues up the organization.

Their PM lacks time/skill/authority: . . . You have to have someone [on the client's side] who is given the authority to run the project . . . to control it. It may be that you have to go up the organization to get the name of someone lower down. Lack of time and skill can be worked around . . . [but] they must have authority . . . [if not resolved] I think I'd bail out.

Unattributable: Don't go further if there's no owner with authority. Walk out. you're going to fail . . .

#3
If the client project manager hasn't the needed time or skill (but has the needed authority), try to get him/her support/training. If this doesn't work, ask for a suitable alternative person, or try to work around him/her.
Number of PMs mentioning: 5   *Elicited by:*   *Their PM lacks time/skill/authority (5)*   *No real owner (1)*

The Evidence

BOB

Their PM lacks time/skill/authority: . . . If their main project person isn't available to you . . . doesn't have the skill . . . to implement change . . . It could end up in rows, and the delivered product being not what they expect . . . I'd request a meeting with more senior people. I'd try to be as apolitical as possible and I'd say "We feel this guy isn't giving us the needed support or whatever. Can we change the person?"

MIKE A

Their PM lacks time/skill/authority: If it was a lack of skill, I'd broaden my contacts [with] the users . . . put more reliance on them. I'd try to find someone on that front who had the skills. If it's lack of time, . . . highlight this to their management . . .

OWEN

Their PM lacks time/skill/authority: ... Go back to top management and educate them as to the requirements and needs of that particular individual ... If time can be provided, that's one hurdle overcome. If it's a lack of skill, you can educate him or her. But we cannot give him or her authority. That has to come from within the organization ... from the top.

TOMMY

Their PM lacks time/skill/authority AND No real owner: ... I'd sit the client down and have some hard face-to-face conversations about it ... Once the problem is accepted as a problem, it can sometimes be solved by bringing in some third party, someone from your own side, or someone else, ... to free up some time for the client or his rep ... or to equip him to be in a better position to argue the case for the project within the organization ... Anyway, the earlier it's addressed the better.

SUSAN B

Their PM lacks time/skill/authority: ... if he's giving us the wrong information, or not giving us any feedback, I would have to raise this officially and get him ousted because he is jeopardising the project.

#4

Put more reliance on key users and other key managers and less reliance on the client project manager or official project "owner".

Number of PMs mentioning: 3

Elicited by:

Their PM lacks time/skill/authority (2)

No real owner (1)

Unrealistic expectations (1)

Real agenda hidden (1)

The Evidence

ANNE

No real owner: Without real ownership from senior people . . . work in tandem with the users . . . get to know the users well . . .

MIKE A

Unrealistic expectations AND their PM lacks time/skill/authority: Broaden the base of my contact with the company. If lack of authority, look upwards to find someone with authority to support the guy I've to deal with. If skill shortage, broaden my contacts with the users . . . put more reliance on them . . .

Their PM lacks time/skill/authority: Get in tight with the users. They seem to want the system, so establish good relations with them. As [their] main project person isn't in a position to help you very much, then the users are key . . .

PAUL

Real agenda hidden: . . . conduct interviews with as many people as you can, without committing yourself to one side or the other . . . far less serious when the people most affected really want [the new system] . . . even if there is another agenda, it doesn't have to be your concern. If the people affected want it, you can work with them and make it a success.

> **#5**
>
> **Recalibrate unrealistic expectations about cost, timescales, or what's "doable" up front. Try an educational strategy . . . show them what their competitors are doing . . . run workshops on the state of the art, etc. Give examples of what might be achievable. Maybe have them bring in an independent consultant to give objective advice. Walk away if all this doesn't work.**
>
> *Number of PMs mentioning: 8*
>
> *Elicited by:*
>
> *Unrealistic expectations (8)*
>
> *They're inexperienced in running computer projects (2)*

The Evidence

BOB

Unrealistic expectations: Describe previous histories of any similar projects. If no history, explain you're breaking new ground.

CANICE

Unrealistic expectations: . . . have a workshop to drill down into needs . . . into what's really important and the real reasons for these . . . this is a show-stopper. Until it's sorted out, there's not much point in trying to address other issues . . . I think the first thing is to invest time in working through with the customer exactly where the project is at the moment, what is realistic, and in what time-frame and at what cost. If you don't get through that exercise to everyone's satisfaction, just walk away.

MIKE A

Unrealistic expectations: I'd tell them at the pre-contract stage what I think is doable. If they don't buy this, I'd bail out . . . it's an ongoing education process.

OWEN

Unrealistic expectations: . . . educate them as to what the reality is, i.e. get them to talk to other clients of ours in their industry so they see what's involved. Factor this education into the price.

PADRAIG

Unrealistic expectations: I would talk to them face to face and explain why their ideas were unrealistic. I'd give examples of what might be achievable.

PAUL

Unrealistic expectations AND They're inexperienced in running computer projects: I'd explain why, in my view, their expectations were unrealistic. I'd keep at this until one of two things happened . . . they changed their expectations, or I'd reckoned I was on a loser and I'd just walked away . . . everybody has to understand that everything costs money . . . takes time . . . I'd find a way of explaining this to them using non-IT examples, like building a house.

TOMMY

Unrealistic expectations: Meet the customer and reset those expectations. Hold workshops involving key people from the customer's side and our side where we learn to speak one another's language. You can get communication going . . . get debate going . . . people begin to understand what's on the other side of the fence.

TONY

Unrealistic expectations AND They're inexperienced in running computer projects: there's an educational process to be gone through. So, get them to bring in a consultant or some other facilitator to get their needs sorted out . . . to get some objective advice.

> **#6**
>
> **Get early feedback on your ideas for the solution. Make your ideas for the solution as concrete as possible for the client and users. Help people see what your solution entails for them. Ideally, build a working prototype. If this is not feasible, build some form of mock-up/simulation to test proof of concept.**
>
> *Number of PMs mentioning: 9*
>
> *Elicited by:*
>
> *Major change for the customer (4)*
>
> *People most affected don't want it (2)*
>
> *System must go right first time (2)*
>
> *Mission-critical application (2)*
>
> *Unrealistic expectations (1)*
>
> *Project duration >three months (1)*
>
> *Real agenda hidden (1)*
>
> *Unattributable (1)*

The Evidence

ANDRE

Major change for the customer AND People most affected don't want it: Possibly you will have to show them some sort of prototype.

ANNE

Major change for the customer: I'd set up meetings with users and discuss the changes with them . . . maybe put a prototype together to show them the type of thing envisaged . . . you should sit down with them and prepare the way for it before you get stuck-in.

CANICE

Unrealistic expectations: . . . sell them on the idea that the first revenue-earning phase should deliver a document on [their] needs and rationale behind each, to their satisfaction . . . second phase deliverable should be prototype, or some form of proof of concept . . . if they won't accept an incremental path towards clarification, you just walk away! . . . be very clear about what is to be delivered . . .

COLIN

System must go right first time: I'll assume you mean that a parallel run is not possible. This puts a big strain on things. Obviously you would have to build a simulation model or something that will allow you to test the ideas very thoroughly and rigorously. . . . something that would say "This is what it will be."

GERRY

Project duration >three months: . . . approach the prototyping more seriously . . . Prototyping is very important. If we can't show the client a prototype . . . then we will have to go back to old-fashioned printed documentation . . . draft some sample windows . . . draw some pictures for the client to show them what it was going to look like . . . so at least the client can see exactly how everything is going to work.

Unattributable: We like to produce a fully developed front end with all screens painted but no code behind these . . .

MICHAEL B

People most affected don't want it: If they hated the whole thing, if I was stuck in the middle, I'd work really, really hard to get a good relationship with these people . . . by being on site . . . by showing them prototypes . . . by being personal . . . by explaining that the system will make things easier for them.

PADRAIG

Major change for the customer: If possible, prototype . . .

PHILIP

Mission critical application AND Can't show a prototype: . . . you'd do your damdest to find a way of expressing to the client what the system was going to deliver . . . graphically or in some other form . . . to get some confirmation back. You'd need the client's sign-off on something to give you some comfort.

SUSAN B

Mission-critical application OR Major change for the customer: . . . you have to insist on prototyping it . . . piloting it, not expecting it to go right first time . . .

Real agenda hidden: . . . get customer sign-offs on everything . . . req spec, system spec, detailed criteria for acceptance testing. we'd mock up screens in advance so they'd know exactly what they were getting . . . that's how we have protected ourselves in the past.

System must go right first time: . . . We'd set up a test environment here that mimicked their environment. we'd prototype it . . . bring them in to check it out . . . gain their acceptance of the prototype.

#7

Ensure that organizational-development issues (restructuring, IR, etc.) and people-centred issues/obstacles (disagreement, resistance to change, etc.) are addressed before getting into the "nitty-gritty" of the project. Sit down with the people who'll be impacted and prepare the way ahead before getting stuck in.

Number of PMs mentioning: 6

Elicited by:

Major change for the customer (3)

People most affected don't really want it (2)

They disagree amongst themselves (1)

The Evidence

ANDRE

Major change for the customer: . . . we'd want to be sure that things like user training, union negotiations, restructuring, etc. which were critical to the project would all start very early on and would be clearly agreed to be part of the client's responsibility.

ANNE

Major change for the customer: If you have to introduce change in the customer's workflow, it can be stressful . . . this takes the project beyond being just about software development . . . it takes the project into the realms of people management . . . organization development and business process re-engineering. These aspects have to be dealt with before you get stuck into the nitty-gritty of the project . . . I'd set up meetings with users and discuss the changes with them. Maybe put a prototype together to show them the type of thing envisaged. Sit down with them and prepare the way for it before you get stuck in.

BOB

Major change for the customer: . . . get the people involved from the different levels . . . who are involved in the workflow . . . and educate them . . . get them to accept that there are going to be changes for the benefit of the overall company.

CANICE

People most affected don't want it: I'd want it sorted out before sign-up. I'd dig in a bit to find out the reasons . . . Maybe users don't want it because they perceive it's going to cause them extra work. It's often a matter of ignorance or misperception on someone's part. A perceives it's bad . . . B perceives it's good. Who's right? Who's wrong? So my first call would be an educational one . . . to try to make sure that everyone has the same facts and to try to straighten out misperceptions about the reasons for the system, and so on.

MERVYN

People most affected don't want it: This could be one to be worked on early on . . . you need to track down reasons . . . If the root cause is that half a dozen people are going to lose their jobs, then it's outside your control . . . if it's cost or non-job losing stuff, you can sell them the advantages of the new system . . . [if the former] there's nothing you can tell these people that will cheer them up, except that it's not your doing . . . it's the bosses who made the decision.

TONY

They disagree amongst themselves: You have to facilitate reaching an agreement . . . to get a consensus on what the project is about . . . and to define it. If it was a big project, we'd suggest they bring in an independent consultant to advise on their needs. Then we'd pick up from there.

#8

Ensure careful, early and detailed implementation planning. Be very clear about implementation tasks and responsibilities. Strengthen user training/user preparation. Plan details of roll-out very carefully. Resource roll-out very well. Roll out in controllable phases. Agree a precise handover point.

Number of PMs mentioning: 6

Elicited by:

Mission-critical application (3)

Major change for the customer (2)

They disagree amongst themselves (1)

People most affected don't want it (1)

Client unable/unwilling to drive implementation (1)

Inexperienced computer users (1)

System must go right first time (1)

Unattributable (1)

The Evidence

ANDRE

Mission-critical application AND Major change for the customer: Spell out line by line who is responsible for ancillary activities like training, implementation, . . .

MERVYN

They disagree amongst themselves OR People most affected don't want it AND Client unable/unwilling to drive implementation: Draw up a detailed implementation plan. Get some authority from the client. Make sure the project leader on the client's side will help us enforce implementation decisions.

PADRAIG

Mission-critical application: Developers to remain on the project right through to handover to help our support people handle the implementation effectively. Plan the roll-out very carefully . . . the details of how the system will go live.

Major change for the customer: Put in a formal training plan and allow the requisite time and resources to get the users on board . . . Lengthen the roll-out of the parallel run . . . Plan the implementation very carefully . . . Roll out in phases.

SUSAN A

Inexperienced computer users: [decide on how] to prepare for any beta testing by the users, familiarize them with the operating system to be used. Maybe release any early versions for them to play with.

SUSAN B

System must go right first time: . . . we'd install it in a small group of users, bed it in with them, then expand out.

TONY

Mission-critical application: you'd be looking for clarity on the issues and arrangements for handing the product over . . . where responsibilities lie, precisely when does the project . . . finish . . . Agreeing a precise handover point also . . .

Unattributable: Define the implementation job carefully and put the tasks and responsibilities into the contract.

> **#9**
>
> **Where there is disagreement, unwilling users or negative politics, try to resolve it through an educational/facilitating strategy. If there have to be winners and losers, pass the problem to the client's power structure for resolution. Don't get sucked into the problem yourself. Tell them to get expert consultancy help if needed.**
>
> *Number of PMs mentioning: 12*
>
> *Elicited by:*
>
> *They disagree amongst themselves (8)*
>
> *People most affected don't want it (6)*
>
> *Real agenda hidden (2)*
>
> *Major change for the customer (1)*
>
> *We must satisfy multiple groups with different needs (1)*

The Evidence

ANDRE

People most affected don't want it AND Major change for the customer: . . . if you have lower-level managers who are going to resist things, then you will have to do a lot of training . . . a lot of talking to these people to turn them around to your way of thinking . . . have to run a lot of workshops . . . if you are an outsider, you can't go into a user area and tell them what they need . . . those days are gone.

CANICE

People most affected don't want it: Maybe users don't want it because they perceive it's going to cause them extra work. It's often a matter of ignorance or misperception on someone's part. A perceives it's bad . . . B perceives it's good. Who's right? Who's wrong? So my first call would be an educational one . . . to try to make sure that everyone has the same facts and to try to straighten out misperceptions . . .

271

MERVYN

They disagree amongst themselves: I'd summarize the issues from the different camps . . . what they want in . . . what they want out . . . and I'd take this to the person who has ownership. I'd pass the buck to him. He must decide. I'd be guided by him.

MIKE A

People most affected don't want it: [this] reduces your chances of success hugely. Having committed users is vital. If pushed into this situation, you need someone with clout on the client's side to push things through . . . it's doable provided the senior guy stays with the project and remains committed.

They disagree amongst themselves: . . . get someone further up the line to steamroller it through.

MICHAEL B

People most affected don't want it: If they hated the whole thing, if I was stuck in the middle, I'd work really, really hard to get a good relationship with these people . . . by being on site . . . by showing them prototypes . . . by being personal . . . by explaining that the system will make things easier for them . . . [if this didn't work] we'd go on with the system regardless and just hope it would turn out OK.

OWEN

The people most affected don't want it: You would need to seek leadership and ownership for the project from within the organization . . . someone with real clout . . . because, from my experience, if they can't create the right environment, we certainly wouldn't be able to.

PADRAIG

They disagree amongst themselves: . . . I'd talk to the main project guy on their side and put forward suggestions . . . compromises . . . and look to him to provide the necessary decision making to get things done. Align with whoever is the strongest . . . Emphasize that "good enough" is what's required.

PAUL

Real agenda hidden AND People most affected don't want it: Conduct interviews with as many people as you can, without committing yourself to one side or the other . . . show you're not pushing the system, but just trying to understand the problem.

We must satisfy multiple groups with different needs AND They disagree amongst themselves BUT There's a real owner with authority: . . . have a heavy session with the heads of these groups of people. Explore why they can't agree. If its conflicting requirements or different goals, they need a consultant type to work with them to sort it out . . . If they have similar goals, this disagreement can usually be resolved by an IT type.

SUSAN A

They disagree amongst themselves BUT Their PM has time/skill/authority: That's an issue they need to sort out. The main client guy looks good so he can take on the job of sorting them out.

SUSAN B

They disagree amongst themselves AND real agenda hidden: . . . escalate it to their main project guy. Tell him to bang their heads together.

TOMMY

They disagree amongst themselves: I'd put in place a procedure to make sure that everyone reaches agreement. There are various sorts of methodologies out there to help. Structured debates and the like. There are lots of methods consultants can use to handle this sort of thing.

TONY

They disagree amongst themselves: You have to facilitate reaching an agreement . . . to get a consensus on what the project is about . . . and to define it. If it was a big project, we'd suggest they bring in an independent consultant to advise on their needs. Then we'd pick up from there.

> **#10**
>
> **Ensure the client accepts overall responsibility for managing organizational change . . . for preparing the organization for the new system. Be very explicit with the client about any changes to internal processes, etc. entailed by the new system. Ensure preparations for change (restructuring, IR, user training) start at an early stage in the project**
>
> *Number of PMs mentioning: 3*
>
> *Elicited by:*
>
> *Major change for the customer (3)*

The Evidence

ANDRE

Major change for the customer: . . . we'd want to be sure that things like user training, union negotiations, restructuring, etc., which were critical to project, would all start very early on and would be clearly agreed to be part of the client's responsibility.

PADRAIG

Major change for the customer: Most organizations realize that it is their responsibility to ensure that the organization is ready for the new system. You can only point out what they need to do. The responsibility must be made to rest on the customer's side.

SUSAN A

Major change for the customer: The client may not have bargained for changing their internal processes so you need to make sure they are on board . . . you must be very explicit about what has to change . . . You just can't release the product and hope they'll change their internal procedures and workflow. You need to get their involvement on this issue very early on so they can start to think it through and prepare the ground.

#11
Restrict project scope to match the client's capacity for absorbing change.
Number of PMs mentioning: 2   *Elicited by:*   *Major change for the customer (1)*   *Client unwilling/unable to drive implementation (1)*

The Evidence

COLIN

Major change for the customer: . . . If there will not be major changes you will be designing a system to fit in with the known . . . it's all relatively controllable. If there are going to be major changes, nobody can predict how things will pan out . . . it is totally outside of your control . . . you have to break the implementation into stages. You implement stage one. If it works . . . if it's practical . . . then you can implement stage two, etc. If you don't do it like this, you can paint yourself into a corner.

MICHAEL C

Client unable/unwilling to drive implementation: . . . We had one case like this recently. We knew that implementation would involve a massive amount of data entry, correction and standardization, and so on right across the organization. At the outset we said "In our view, you are not ready for this new system. You don't have the basic procedures in place."

275

#12

Restrict project scope/content to what's reliably "doable" by you in time, cost and technical sense.

Number of PMs mentioning: 3

Elicited by:

Unrealistic expectations (2)

Mission-critical application (1)

Unfamiliar platform/environment (1)

Unfamiliar languages/tools (1)

Tight imposed timescales (1)

Unattributable (1)

The Evidence

ALAN

Mission critical application: If it's mission-critical it's a big risk to us because we're touching something which, if it breaks, will have a serious impact on the client ... [so] lower requirements ... be less ambitious ... focus on what's reliably "doable". No rocket science!

MIKE A

Unrealistic expectations: We would try to change the goalposts ... to make it doable ... cost-affordable ... it's an ongoing education process. I'd tell them ... what I think is doable.

Unfamiliar platform/environment OR Unfamiliar languages/tools AND Tight, imposed timescales: [this] would be an excruciating combination ... Unless I could re-scope the project to reduce risk, I'd definitely walk away ...

Unattributable: Try to minimize the scope of the project ... go for the smallest possible task in the longest possible timescale ... aim to get an initial limited functionality working with a number of follow-on phases, because all the indications here suggest that you will want that limited functionality to go in on time.

PADRAIG

Unrealistic expectations: . . . I'd come back with something more realistic that would invariably involve narrowing the scope of the project . . . I'd say "Let's achieve this over the next three to six months. Then let's review things and go on to a second phase."

#13

Use an incremental/evolutionary life-cycle. Scope the project into multiple phases, each with a mini-implementation. Roll out the least risky or most urgent infrastructure/functionality first. Then review progress and decide where to go next.

Number of PMs mentioning: 4

Elicited by:

Unrealistic expectations (2)

Tight, imposed timescales (2)

Major change for the customer (1)

Unattributable (1)

The Evidence

COLIN

Major change for the customer: If there will not be major changes you will be designing a system to fit in with the known . . . it's all relatively controllable. If there are going to be major changes, nobody can predict how things will pan out . . . it is totally outside of your control . . . you have to break the implementation into stages. You implement stage one. If it works . . . if it's practical . . . then you can implement stage two, etc. If you don't do it like this, you can paint yourself into a corner.

Unrealistic expectations: . . . advise them that the project should be broken down into mini projects, and that if they expect a lot from any one project it will probably go wrong because no one will have understood the complexities of the thing at the outset. Get the first mini-project going then review the situation after its implementation.

Tight, imposed timescales: . . . No matter what anyone says, the "big bang" theory just doesn't work. Things are more likely to go wrong . . . I like to be able to ask "what do you need next week? What can wait?" So you can tackle the critical bits first. The ancillary or "nice-to-have" features can be added later . . . Ask "What do you need next week? What can wait?"

MIKE A

Unattributable [very unfavourable situation]: Try to minimize the scope of the project . . . go for the smallest possible task in the longest possible timescale . . . aim to get an initial limited functionality working with a number of follow-on phases, because all the indications here suggest that you will want that limited functionality to go in on time.

PADRAIG

Unrealistic expectations: . . . I'd come back with something more realistic that would involve narrowing the scope of the project . . . I'd say "Let's achieve this over the next three to six months. Then let's review things and go on to a second phase."

SUSAN B

Tight, imposed timescales: . . . what we'd actually do is to try to reset their expectations about the time needed. we'd suggest a two-phase installation. we'd say "Let's put the infrastructure in place and do the easy things in the time available in phase one, then see where we've got to, and then build on the rest of the functionality in phase two."

#14		
Negotiate the flexibility to juggle timescales and deadlines.		
Number of PMs mentioning: 2		
Elicited by:		
Mission critical application (2)		
Major change for the customer (2)		

The Evidence

ANNE

Mission-critical application: . . . need flexibility to juggle with timescales . . . rather be right and be late . . .

SUSAN B

Major change for the customer: Need flexibility in timescales.

Mission-critical application OR Major change for the customer: You must insist on . . . some flexibility in timescales.

> #15
>
> **When there's a lot of change for the client, or when there are client people-related issues to be handled (e.g. disagreement, politics, etc.), put people-oriented people on your team (good listeners, communicators, etc.)**
>
> *Number of PMs mentioning: 2*
>
> *Elicited by:*
>
> *Major change for the customer (1)*
>
> *People most affected don't want it (1)*
>
> *We must satisfy multiple groups with different needs (1)*
>
> *Unrealistic expectations (1)*

The Evidence

ANDRE

Major change for the customer AND People most affected don't want it: . . . and if you have lower-level managers who are going to resist things, then you will have to do a lot of training . . . a lot of talking . . . to turn them around to your way of thinking . . . the people you would have to choose on that project would have to be people who can handle the human side of things.

PAUL

Unrealistic expectations AND Must satisfy multiple groups with different needs: . . . put in a good communicator . . . a good listener . . .

#16

If a project involves a big learning curve for you, view the choice of whether or not to get involved as a strategic decision. In particular, only take the financial "hit" yourself if the learning is of future strategic benefit.

Number of PMs mentioning: 6

Elicited by:

Unfamiliar languages/tools (5)

Unfamiliar platform/environment (3)

We've little/no knowledge of their industry (2)

The application is new to us (1)

The Evidence

ANDRE

Unfamiliar languages/tools: The question becomes is this an opportunity for us to train people or is it something that's deadbeat with no future. If it's an opportunity for the future, it's a cost we will find ourselves . . . it would be an investment . . . a commercial decision.

CANICE

Unfamiliar platform/environment OR Unfamiliar languages/tools: If we were learning Java for the first time but we saw a spectrum of future stuff coming from this, we'd take the hit. But if it was esoteric, "We'll have to charge you for our learning it."

MIKE A

Unfamiliar platform/environment OR Unfamiliar languages/tools AND Tight, imposed timescales: [this] would be an excruciating combination . . . we wouldn't adopt something that we hadn't seen proven in practice . . . it would be a strategic investment for us, and not taken on lightly . . . Unless this is a very strategic project, one should walk away . . .

281

PADRAIG

Unfamiliar languages/tools: Budget for the learning curve . . . even up to fifty per cent if it's completely new. The reality in bidding . . . generally tied to fixed-price contract . . . you'd swallow most of this cost and put it down to training. Justify as an investment in moving yourself up the learning curve, if it's an area you want to get into.

We've little/no knowledge of their industry: Have to put more into the specification stage. This would be a learning phase, so you would need to budget for this. If you want to get into their industry, you'd take the hit for this.

PATRICK

The application is new to us: If the application is new to us, we'd have to spend more time learning about the business . . . being up against a competitor . . . we would have to carry the cost ourselves. If it's an abstruse area, it [might] cost us too much to educate ourselves . . . You have to make a judgement on how familiar it all is . . . .you might decide you wanted to go into that market anyway . . . maybe decide to swallow that overhead yourself.

Unfamiliar languages/tools: it's three-month overhead. Strategic decision to swallow it yourself . . .

PHILIP

We've little/no knowledge of their industry AND Unfamiliar platform/ environment:

The combination . . . new industry . . . new platform . . . they're strong negatives. It depends from a business point of view, on whether you still want to pursue the project . . .

> **#17**
>
> **If there is a critical learning curve for the developer around some aspect of the project, structure the project to build this learning in early on. Get up to speed before embarking on the "main" project. Don't risk learning on-the-fly.**
>
> *Number of PMs mentioning: 5*
>
> *Elicited by:*
>
> *Unfamiliar languages/tools (3)*
>
> *We've little/no knowledge of their industry (3)*
>
> *Unfamiliar platform/environment (2)*
>
> *The application is new to us (1)*
>
> *Unrealistic expectations (1)*

The Evidence

COLIN

Unfamiliar languages/tools OR Unfamiliar platform/environment: Structure project to build in a learning curve . . . Try to shape up a small project first to get the needed experience before you get into the main project.

MICHAEL B

Unfamiliar languages/tools OR Unfamiliar platform/environment: We wouldn't pitch for something if we didn't have the expertise. But if we were forced to, we'd buy in the skills . . . to train our people. But we wouldn't write the application and try to learn at the same time.

PADRAIG

Unfamiliar languages/tools: Main way would be to get training before undertaking the project. Budget for the learning curve . . . even up to fifty per cent if it's completely new.

We've little/no knowledge of their industry: . . . Have to put more into the specification stage. This would be a learning phase so you would need to budget for that . . . Try to stretch the timescale of the specification stage to give yourself time to become familiar with the industry.

283

PHILIP

We've little/no knowledge of their industry AND The application is new to us: there's a learning exercise to be done . . . You'd include an allowance for this in your project proposal under the first phase to do the functional spec. The learning and the functional spec would go hand in hand.

TONY

We've little/no knowledge of their industry AND Unrealistic expectations: Look for a front-end loading to the contract to learn their business . . . there's a learning curve going into the project.

#18

If there is a lot of technical risk around some aspect of the project, resolve this up front with a separate investigation task/phase with its own budget. Don't make any commitments around this aspect of the project until the risk is quantified or resolved.

Number of PMs Mentioning: 6

Elicited by:

We must change another developer's code (3)

Some tricky interfacing (2)

Unfamiliar languages/tools (1)

The Evidence

ANDRE

Some tricky interfacing with an existing application: Treat the question "do we have to write an interface" as a separate fixed charge in the contract. Have a separate section in the contract detailing this point, full of qualifiers about the standards used, etc. Depending on the answers, reserve the right to quote writing interface as a separate fixed charge or as a time and materials charge.

284

CANICE

We must change another developer's code: Up front, I'd inspect their code . . . standards, documentation, etc . . . You'd be crazy to take it on a fixed-price basis . . . Try to wrap it instead of opening it up. Get clear understanding with the customer on "who's going to support it after we've been into it or wrapped it?" . . . Ideally you should look for a phase one exercise which analyzes the code and software, and which the customer pays for.

MIKE A

Unfamiliar languages/tools: Check very carefully with people already using these tools in the same environment. Check out the back-up/support available for these . . . [Given that the development environment is unfamiliar] go for a phased contract. First phase initial study. Fixed price. Postpone fixing later phase costs until initial study done.

PADRAIG

We must change another developer's code: . . . avoid giving any estimates until we've seen the code. Don't give ballpark estimates in advance of this . . . Allocate a fixed number of days in the contract to reviewing and assessing the code. Then come back with estimates as to what changes are required and what's involved.

Some tricky interfacing with an existing application: If it wasn't all very straightforward, . . . an investigation might be needed . . . and budget separately for this.

PHILIP

We must change another developer's code: . . . make a quick assessment of how well it's written before you commit.

SUSAN A

Some tricky interfacing with an existing application: . . . find out exactly what's involved up front. If we don't have the expertise in-house, buy it in or maybe go for training. If it's simple and straightforward, no problem . . . it [up-front investigation] cuts down that risk.

> #19
>
> **Plug any skills gaps on your side with imported training, consultancy, contract staff, etc. But don't disrupt/unsettle your team by importing too many "outsiders". If this is a risk, subcontract out or structure the project as a joint venture with another developer.**
>
> *Number of PMs mentioning: 8*
>
> *Elicited by:*
>
> *Unfamiliar languages/tools (6)*
>
> *Unfamiliar platform/environment (3)*
>
> *Some tricky interfacing (3)*
>
> *Complex application (2)*
>
> *Application is new to us (1)*

The Evidence

ALAN

Unfamiliar platform/environment OR Unfamiliar languages/tools: We're back to contracting. It's about getting experienced people that you know know the technology. But also who can relate to people. You don't want tech-noheads who know it all . . . but who can't relate to other people in the group . . .

Some tricky interfacing with an existing application: it's about getting the people [contractors] who really understand the interfaces . . . the experts! you'll have to pay more!

MERVYN

Some tricky interfacing with an existing application: . . . if you are [contracting] because there are one or two small technical interfaces that you don't know how to do, or something like that, that need not be a big problem . . . if you're taking in a single [contractor] into your own team of, say, five people, that's OK. But if you're taking in ten . . . then you're heading for a nightmare because you'll have them changing . . . coming and going . . . they all have mobile phones . . . they're all worrying about their next contract . . . they're not as focused and dedicated . . . they have nicer cars . . . they can afford more drink on a Friday night . . . so it makes your own full-

286

time people very uneasy . . . if lots of people are required, run the project jointly with another software house.

MICHAEL B

Unfamiliar platform/environment OR Unfamiliar languages/tools: We wouldn't pitch for something if we didn't have the expertise. But if we were forced to, we'd buy in the skills . . . to train our people. But we wouldn't write the application and try to learn at the same time.

PADRAIG

Unfamiliar languages/tools: . . . The main way we would address unfamiliar tools would be to get the requisite training before undertaking the project.

SUSAN A

Complex application: . . . we're into a big educational thing for us . . . maybe send people on courses or some sort of training . . . to speed up the learning curve.

Some tricky interfacing with an existing application: If we don't have the expertise in-house, buy it in or maybe go for training.

SUSAN B

Unfamiliar Languages/Tools: we'd have to bring in subcontractors. there's no other way around it. Or you have a choice of not bidding for the business . . . You've to walk away from business that's not your core business.

Complex Application: we'd bring the expertise in-house or we'd outsource it.

TOMMY

The application is new to us AND Unfamiliar platform/tools AND Unfamiliar languages/tools: I'd start running now! I'd go to the market for the technical skills and get them involved at the earliest possible stage . . . On the application side, I'd get an application consultant who understands the area.

TONY

Unfamiliar languages/tools: . . . we'd front load the project because we'd have to bring in training or contract in new skills.

#20

Learn the client's industry/business/application by spending time on-site with the client's people, including the key users, and observing how they currently do things. Learn by getting them to document what they want the new system to do. Also look at other developers' solutions to the same problems in similar companies.

Number of PMs mentioning: 3

Elicited by:

We've little/no knowledge of their industry (3)

The application is new to us (3)

The Evidence

MERVYN

We've little/no knowledge of their industry BUT There is a committed project "owner" AND They don't disagree amongst themselves: Get them to document clearly what they want to be done. The more detail we can get from the users in that spec, guided by their main leader, the better. This will document all we need to know about the industry . . . spend as much time as possible at the start on the client's site, and learn the business.

MICHAEL B

We've little/no knowledge of their industry: Get some consultancy help or "lessons" from someone in the industry. Look at competitors' software products, brochures aimed at the industry.

The application is new to us: . . . work with Cecil on a day-to-day basis . . . or whoever would be running the application . . . we'd gen ourselves up on the application this way.

PHILIP

The application is new to us: Need to make time to learn the application with the people in the business.

We've little/no knowledge of their industry AND The application is new to us: there's a learning exercise to be done. So I'd spend time at the client's site. At his expense. Watching how all the functions that you have to provide within your system are currently carried out ... plus background reading ... talking to certain people. You'd include an allowance for this in your project proposal under the first phase to do the functional spec. The learning and the functional spec would go hand in hand.

#21

Agree a time-and-materials deal (or, at least, variation clauses) for aspects of the project which involve a lot of learning, aspects over which you don't have full control, or where there is disagreement, unfavourable politics, or other big "human" or technical uncertainties. "Package up" such aspects separately in the contract. Only accept a fixed price if you can add a big contingency figure, or if the project is of key strategic importance to you.

Number of PMs mentioning: 8

Elicited by:

People most affected don't want it (3)

We must change another developer's code (2)

They disagree amongst themselves (2)

Client unable/unwilling to drive implementation (2)

Major change for the customer (1)

Some tricky interfacing (1)

Unfamiliar languages/tools (1)

Unattributable (2)

The Evidence

ALAN

We must change another developer's code: In scoping the project, separate out the new programs to be written from the programs to be changed. For the stuff to be changed ... try for time-and-materials deal on that deliverable. If we had to quote fixed price, err on the side of extreme caution and bump up our figures.

ANDRE

Major change for the customer AND People most affected don't want it: You would need a good contingency figure built into the systems definition stage of the project.

Some tricky interfacing with an existing application: Treat the question "do we have to write an interface" as a separate fixed charge in the contract. Have a separate section in the contract detailing this point, full of qualifiers about the standards used, etc. Depending on the answers, reserve the right to quote writing interface as a separate fixed charge or as a time and materials charge.

MERVYN

They disagree amongst themselves OR People most affected don't want it AND Client unable/unwilling to drive implementation: I would make sure that the contract stated that implementation costs were to be on a time and materials basis ... Even if you feel people are keen to put the system in, implementation is the phase where timescales can go absolutely crazy.

MICHAEL B

Client unable/unwilling to drive implementation: Put in a hard-nosed non-programmer type as implementation person ... "I'm here to get things done.". .. If we did this, it would be on a time-and-materials basis. If you're not charging the client, and if they don't have the drive to manage it themselves, three days becomes a week then two weeks then three weeks. If you charge them £$%^ a day, they're going to take it a bit seriously.

MICHAEL C

They disagree amongst themselves OR People most affected don't want it: One strategy is to think of a price for the contract, then double or treble it ... it gives you enough of a cushion to deal with these kinds of issues. But it's not a very moral way to do things. Honest guys would walk away.

Unattributable [almost all poles nasty!]: ... You're into the self-protection business. If they insist on a fixed-price contract, walk away. Get the conditions of contract right ... proper variation clauses to cover the unpredictable problems you could find ... Draw up two contracts: a project management one on a time-and-materials basis to cover variable, less-defined things like specifying requirements. This leading into a point where we can do a proper contract for the software delivery.

OWEN

Unattributable [all poles nasty!]: Oh, Dear! . . . Ideally, time-and-materials contract. If it has to be fixed price, load it!

PHILIP

We must change another developer's code: Could be a reason for walking away! . . . this third-party code aspect would be a good candidate for time and materials . . . maybe parcel it up as a separate project.

TONY

Unfamiliar languages/tools: We'd front load the project because we'd have to bring in training or contract in new skills. We wouldn't be able to fix our costs until the technical spec was completed and signed off. So, time and materials up to then.

#22
Behave bureaucratically/Put everything in "black and white"/Make everything explicit/ Break everything down to a detailed level/Pin it down!/Tie it up with a pink ribbon.
Number of PMs mentioning: 8
Elicited by:
Unrealistic expectations (4)
They disagree amongst themselves (3)
No real owner (2)
Mission-critical application (2)
People most affected don't want it (1)
Real agenda hidden (1)
Major change for the customer (1)
Their PM lacks time/skill/authority (1)
They are inexperienced in running computer projects (1)
Unattributable (3)
This theme is also reflected in many of the other strategies. Here, I'm bringing together instances of explicit, generic expressions of this sentiment.

The Evidence

ALAN

Unrealistic expectations AND No real owner: If no one will sign off on [project scope], then we'd have to walk away, because things aren't tied down tightly.

Real agenda hidden AND No real owner: . . . you're talking about getting as much coverage of your rear as possible . . . everything should be done in triplicate and signed off before you go any further with anything . . .

ANDRE

Mission-critical application: . . . be extremely careful in delimiting the boundaries of the project . . . be very specific about what the project will do and what it will not do.

292

Mission-critical application AND Major change for the customer AND People most affected don't want it: . . . be very careful on all your documentation . . . everything to be pinned down exactly . . . spell out line by line who is responsible for [what] . . .

They disagree amongst themselves: . . . tie it [project] up in a pink ribbon . . . sign-offs at every step of the way. This is self-protection . . .

They are inexperienced in running computer projects AND Unrealistic expectations: Make everything very explicit, bureaucratic . . . break it down to a very detailed level . . . pin it down.

CANICE

Unrealistic expectations OR They disagree amongst themselves: Be very clear about what is to be delivered . . . spec must be at a fine level of detail . . . nothing vague . . . customer sign-offs all the way.

MIKE A

Unattributable [generally unfavourable situation]: Document everything carefully . . . every step of the way. Sign-offs . . . the lot.

MICHAEL B

Unrealistic expectations: . . . document very clearly what is doable, and at what cost, and on what timescale . . . A lot of this would be self-protection.

Their PM lacks time/skill/authority: . . . very clearly document everything . . . You need everything in black and white.

OWEN

Unattributable [very unfavourable situation]: We would make everything very explicit . . . what we would do . . . what they would have to do . . . [etc.]

PADRAIG

They disagree amongst themselves: . . . hammer down the functional spec.

PAUL

Unattributable [unfavourable situation]: . . . write everything down . . .

293

> **#23**
>
> **Document and agree project scope/boundaries with precision . . . what the project includes . . . what it excludes, where it starts . . . where it finishes. All "extras" to be treated as change requests with their own additional budget. "Ring-fence the project" by erecting barriers against creeping scope.**
>
> *Number of PMs mentioning: 11*
>
> *Elicited by:*
>
> *Unrealistic expectations (3)*
>
> *Mission-critical application (2)*
>
> *Tight imposed timescales (1)*
>
> *Real agenda hidden (1)*
>
> *They disagree amongst themselves (1)*
>
> *Complex application (1)*
>
> *We've little or no knowledge of their industry (1)*
>
> *Unattributable (6)*

The Evidence

ALAN

Tight, imposed timescales: So again this comes back to defining the scope . . . defining as clearly as possible what we're going to do and when.

Unattributable: The first thing to do is to define the scope of the project, what we're going to do, early on and stick with it. If there is any change to this, handle it as a change request . . . in a project like this that has a potentially creeping scope.

ANDRE

Mission critical application: You would have to be extremely careful in delimiting the boundaries of the project . . . be very specific about what the project will do and what it will not do.

BOB

Real agenda hidden: If there was a power struggle in the organization, you'd walk away from them if possible. If you couldn't walk away, you'd make sure that people saw exactly what's being contracted for.

CANICE

Unrealistic expectations OR They disagree amongst themselves: . . . be very clear about what is to be delivered . . . nothing vague . . .

GERRY

Unattributable: Get agreement at the outset on a brief that identifies the key elements of what you are going to try to achieve, and get agreement that anything outside that brief will be an extra charge . . . draw a line under these and say "This is what we are going to do for this amount of money. Anything beyond this will be charged for on a time-and-materials basis." We would have at least some damage-limitation protection . . . document the minimum requirements for the project in such a way that these can be measured in a month's time, two months' time, etc. . . . you really have to protect yourself.

MICHAEL B

Unrealistic expectations: . . . We would document very clearly what is doable, and at what cost, and on what timescale. We would document the limits, what the system will do, what it won't do, where it finishes . . . A lot of this would be self-protection.

MICHAEL C

Unattributable: . . . you're into the self-protection business . . . the most critical thing is to get the conditions of contract right . . . proper variation clauses to cover the unpredictable problems you could find . . . contract must define precisely what you will do and what you will not do . . .

OWEN

Unattributable: . . . We would make everything very explicit . . . what we would do . . . what they would have to do . . .

PADRAIG

Complex application: . . . with the best will in the world, sometimes what people define up front isn't actually what they need . . . especially in complex systems . . . other requirements may surface [later] . . . One approach is to nail things down by getting agreement on a budget for requirements that are visible up front, and getting agreement that requirements that surface later will be treated as enhancements, with their own additional budget.

PAUL

Unattributable: Scope your project very clearly . . . write everything down.

TONY

Mission-critical application: . . . you'd be looking for a very clear definition of what the project is, what it's supposed to achieve . . . where responsibilities lie, precisely where does the project start and finish . . . you'd be trying to ring-fence the project . . .

Unrealistic expectations AND We've little/no knowledge of their industry: . . . You are looking for a front end loading to the contract to learn [their] business and to establish and pin down the scope of the project.

Unattributable: . . . I'd insist on a very clear understanding around the contract, what it includes, and most importantly, what it excludes, and . . . define each parties responsibilities very clearly . . .

> **#24**
>
> **Negotiate a separate contract for a first phase to agree project scope, requirements and functional specification.**
>
> *Number of PMs mentioning: 8*
>
> *Elicited by:*
>
> *Unrealistic expectations (2)*
>
> *They disagree amongst themselves (2)*
>
> *They are inexperienced in running computer projects (1)*
>
> *Unattributable (4)*

The Evidence

CANICE

Unrealistic expectations: . . . have a workshop to drill down into needs . . . into what's really important and the real reasons for these. Sell them idea that first revenue-earning phase should deliver a document on these needs and rationale behind each, to their satisfaction. Second phase deliverable should be prototype or some form of proof of concept.

COLIN

Unattributable [overall, an unfavourable situation]: Any major contract is tricky . . . make sure you have the customer pinned down . . . always try to split it into two phases. In the first phase do a very detailed spec . . .

MIKE A

Unattributable [overall, an unfavourable situation]: Go for a phased contract. First phase initial study.

MICHAEL C

Unattributable [overall, an unfavourable situation]: . . . You're into the self-protection business . . . Draw up two contracts: a project management one on a time-and-materials basis to cover variable, less-defined things like specifying requirements. This leading into a point where we can do a proper contract for the software delivery.

PADRAIG

They disagree amongst themselves: . . . A lot of it comes back to scoping . . . agreeing what this should be, and making sure this meets the most important requirements. Hammer down the functional spec. Treat doing this as the first phase of the project. Initially bid just for this phase.

PATRICK

They disagree amongst themselves: . . . extra front loading in the contract in terms of specification . . . getting things clear . . . getting agreement. Need to say "We'll have a formal charge for agreeing things and from what we've seen so far this phase will cost X." It's really a case of splitting the contract into project phases and deliverables that begins with clarifying what they want.

TOMMY

Unattributable [overall, an unfavourable situation]: I'd start with the functional spec. This task should be charged for separately on a fixed price basis. When this is agreed and signed off, then give estimates for subsequent phases.

TONY

Unrealistic expectations AND They are inexperienced in running computer projects: . . . first produce the functional specification, which defines the business application . . . really have to get [this] agreed and tied down . . .

#25

The requirements analysis, functional specification and system specification must be particularly rigorous and detailed.

Number of PMs mentioning: 7

Elicited by:

They disagree amongst themselves (3)

Unrealistic expectations (1)

Real agenda hidden (1)

System must go right first time (1)

Mission-critical application (1)

We'll have to subcontract (1)

Need >two people on our team (1)

The Evidence

CANICE

Unrealistic expectations OR They disagree amongst themselves: . . . sell them on the idea that the first revenue earning phase of the project should deliver a document that tries to capture these needs and rationale behind each, to their satisfaction . . . be very clear about what is to be delivered . . . spec really has to be at a fine level of detail . . . nothing vague . . .

Real agenda hidden: Be as rigorous as you can in specifying what the system is to do.

GERRY

Need >two people on our team: . . . Need a rigid specification . . . everybody needs to know exactly what they are doing . . .

MERVYN

System must go right first time: All you can do is make sure you've a clear picture of what you are doing . . . write your specs in detail . . . be as professional as you can . . .

PADRAIG

They disagree amongst themselves: A lot of it comes back to scoping . . . agreeing what this should be, and making sure this meets the most important requirements . . . hammer down the functional spec. Treat doing this as the first phase of the project . . . Initially, just bid just for [this].

PATRICK

They disagree amongst themselves: . . . extra front loading in the contract in terms of specification . . . getting things clear . . . getting agreement . . . that begins with clarifying what they want . . .

SUSAN A

We'll have to subcontract: . . . make sure the communications are right . . . the objectives clear . . . doing proper requirements documents . . .

SUSAN B

Mission critical application: . . . you'd tell the client "Don't put in something cheap and nasty just to plug the hole . . . do a proper analysis . . . a proper systems spec."

> **#26**
>
> **Make both the developer's AND client's responsibilities/commitments explicit. Get agreement and clarity on where responsibilities lie . . . "what, and by whom, and by when". . . and on the resources the client will need to commit, and by when.**
>
> *Number of PMs mentioning: 7*
>
> *Elicited by:*
>
> *Mission-critical application (2)*
>
> *Major change for the customer (2)*
>
> *Their PM lacks time/skill/authority (2)*
>
> *People most affected don't want it (1)*
>
> *Unrealistic expectations (1)*
>
> *They are inexperienced in running computer projects (1)*
>
> *Unattributable (4)*

The Evidence

ANDRE

Mission-critical application AND Major change for the customer AND People most affected don't want it: . . . be very careful on all your documentation . . . everything to be done . . . responsibilities and so on . . . to be pinned down exactly. If it's mission-critical with a lot of change, there will be a lot of ancillary activities . . . training, implementation, maybe union negotiations. All of this will have to be spelt out, line by line, saying who is responsible for what.

MIKE A

Unrealistic expectations AND Their PM lacks time/skill/authority: If it's lack of time, . . . highlight this to their management and carefully monitor what they actually do vis-à-vis what they are supposed to do . . . check if the time is actually being put in. Be very careful to document what they are supposed to do, what's actually done, by whom and when. This is just covering one's $£&.

MIKE C

Unattributable: When you're into a project like this, you're into the self-protection business. The most critical thing is to get the conditions of contract right . . . The contract must define precisely what you will do and what you will not do . . .

OWEN

Unattributable: . . . We would make everything very explicit . . . what we would do . . . what they would have to do . . . so the customer couldn't come back down the line and say he didn't realize or didn't understand . . .

PADRAIG

Their PM lacks time/skill/authority: . . . point out the dangers . . . and document your case . . . put assumptions in agreed plan about people agreeing designs, for example, by a specific date. If those deadlines are not met because of somebody on the customer's side, at least we've the justification for ensuring we get paid for the work that's been done by us.

Major change for the customer: . . . [point out] that it is their responsibility to ensure that the organization is ready for the new system. You can only point out what they need to do.

TOMMY

They're inexperienced in running computer projects: . . . A customer without experience often expects the supplier to come in, do everything, and walk away with everything done. So [it's important] that the customer's responsibilities be clearly outlined, up front . . .

Unattributable: Give them a detailed project plan showing what resources they will need to commit and when.

TONY

Mission-critical application: you'd also be looking for great clarity on . . . where responsibilities lie . . .

Unattributable: I'd insist on a very clear understanding around the contract, what it includes, and most importantly, what it excludes, and what the responsibilities of the customer are . . . define each parties responsibilities very clearly . . .

> **#27**
>
> **Keep a record of all failures on the client's part to meet agreed responsibilities, commitments, deadlines etc. and of any other "problems" for the project which originate in the client organization.**
>
> *Number of PMs mentioning: 3*
>
> *Elicited by:*
>
> *Their PM lacks time/skill/authority (3)*
>
> *Unrealistic expectations (1)*

The Evidence

MIKE A

Unrealistic expectations AND Their PM lacks time/skill/authority: . . . carefully monitor what they actually do vis-à-vis what they are supposed to do . . . check if the time is actually being put in. Be very careful to document what they are supposed to do, what's actually done, by whom and when. This is just covering one's $£&.

MIKE B

Their PM lacks time/skill/authority: . . . very clearly document everything . . . what we've done this week . . . what we're going to do next week. So [if things are delayed], for example, you can demonstrate exactly what happened . . . "No help from Mr X". . . You need everything in black and white. Self-protection.

PADRAIG

Their PM lacks time/skill/authority: . . . put assumptions in agreed plan about people agreeing designs, for example, by a specific date. If those deadlines are not met because of somebody on the customer's side, at least we've the justification for ensuring we get paid for the work that's been done by us.

> **#28**
>
> **Ensure that project "success" measures, including acceptance-testing criteria, are well defined and agreed in advance.**
>
> *Number of PMs mentioning: 3*
>
> *Elicited by:*
>
> *Unrealistic expectations (1)*
>
> *They disagree amongst themselves (1)*
>
> *Mission-critical application (1)*
>
> *Unattributable (1)*

The Evidence

ANNE

Unattributable: Make sure the acceptance criteria are very well defined and agreed in advance.

CANICE

Unrealistic expectations OR They disagree amongst themselves: . . . be very clear about what is to be delivered . . . spec really has to be at a fine level of detail . . . nothing vague . . . the acceptance test must mirror this spec exactly . . .

TONY

Mission-critical application: . . . you'd be looking for agreement on definite, measurable end results . . . you'd be trying to ring-fence the project and find out and agree the measures which will demonstrate to everybody that the project has been completed to the customer's satisfaction.

#29

Get customer sign-offs on every deliverable and on each stage of the project. Don't proceed without sign-offs.

Number of PMs mentioning: 8

Elicited by:

They disagree amongst themselves (4)

Unrealistic expectations (3)

Real agenda hidden (3)

No real owner (1)

People most affected don't want it (1)

Mission-critical application (1)

Can't show a prototype (1)

Unattributable (2)

The Evidence

ALAN

Unrealistic expectations AND No real owner: there's a train of thought that says we should walk away. What we would more likely do is to try to define the scope for the project ourselves . . . if they agree with what we say we're going to do, we'd do it. If no one will sign off on [this], then we'd have to walk away, because things aren't tied down tightly. Walk away if they won't sign off because things aren't tied down tightly.

Real agenda hidden AND No real owner: . . . You'd insist on sign-offs on proposals, specifications . . . EVERYTHING . . . you're talking about getting as much coverage of your rear as possible . . . everything should be done in triplicate and signed off before you go any further with anything . . .

ANDRE

They disagree amongst themselves: This is looking very bad. It may not be solvable. Project definition . . . stages, deliverables and so on . . . will take a long, long time because you will have to tie it up in a pink ribbon and build in sign-offs at every step of the way. This is self-protection.

CANICE

Unrealistic expectations OR They disagree amongst themselves: . . . get them to sign off on functional spec and the project plan . . . And customer sign-offs all the way.

Real agenda hidden: Be as rigorous as you can in specifying what the system is to do. Make sure the person signing off has lots of clout. Then, at the end of the day, if that person commissions a white elephant, that's their problem.

MIKE A

People most affected don't want it: If one was pushed into this situation, then you'd need someone with sufficient clout on the client's side to push things through and to sign off at the completion of each stage of the project . . .

They disagree amongst themselves: . . . get someone further up the line to steamroller it through. But even if you can, you may find yourself trying to build a system that's very hard to pin down . . . lots of change requests . . . thrashing around. So you would need to be very careful about getting sign-offs at every stage.

Unattributable [very unfavourable situation]: Sign-offs . . . the lot!

PHILIP

Mission critical application AND Can't show a prototype: . . . you'd do your damnedest to find a way of expressing to the client what the system was going to deliver . . . graphically or in some other form . . . to get some confirmation back. You'd need the client's sign-off on something to give you some comfort.

SUSAN A

They disagree amongst themselves: You must get them involved in feedback and sign-off on requirements, the functional spec, and on the detailed design if necessary. If they're signing off at all stages, I don't think you can go wrong.

SUSAN B

Real agenda hidden: . . . get customer sign-offs on everything . . . req spec, system spec, detailed criteria for acceptance testing . . . That's how we have protected ourselves in the past.

TOMMY

Unrealistic expectations: In this situation good project management relies on sign-offs at different phases in the project . . . on requirements, specifications, . . .

Unattributable [Very unfavourable situation]: If we don't fully sign off on a phase before we start the next one . . . we should recognise this and know what new risks we are bringing in.

#30

Manage your subcontractors at least as tightly as the client is managing you. Include non-performance penalty clauses in their contract. Insist on sign-offs on all their deliverables. Make sure communications/interface with them is right. Get clarity on respective roles/responsibilities. Research their background, experience, and compatibility with the way you do things.

Number of PMs mentioning: 4

Elicited by:

We'll have to subcontract (4)

The Evidence

ANNE

We'll have to subcontract: . . . need to define your relationship with these other people very well.

BOB

We'll have to subcontract: . . . check them out . . . are they professional? . . . have they a track record? . . . Can we trust them as people? . . . Make sure you have penalty clauses in [their] contract . . . Make sure to liaise well with their main project person.

PHILIP

We'll have to subcontract: it's probably manageable. But it's something I'd prefer not to have to do. Someone else might look on this as a plus . . . "we can subcontract the risk to someone else". . . but you're still carrying the risk because you have to answer to the client. It's about managing them very tightly.

SUSAN A

We'll have to subcontract: Preferably, I'd rather not subcontract because it's out of our control once we hand it over. The issues between the subcontractor and us, and between us and the client, are much the same. In both cases, . . . make sure the communications are right . . . the objectives clear . . . doing proper requirements documents . . . ensuring everyone knows their role and their task . . . basically to run a tight ship . . . regular communication . . . the right [communication channels] are open . . . that we're involved in signing off on what they're doing . . . the same way that we involve the client.

#31
If there are third parties involved in the project, e.g. other consultants, ensure their roles, their responsibilities, and their relationships with you are very clearly defined. Research their background, experience, and compatibility with the way you do things.
Number of PMs mentioning: 5
Elicited by:
Must share control with a third party (5)
We'll have to subcontract (1)

The Evidence

ALAN

Must share control with a third party: Once we've to subcontract, or share control with a third party, there's the risk to us that they won't do the job properly . . . clarify roles, interdependencies, interfaces with any third parties. How do they control their people and their processes? Have they done it before? Their references? Can we work with them?

308

ANNE

We'll have to subcontract OR Must share control with a third party: . . . need to define your relationship with these other people very well.

CANICE

Must share control with a third party AND Real agenda hidden: . . . if you've to share control with some sort of consultant, that consultant could very much impede the process, or there may be politics or rivalry brought in . . . be very explicit up front about roles and responsibilities. I'd meet with the third party to gauge their attitudes and perspective. I'd look at background and experience.

COLIN

Must share control with a third party: If you have a third party with their own personality involved . . . depending on their behaviour which might range from very bad to very good . . . all that's going to have a major impact on the project . . . If there's professional jealousy, lack of cooperation . . . a bit of obstruction here and there you have obviously got big problems . . . I'd have a long, long talk with these people before I got trapped into the project . . . I would have a very good agreement with them with trigger clauses, so if they failed in their obligations, something [nasty] would happen.

MICHAEL C

Must share control with a third party: We will NOT share control of a project with a third party . . . simply NO! Any time we have done it, it has caused us trouble . . . their agenda was different from our agenda . . . they would promise the client anything to keep them happy . . . a definite "walk-away" job.

> **#32**
>
> **Don't open up another developer's or supplier's artefact (code, interface etc.) if you can avoid it. Treat it as a potential "Pandora's box". If you can't "wrap it", and must open it up and rework it, try if possible to have the original developer/ supplier/maintainer take responsibility for the work, or to sign off on the changes you'll make. If this is not possible, unless a very straightforward change, rewrite or redevelop from scratch. Do a lot of testing . . . trying to crash it. Get clear agreement on "Who's going to support it after we've been into it or wrapped it."**
>
> *Number of PMs mentioning: 6*
>
> *Elicited by:*
>
> *We must change another developer's code (5)*
>
> *Some tricky interfacing (3)*

The Evidence

ANNE

Some tricky interfacing with an existing application: Make sure lines of responsibility vis-à-vis the original developer are clearly defined.

CANICE

We must change another developer's code: Up front, I'd inspect their code . . . standards, documentation, etc. . . . You'd be crazy to take it on a fixed-price basis . . . Try to wrap it instead of opening it up. Get clear under-standing with the customer on "who's going to support it after we've been into it or wrapped it?"

COLIN

We must change another developer's code: This could be a nightmare! If it was just a few lines of code, I'd probably just rewrite it . . . goodness knows what problems you'd face there . . . is the other developer available? . . . is it docu-mented? . . . how well is it structured? . . . you are usually better off to look at what they are trying to do and to rewrite it yourself in your own way.

Some tricky interfacing with an existing application: . . . get as much help from the original supplier as you can. Maybe arrange for one of their people to be available at critical stages. Do a lot of testing . . . trying to "crash" it, find the weaknesses.

MERVYN

We must change another developer's code: You have to get the other developer on side. Get him to agree what you're going to change . . . what your not going to change. Make sure he is happy with that and get him to sign off on it . . . release any changes we make to this other company's software back to them, not directly to the client. This other developer then tests it to satisfy themselves. Then THEY ship to the client.

PADRAIG

We must change another developer's code: Have the supplier of the existing system keep ownership of the code and channel the required changes to them.

Some tricky interfacing with an existing application: you'd have to liaise with the developer, supplier or maintainer of the existing system . . . Testing becomes more complex because you have to schedule not only your own resources, but the customer's resources and the third party's resources.

PHILIP

We must change another developer's code: If it's not worth changing, throw it out and rewrite it.

#33
Strengthen quality assurance/increase the level of formality of the development process.
Number of PMs mentioning: 9
Elicited by:
System must go right first time (4)
Mission critical application (3)
We'll have to subcontract (2)
Some tricky interfacing (2)
Project duration >three months (1)

The Evidence

ALAN

We'll have to subcontract: The danger with significant subcontracting is that you don't own the people . . . The key is to have a well-defined development process so that, if someone falls off the manpower list, and we bring in someone else, they can slot in easily.

Mission-critical application: . . . you'd have to plan to beef up your testing effort . . .

ANNE

Mission-critical application: . . . beef up your quality control . . . beef up your quality assurance procedures.

System must go right first time: Beef up your testing and get users more involved in this . . . concentrate on making sure the testing effort is very well planned, executed and managed.

COLIN

Some tricky interfacing with an existing application: . . . Do a lot of testing . . . trying to "crash" it and find any weaknesses.

GERRY

Project duration >three months AND We'll have to subcontract: . . . have a much more rigorous review process than we might have with a smaller project . . .

MERVYN

System must go right first time: All you can do is make sure you've a clear picture of what you are doing . . . write your specs in detail, write your code properly and test the hell out of it before you release it. You have to be as professional as you can . . .

OWEN

Some tricky interfacing with an existing application: . . . we'd need the technical expertise to handle it. It certainly would extend time and people estimates . . . and the time needed for testing.

PADRAIG

Mission-critical application: . . . and you need to ensure that all the necessary testing is done . . . so the risk is minimized when you actually go live.

PATRICK

System must go right first time: You would need to be much more conscious about your quality assurance and project-management procedures, and you'd have to charge extra for this . . . you have to build a more formal method of controlling things . . . "No seat of the pants!". . . need more bureaucracy and explicitness . . . more QA than you would normally rely on . . .

SUSAN B

System must go right first time: . . . We'd set up a test environment here that mimicked their environment . . . We'd do application-acceptance testing and technical-acceptance testing prior to installation.

#34
Intensify the level of user input into business test-case generation and testing.
Number of PMs mentioning: 4 *Elicited by:* *System must go right first time (2)* *Mission-critical application (1)* *Major change for the customer (1)*

The Evidence

ALAN

Mission critical application: . . . If it's mission-critical it's a big risk to us because we're touching something which, if it breaks, will have a serious impact on the client . . . You'd have to set the expectation that users would test it for you . . . help us to generate and apply business test cases . . . you'd have to plan to beef up your testing effort . . .

ANNE

System must go right first time: . . . build a good relationship between whoever is testing on your side and the users because each will bring their own perspective to testing. Beef up testing and get users more involved in this.

MERVYN

System must go right first time: . . . test the hell out of it before you release it. You have to be as professional as you can . . . get some of the users onto your test team . . . get them to provide as much realistic test data as they can . . . get them to give you test cases . . . get somebody who works in that industry to do the testing because they know the real pitfalls . . . make the testing as realistic as possible . . . test the hell out of it.

PADRAIG

Major change for the customer: . . . budget for more user testing than normal.

#35
If the application is mission-critical for the client, ensure there is a high level of technical competence and application experience on your team.
Number of PMs mentioning: 2
Elicited by:
Mission-critical application (2)

The Evidence

ANNE

Mission critical application: . . . be a lot more careful about putting your team together . . . competent, experienced people . . .

PHILIP

Mission critical application: . . . you'd better have an experienced development team . . .

> **#36**
>
> **Increase the formality and rigour of project management. Manage the project more formally, more tightly. Control by deadlines and deliverables. Lots of supervision and control.**
>
> *Number of PMs mentioning: 5*
>
> *Elicited by:*
>
> *Need >two people on our team (4)*
>
> *Project duration >three months (1)*
>
> *Unfamiliar platform/environment (1)*
>
> *Unfamiliar languages/tools (1)*
>
> *Must go right first time (1)*
>
> *Must change other developer's code (1)*

The Evidence

ALAN

Unfamiliar platform/environment OR Unfamiliar languages/tools: it's about getting experienced people that you know know the technology. But also who can relate to people. You don't want technoheads who know it all . . . but who can't talk to other people! . . . If you can't find the right people, you just have to manage it more closely . . . regular weekly meetings with the team . . . To say "Tell me what's deliverable next week . . . and next week I'll ask you did you do it, and if you didn't, you'll tell me why!" It's those kinds of things.

BOB

Need >two people on our team: . . . If you need three or more people, you have to make sure that everyone is singing from the same hymn book. With only one or two people, you can manage through informal chats. But with three or more, you need to have formal reviews of progress, etc.

GERRY

Need >two people on our team: . . . Need a rigid specification . . . everybody needs to know exactly what they are doing . . . Basically, you would need a more controlled project environment.

Project duration >three months AND need >two people on our team AND Must change other developer's code: . . . It's going to need a lot of supervision and control . . . we would need a full-time project manager who does nothing except manage the project.

PATRICK

Must go right first time: . . . You would need to be much more conscious about your quality assurance and project-management procedures, and you'd have to charge extra for this . . . you have to build a more formal method of controlling things . . . "No seat of the pants!". . . need more bureaucracy and explicitness . . . more QA than you would normally rely on . . .

PHILIP

Need >two people on our team: . . . It needs to be managed more tightly I think. More formality of reporting. Logging of time and deadlines. there's more management overhead because you've got more people.

#37
Unless it's a very strategic project for you, walk-away if . . .
Number of PMs mentioning: 14
Elicited by:
<defies easy analysis! . . . see below.>

The Evidence

ALAN

Unrealistic expectations AND No real owner: What we would more likely do is to try to define the scope for the project ourselves . . . if they agree with what we say we're going to do, we'd do it. If no one will sign off on [this], then we'd have to walk away, because things aren't tied down tightly.

Real agenda hidden AND No real owner: I'd be suspicious that there's something else going on . . . maybe someone has taken us into the company to act as a scapegoat . . . or maybe getting a free feasibility study . . . or maybe using the project to force change on somebody else . . . it's too risky. We would walk away very quickly . . . Of course, it's a public profile thing . . . it's hard to walk away from a prestigious contract with one of the big banks or something . . . so [maybe] you'd have to drive it from your end . . . fix the scope yourself . . . work on the unrealistic expectations . . . forget the agenda, hidden or not.

ANNE

Their PM lacks time/skill/authority AND No real owner AND People most affected don't want it: [You could] stick with the project without real owner-ship from senior people [by] working around the ownership problem . . . I'd work in tandem with the users [if they really wanted the new system]. Otherwise I'd walk away.

Mission-critical application AND Tight, imposed timescales: I want out!

No real owner AND Unrealistic expectations AND Mission critical applica-tion: I just wouldn't do it under these conditions.

BOB

Real agenda hidden: If there was a power struggle in the organization, you'd walk away from them if possible. If you couldn't walk away, you'd make sure that people saw exactly what's being contracted for.

CANICE

Unrealistic expectations: If they won't accept an incremental path towards clarification [of their requirements], walk away!

COLIN

No real owner: . . . go to the top and say, sort this out or forget it.

Unfamiliar languages/tools AND No real owner: Look for some other busi-ness quickly!

Unfamiliar languages/tools AND System must go right first time: . . . totally off-the-wall!

MERVYN

No real owner: I'd try to highlight this to whoever asked me to look at the area in the first place. To say, face to face to them, "Do you REALLY want this system? Is what we're proposing what you REALLY want?" If he says "Yes. This is REALLY where we want to go," then you're starting to create ownership. If he says "Well, it's not really what we want", he'll probably talk himself out of doing it at all. At that stage, you're probably better off walking away, if you can do that.

We've little/no knowledge of their industry AND ["if [the project] is very big"]: If something is very big, and you've no knowledge of it, you should simply walk away.

MIKE A

Unfamiliar platform/environment OR Unfamiliar languages/tools AND Tight, imposed timescales: [This] would be an excruciating combination . . . Unless this is a very strategic project, one should walk away.

Unfamiliar languages/tools AND Tight, imposed timescales AND Must satisfy different groups with different needs: . . . it would definitely be time to leave the party!

MICHAEL B

No real owner: . . . we're on a loser if someone isn't guiding things from the client's side . . . if there's no real ownership . . . it's usually been a disaster in terms of timescales and costs, and the client not really getting what they wanted. Ideally, I'd pull out . . . If we couldn't pull out, I would get them to encourage someone less senior but very enthusiastic to take it on . . . someone who wants to develop their computer skills.

MICHAEL C

They disagree amongst themselves: This is the single most important one. Disagreement is an absolute show-stopper as far as I'm concerned . . . We now have a policy of actually walking out. You cannot make them agree, so you've no countermeasure.

They disagree amongst themselves OR People most affected don't want it: . . . one strategy is to think of a price for the contract, then double or treble it! . . . it gives you enough of a cushion to deal with these kinds of issues. But it's not a very moral way to do things. Honest guys would walk away.

Must share control with a third party: We will NOT share control of a project with a third party . . . simply NO! Any time we have done it, it has caused us trouble . . . their agenda was different from our agenda . . . they would promise the client anything to keep them happy . . . a definite "walk-away" job.

No real owner AND Their PM lacks time/skill/authority: . . . my advice would [be] to walk away.

PATRICK

Their PM lacks time/skill/authority: You'd have to [walk out]. Lack of time, even skill, one could live with, but if he/she doesn't have the authority, there's no real contract.

No real owner: . . . that would be that! [i.e. walk away]

Mission-critical application AND They disagree amongst themselves: . . . the project can't go ahead because you will end up with one side refusing to cooperate. They'll say "That was THEIR specification, not ours." If it isn't mission-critical, you can normally go ahead on the basis that one side is enough to sign a cheque!

PAUL

No real owner: You have to find someone who'll say "Yes" [to your proposals, ideas, etc.]. Otherwise you have to go up and up, even to the board. If not resolved, bail out!

Their PM lacks time/skill/authority: . . . lack of time and skill can be worked around . . . but they must have authority. It may be that you will have to go up the organization to get the name of someone lower down . . . who can decide/is given authority. . . . [if not resolved] I think I'd bail out.

Must satisfy different groups with different needs AND They disagree amongst themselves AND No real owner: I'm out of here!

Unrealistic expectations AND They are inexperienced in running computer projects: I'd explain why, in my view, their expectations were unrealistic. I'd keep at this until one of two things happened . . . they changed their expectations, or I'd reckoned I was on a loser and I'd just walked away . . .

PHILIP

We must change another developer's code: . . . make a quick assessment of how well it's written before you commit. This third-party code aspect would be a good candidate for time and materials. Maybe parcel it up as a separate project. If it's not worth changing, throw it out and rewrite it. But it would have to be a language you're familiar with . . . That could be reason for walking away.

We've little/no knowledge of their industry AND Unfamiliar platform/ environment: The combination . . . new industry . . . new platform . . . they're strong negatives. It depends from a business point of view, on whether you still want to pursue the project . . .

Tight, imposed time scales AND We must change another developer's code: . . . you may have to walk away.

No real owner AND Mission critical application: . . . confront the client directly and say "We need a senior manager . . . the board . . . to approve . . . underwrite this project." If that didn't work, then it's goodbye time.

SUSAN B

Unrealistic expectations: . . . We'd probably walk away from the business to be honest . . . if you can't reset their expectations, you have to walk away.

The application is new to us AND System must go right first time: . . . do an initial requirements spec, check if we had the needed skills in-house . . . whether it's really our bread and butter or not. Then we'd decide if we wanted the business.

Unfamiliar languages/tools: we'd have to bring in subcontractors. there's no other way around it. Or you have a choice of not bidding for the business . . . You've to walk away from business that's not your core business.

TOMMY

Their PM lacks time/skill/authority AND No real owner: we're going down the tubes rapidly here! . . . I'd ask myself do I REALLY want this project? . . . Is this a strategic project for me?

The application is new to us AND Unfamiliar platform/environment AND Unfamiliar languages/tools: I'd start running now!

References

Chapter 1

Argyris C and Schön DA (1978) *Organizational Learning: A Theory of Action Perspective*, Addison-Wesley Publishing Company, London.

Bell J and Hardiman RJ (1988) Chapter 2 in Dan Diaper (ed.) *Knowledge Elicitation: Principles, Techniques and Applications*, Ellis Horwood, Chichester, UK, pp. 57–69.

Gluch DP (1994) "A Construct for Describing Software Development Risks", Technical Report CMU/SEI-94-TR-14, Software Engineering Institute, Carnegie Mellon University, July.

Schön, DA (1983) *The Reflective Practicioner: How Professionals Think in Action*, Basic Books Inc., New York.

Terkel S (1997) *Working: People Talk About What They Do All Day and How They Feel About What They Do*, The New Press, New York.

Chapter 2

Bannister D and Fransella F (1989) *Inquiring Man: The Psychology of Personal Constructs* (3rd edition), Routledge, London.

Stewart V and Stewart A (1981) *Business Applications of Repertory Grid*, McGraw-Hill, London.

Chapter 3

Barki H, Rivard S and Talbot J (1993) "Toward an Assessment of Software Development Risk", *Journal of Management Information Systems* (10), 203–225.

Bieri J (1955) "Cognitive Complexity–Simplicity and Predictive Behaviour", *Journal of Abnormal Social Psychology* (51), 263–268.

Boehm B (1989) *Software Risk Management*, IEEE Computer Society Press, Los Alamitos, CA.

Carr MJ, Konda SL, Monarch I, Ulrich FC and Walker CF (1993) *Taxonomy-based Risk Identification*, SEI-93-TR-006, Software Engineering Institute, Pittsburgh.

Healy MJR (1988) *GLIM: An Introduction*, Clarendon Press, Oxford.

Maister DH (1993) *Managing the Professional Services Firm*, The Free Press, New York.

Chapter 27

Beckhard R and Harris RT (1987) *Organizational Transitions: Managing Complex Change* (2nd edition), Addison-Wesley, New York.

Eisenhardt KL (1989) "Agency Theory: An Assessment and Review", *Academy of Management Review* 14(1): 57–74.

Harrison MI (1994) *Diagnosing Organizations: Methods, Models and Processes* (2nd edition), Thousand Oaks, California, Sage Publications.

Javidan M (1998) "Core Competence: What Does it Mean in Practice?", *Long Range Planning* 31(1): 60–71.

Markus ML and Benjamin RI: "Change Agentry – the Next IS Frontier", *MIS Quarterly* 20(4): 385–407.

Sharma A (1997) "Professional As Agent: Knowledge Asymmetry In Agency Exchange, *Academy of Management Review*, **22**(3) 1997, pp. 758–798.

Thompson JD (1967) *Organizations in Action*, McGraw-Hill, New York.

Williamson OE (1985) *The Economic Institutions of Capitalism*, Free Press, New York.

Zaheer A, McEvily B and Perrone V (1998) "Does Trust Matter? Exploring the Effects of Interorganizational and Interpersonal Trust on Performance", *Organization Science* 9(2): 141–159.

Chapter 28

Burns RN and AR Dennis (1985) "Selecting the Appropriate Application Development Methodology", *Data Base* (Fall): 19–23.

Davis GB (1982) "Strategies for Information Requirements Determination", *IBM Systems Journal* 21(1): 3–30.

Nidumolu SR (1996) "Standardization, Requirements Uncertainty and Software Project Performance, *Information and Management* 31: 135–150.

Stork D and Sapienza AM (1995) "Uncertainty and Equivocality in Projects: Managing Their Implications for the Project Team, *Engineering Management Journal* 7(3): 33–38.

Chapter 29

Azjen I (1988) *Attitudes, Personality and Behaviour*, Dorsey Press, Chicago.

Alavi M and Leidner DE (2001) "Knowledge Management and Knowledge Management Systems: Conceptual Foundations and Research Issues, *MIS Quarterly* 25(1) March: 107–136.

Maister DH (1993) *Managing the Professional Services Firm*, The Free Press, New York.

Mills PK and N Margulies (1980) "Towards a Core Typology of Service Organizations", *Academy of Management Review* 5(2): 255–265.

Moynihan T (1996) "An Inventory of Personal Constructs for Risk Researchers", *Journal of Information Technology* 11: 359–371.

Nonaka I (1994) "A Dynamic Theory of Organizational Knowledge Creation", *Organization Science* 5(1) February: 14–37.

Priem RL and Rosenstein J (2000) "Is Organization Theory Obvious to Practicioners? A Test of One Established Theory", *Organization Science* 11(5) Sept–Oct: 509–524.

Schenhar AJ (2001) "One Size Does Not Fit All Projects: Exploring Classical Contingency Domains", *Management Science* 47(3) March: 394–414.

Schmidt R, Lyytinen K, Keil M and Cule P (2001) "Identifying Software Project Risks", *Journal of Management Information Systems* 17(4) Spring: 5–36.

Weick KE (1989) Theory Construction as Disciplined Imagination, *Academy of Management Review* 14: 516–531.

Index

PRACTITIONER SERIES

Series Editor: *Ray Paul*
Editorial Board: *Frank Bott, Nic Holt,*
Kay Hughes, Elizabeth Hull,
Richard Nance, Russel Winder and Sion Wyn

These books are written by practitioners for practitioners.

They offer thoroughly practical hands-on advice on how to tackle specific problems. So, if you are already a practitioner in the development, exploitation or management of IS/IT systems, or you need to acquire an awareness and knowledge of principles and current practice in an IT/IS topic fast then these are the books for you.

All books in this series will be clear, concise and problem solving and will cover a wide range of areas including:
● systems design techniques
● performance modelling
● cost and estimation control
● software maintenance
● quality assurance
● database design and administration
● HCI
● safety critical systems
● distributed computer systems
● internet and web applications
● communications, networks and security
● multimedia, hypermedia and digital libraries
● object technology
● client-server
● formal methods
● design approaches
● IT management

All books are, of course, available from all good booksellers (who can order them even if they are not in stock), but if you have difficulties you can contact the publishers direct, by telephoning +44 (0) 1483 418822 (in the UK & Europe), +1/212/4 60/15 00 (in the USA), or by emailing orders@svl.co.uk

www.springer.de   www.springer-ny.com